To Dave Joane:

lots of lively
Albinaise.

Regards,

Bob Logan

Bob Logan's Tales From Chicago Sports

Cubs, Bulls, Bears, and Other Animals

By
Bob Logan

Sports Publishing LLC
www.sportspublishingllc.com

Director of production: Susan M. Moyer
Dust jacket design: Kenneth J. O'Brien
Bob Logan's stories and columns reprinted by permission of the Chicago
Tribune, Daily Herald, Basketball Times, and Baseball Bulletin. Photos
courtesy of the Chicago Cubs, Chicago White Sox, Chicago Bears, Chicago
Bulls, the University of Illinois and Notre Dame Sports Information
Department. Cover photo of Sammy Sosa by Stephen Green. Back cover
photo by James C. Snyder

ISBN:1-58261-470-9

Printed in the United States of America

Sports Publishing LLC
www.sportspublishingllc.com

Other books by Bob Logan

The Bulls and Chicago
Miracle on 35th Street
Cubs Win!
So You Think You're a Die-Hard Cub Fan
Chicago Sports Barroom Analyst

Contents

Preface

The Chicago White Sox once had a pair of catchers named Les Moss and Earl Battey. When former sportswriter and Sox publicist Howie Roberts saw them, he said:

"What the White Sox need is less Moss and more Battey."

No wonder Howie was my pun-ultimate idol. I'm no idle punster, either, as my long-suffering pressbox pals groaningly agree. So, for four-plus decades, I've looked on—and written about—Chicago sports as fun (and pun) in the sun. I figured Howie beamed approval from that Big Bullpun in the Sky some years later, when Mookie Wilson of the Mets took a called third strike in Wrigley Field and I summed up Mookie's misfortune this way:

"Looks like he got caught Mooking."

My 40-year romp through Chicago's playgrounds seems more like 40 minutes. Lots of good people, especially Ron and Deb Coffing, Eric and Ethyl Andersen, Bill and Joyce Harper, helped me reconstruct the fun and games. Here and now, this book is for Ellen, the love of my life.

—Bob Logan

Foreword

by Ron Santo

(Author's note: Ron Santo's lifelong battle with diabetes is only one reason why the former Cubs third baseman has been a Chicago favorite for decades. A humble man with a love for baseball, especially in Wrigley Field that Cub fans relate to, Santo and WGN radio partner Pat Hughes make them part of the fun. His Hall of Fame numbers over 15 big-league years eventually will earn an overdue berth in Cooperstown.)

I saw Wrigley Field on the TV Game of the Week when I was a kid, growing up in Seattle. The electricity of that ballpark came right through to my living room, long before I ever dreamed of playing for the Cubs.

When they called me up to Chicago in 1960, after just one year in the minors, it was the start of a magic carpet ride. I'm a very emotional person, and I couldn't hide my feelings about putting on a Cubs uniform for the first time.

I walked out of the old clubhouse door with Ernie Banks, so I got my first look at Wrigley Field from behind our bullpen, down the left-field line. After all these years, I still can't describe the excitement. Whenever Cub fans talk to me about Wrigley Field, they remember the first time they saw the ivy and the scoreboard.

Those fans make the difference. Even though the Cubs haven't won a lot, they keep coming back to their ballpark. Wrigley

Field is special, but Chicago fans are, too. They support all of our teams, win or lose.

So I was glad to know Bob Logan wrote this book about all the fun we've had in Chicago. I was honest with him and the rest of the writers, no matter what happened on the field. Most of the time, they were fair with me.

And I'm proud to be recognized by the fans. When they say "Hi, Ron," and want to talk baseball, I'm happy to stop and sign an autograph, especially for kids.

Foreword

by Norm Van Lier

(Author's note: Stormin' Norman was an outstanding player for a dozen NBA seasons, most of them in Chicago. He teamed with Jerry Sloan to give the Bulls one of pro basketball's toughest backcourt combos. Now a familiar voice on radio and TV sports programs, Van Lier's competitive fire helps him light the way for young players.)

Bob Logan was the first writer to call me on the day the NBA held the 1969 draft. That was how I found out the Bulls picked me. Chicago was the right place. Our fans dug the way I fit in with a team that took a lot more punishment than we handed out.

Nobody got an uncontested layup against the Bulls when Jerry Sloan and I were the starting guards. But Chet Walker, Bob Love, Tom Boerwinkle, and especially Jerry and I, ended up paying a bigger price. Opponents cried when we didn't step aside and let them go to the basket, so writers in other NBA cities ran their quotes about how the Bulls were dirty.

Logan told both sides of the story. If players tell you they don't read the papers, they're lying. They know the difference between writers who know what's happening and the ones just looking for controversy. Guys like Logan, Bob Markus and Bob Verdi were respected by us.

Bob Logan was there when we traveled, practiced and played. The Bulls worked hard, but we had a lot of fun, and he let the fans know it. I enjoyed reading his stories, so I'm glad his book lets the good times roll again.

1

Sosa's Cubs Not So-So

The pace of change, in and out of the sports world, has accelerated too fast to understand since 1945, when the Cubs last lost a World Series game. Since the terrorist tragedy in New York and Washington, made 9/11/01 a day of infamy, events now move at warp speed.

Thankfully, we can count on the Cubs to do something zany, outrageous, or just plain fun. When times get tough, meaning almost always, their fans can recall the fly ball that got lost in Larry Biittner's cap, bizarre back-stabbing by the revolving College of Coaches, Bill Buckner battered by Lee Elia, and countless other such mini-calamities.

When they're not muttering their "Wait till next year" mantra, worshippers at the Wrigley Field shrine can smile about a favorite fable of futility by their beloved bunglers in Cubbie Blue. My indelible memory is this one—when a leather-lunged bleacherite added his own page to Cubs lore:

I Got It Yes, But Who Are You?
(Chicago Tribune, Aug. 13, 1981)

Add the tale of the Unknown Bellower to Cubs' comedy capers, taking its place with Jose Cardenal's stuck eyelid. The Cubs, proving they're nothing if not versatile, hurt themselves with mental and physical misdeeds in this chapter of the Wrigley Field follies.

Not that they needed help in losing for the third straight time to the New York Mets, this one 7-4 in 10 innings, but a right-field bleacherite got into the act just to make sure.

The fun-loving fan yelled, "I got it!" while Cub outfielders Bobby Bonds and Heity Cruz were pursuing a drive off the bat of Dave Kingman, the Mets' leadoff hitter in the 10th. Both men pulled up and the ball eluded center fielder Bonds for a triple. Kingman scored the decisive run seconds later when Ellis Valentine tripled almost to the same spot. Bonds again failed to track it down.

"One of us should have caught it," Bonds said of the Alphonse-Gaston routine he and Cruz staged in right-center. "Somebody in the stands hollered, 'I got it!' So we both stopped. I thought it was Cruz calling for the catch and he thought it was me.

"It was a cruel hoax, but I remember the same thing happening 10 years ago in San Francisco, when Willie Mays played center and I was in right," Bonds said. "At least I had been with Willie long enough to recognize his voice. This was the first time I've been in center with Cruz in right, so we got screwed up when the guy yelled."

"It's been a while since I got a triple, because the outfielders play me so deep, I can't hit a ball in the gap," said Kingman, the slugger who later led the Cubs in homers for two straight years, swatting 48 for them in 1979 to top both leagues. "I'd rather hit home runs and walk around the bases."

That touch of humor was offered with a smile by the man known as King Kong during his brief Chicago sojourn. It was a dual label, applying to his sour moods as much as Kong's prodigious clouts. For some reason, a lighthearted story by *Sun-Times* writer Joe Goddard, naming Kingman worst dressed on the team

Wrigley Field's ill winds often make Cub fans ill while outfielders chase, collide and sometimes even catch elusive fly balls. Billy Williams (left) and Adolfo Phillips try to figure out why another drive got away.

in a poll of the players, drove him into a raging silence. Hungry for a superstar, Cub fans would have made Kingman their favorite animal, but Kong stayed true to his surly self.

Bobby Bonds was a different story. A big, pleasant man, he had a charismatic gene that obviously skipped a generation when his slugging son, Barry, was born.

Way back when writers traveling with the Cubs were allowed to ride on the team bus, I used to sit next to Bobby, just to hear his offbeat perspective on baseball and life in general.

Although the elder Bonds had been victimized by the racial slurs and snubs of ignorant teammates in the minor leagues, he was not embittered by that ordeal.

When Barry Bonds came to Wrigley Field for the 1990 All-Star game, I was delighted to find the father-son combo in the clubhouse. Bobby and I talked about the Bad Old Days of 1981, his only Chicago season, and Barry even opened up a bit.

Just a few days after the '90 All-Star game, another of those wild Wrigley weirdathons hinged on Cubs left fielder Dwight Smith misjudging a liner by Terry Pendleton of the Cardinals, watching it sail over his head for a two-run triple. After St. Louis survived, 8-7, Cards manager Whitey Herzog put it in perspective.

"I know the reason why the Cubs and Cards play so many crazy games here, but I'd better not tell you," Herzog said. "I'd have about 20 pitchers coming after me."

As usual, the White Rat was right. When the wind blows in, out or sideways at Wrigley Field, pitchers age rapidly, though not gracefully, while their fielders stagger around in futile pursuit of anything hit in the air. It's a three-ring circus—howling wind, glaring sun and hysterical fans—unlike anything Barnum & Bailey offers.

Herzog turned off many writers with his no-nonsense approach. Diamond scribes prefer a manager who will schmooze with them, like easygoing Jim Riggleman. Ever since a long conversation in Kansas City with Herzog, when he managed the Royals, I knew he was one of the sharpest minds in captivity, but he seldom got credit for that.

"You have to tailor a team for a place like this," Herzog said of Royals Stadium, where he turned K.C. from AL doormats to contenders.

Andy MacPhail is trying to do the same thing with the Cubs, seeking pitchers who can induce grounders into the thick infield underbrush, rather than popups that become homers when they're lofted into that windblown wild blue yonder.

Slammin' Sammy—from
South Side Reject to Superstar

Sammy Sosa's rise as a home run hero, from an erratic 20-year-old White Sox outfielder in 1989 to one of today's top-shelf superstars, did not happen entirely in the batter's box. He was born with the ability to bash baseballs in the Dominican Republic, but the transformation from an often-erratic ballplayer to one of Chicago's all-time sports heroes has been truly remarkable.

Sosa came to Chicago with untapped potential and just one big-league homer. Soon Sammy will dethrone Ernie Banks as the Cubs' all-time home run king, but a pair of 60-plus homer seasons (66 in 1998, 63 in '99) assures a share of Mr. Cub's undying popularity. They'll need another flagpole, perhaps atop the center field scoreboard, to hoist Super Sam's No. 21 when he retires.

I saw Sosa hit a homer soon after the Sox stole him from the Texas Rangers, a screaming line drive into the upper deck at old Comiskey Park. Unaware that it was a preview of many more, most of them towering fly balls, I sought out the nervous kid in the Sox clubhouse. Understandably, he was not garrulous, speaking in near-inaudible tones.

Less than a year later, I got this startling glimpse of the future from him.

Harold Who?
(Daily Herald, April 15, 1990)

When the Texas Rangers ride into Comiskey Park on April 30, diehard White Sox fans are sure to cut loose with that familiar chant: "Har-old! Har-old!"

Chances are the sound won't make the old park's rusting girders tremble the way it did last season when Sox hero Harold Baines came back for the first time. Time marches on and "Harold!" is history already. The new Sox who came over in the trade that shipped Baines out are turning things around on the South Side.

One of them, 21-year-old Sammy Sosa, showed again Saturday night that he's ready to lead the charge.

Sosa lashed a pair of triples, pacing a 15-hit attack that gave the Sox a 9-4 romp over the Cleveland Indians. The Sosa stampede made it easy for Sox right-hander Melido Perez to pick up his first victory. The crowd of 12,125 went home buzzing about the way Sosa's explosion overshadowed the postgame fireworks show.

"I love to run," Sosa said after burning up the basepaths in his sprint spectacular. "The fans appreciate me because I work hard, and I try to contribute on defense when I'm not hitting.

"I have quick hands, so I can hit the ball where it's pitched," the right-handed swinger said after tapping both triples to the opposite field. "This is the first time I ever got two in one game. It's fun."

A dozen years later, the glee has shifted to the North Side, where Sosa's sentinels stand guard in the right-field bleachers, poised to salaam on cue when their idol makes his ritual pregame inspection tour.

It's much bigger than Gary "Sarge" Matthews Sr. handing out caps adorned with sergeant's stripes to left-field bleacherites in 1984 or the Andre "Hawk" Dawson cult a few years later.

No wonder. Sosa's feats far outshine those two outstanding players. Even more remarkable is the way this Dominican dandy became a spokesman, role model and goodwill ambassador for Chicago and all Latin ballplayers.

Sosa's enjoyment of his job translates easily into English, Spanish and all other languages. He wears his superstar status well. Kids of all ages feel at ease when he strides from the dugout or the batting cage to sign autographs before games. It was a long, rocky road, but the critics who used to claim Sosa's power was overshadowed by his alleged fielding and baserunning flaws are hard to find.

A $72 million contract finally ended years of trade speculation, so Sosa became the unquestioned clubhouse leader, un-

Sammy Sosa's smile lights up Wrigley Field while his bat sparks pennant hopes for the Cubs.

derscored by the departure of popular first baseman Mark Grace. It gave manager Don Baylor a better grip on the club, so the Cubs set out in pursuit of a playoff berth.

Sosa sounded the mantra, over and over: "I want to win." In clubhouse scenes that recalled the Michael Jordan era, Sammy got surrounded daily by the same postgame mob of TV cameras, lights, mikes, tape recorders and notebooks, all seeking The Word from The Man.

Sosa's homer-hammering heroics drove Cub fans in ecstatic frenzy, but in sharp contrast to the MJ six-pack legacy of NBA titles, the Sosa legacy so far is an 0-3 one-peat in the playoffs, after they backed into a 1998 wild card spot. Still in his prime, he's capable of continuing to crack the 60-homer barrier. Before Cub fans crack under a half-century of frustration, can Sammy produce what Ernie, Billy, Fergie, Ron, Ryno, Hawk and the Red Baron couldn't?

Z-Ball and Tall Stories

Honestly, it was more fun covering the Cubs through all those seasons when they made only feeble passes at a division title. Through it all, the slightest hint of a contender in Wrigley Field sends Chicago's blood pressure skyrocketing, its heart pumping and its lungs bellowing.

Yes, the Cubs are loved, win (seldom) or lose (mostly) by the fans who support them through thin and thinner.

When they get tossed a playoff bone every decade or so, those True Believers pounce on it like hungry hounds. From the undying loyalty standpoint, Cub fans are unrivaled.

Yes, if the Bears field another Super Bowl winner sometime in the 21st century, the Art Institute lions will don their helmets again, and their fans will proclaim, "I never gave up on us."

For Cub fans, hope is a way of life, even when there isn't any. Some blind allegiance gene must be passed down to each new generation of them. That's why I enjoyed covering the Cubs more after their annual May malaise, June/July jitters, August angst or September swoon.

Then it was just the writers and the real Cub fans the rest of the season. Gone were the TV cameras and lights, the front-running fat cats in their scalped $200-and-up box seats and the bandwagon riders, clamoring to be born-again boosters. Aside from a minority of gamblers and rowdy drunks, real Cub fans understand baseball better than most, and almost as much as that shrinking corps of lifelong White Sox backers.

But for me, 1989 was an exception. That was fun from start to finish, because it provided a glimpse of real baseball, seldom seen in the Zany Confines. It was produced and directed by Don Zimmer, my favorite Cubs manager.

Zimmer, an old-school, seat-of-the-pants tactician, had the Cubs bunting, running, stealing, squeezing and manufacturing runs any way they could. It was a totally entertaining show, rewarded at last by a Central Division crown. Zim couldn't get past the Billy Goat hex and the San Francisco Giants in the National League Championship Series, but that was a very good year on the North Side. For instance:

Shawon the Man
Daily Herald, Aug. 13, 1989

Red-hot Ryne Sandberg needs a day off? No problem.

Andre Dawson wants to be with his wife for the birth of their first child? Go for it, Hawk.

The way things are working for the Cubs right now, even their junior varsity can do the job. They spotted the Phillies a three-run handicap Saturday in Wrigley Field, then came roaring back for a 9-7 victory.

The first-place Cubs needed the six walks Phils' starter Ken Howell passed out, turning them into a half-dozen runs, but it was shortstop Shawon Dunston's turn to supply the heroics. Dunston had his most productive day in five seasons with a homer, double, single and six RBIs. His double cleared the bases in the first inning, and he did it again in the third, lofting a windblown three-run homer to right.

The Cubs bullpen almost played giveaway, just as in the Phils' 16-13 comeback victory in Thursday's Wrigley wind tunnel.

"If you walk anybody in this park, you're gonna get hurt," said Cubs manager Don Zimmer, echoing the lament of those who've been blown away over the years by Wrigley's wild, wonderful wind.

Meanwhile, Dunston picked up where Sandberg left off Friday, enabling the second baseman to rest before he attempts to break Hack Wilson's 61-year-old Cubs record by homering for the sixth straight game. (Note: Ryno did not break the record, but still shares it with that legendary Hacker.) Dunston suddenly seems to have stopped brooding and started blooming. The slender shortstop credited his daughter Whitney Joi, for the turnabout.

"When I go home and see her, I don't worry about anything," Dunston said.

While Dunston was spreading jubilation among Bleacher Bum refugees, who began saluting him with a handmade "Shawon-O-Meter" to record his batting average, Dawson returned to the dugout with more good news. His wife, Vanessa, had just given birth to a seven-pound, 14-ounce son, Darius de Andre Dawson. Overlooked in Dunston's spree were a pair of singles by sizzling rookie Jerome Walton. The center fielder has hit in 23 straight games, the longest streak for a Cub since 1973.

The good news kept rolling, and so did the Cubs, right into the NL playoffs. Like Walton's batting binge, it was too good to last. The 1989 NL Rookie of the Year demanded a Willie Mays salary, then drifted off into obscurity. Unfortunately, the Cubs beat him to the punch in the NLCS, falling to the Giants in five games.

In pursuit of the last buck from Cub fans eager to pay inflated prices, that series was lengthened to best-of-seven. Still, the ever-versatile Cubs proved that they could revert to form whenever postseason bunting hangs in Wrigley Field. History bears out this sad fact. The Cubs—honest—really did win two straight World Series, right after losing to the Hitless Wonder White Sox in 1906, Chicago's only Crosstown rumble. They had a combined 10-5 record in those three Fall Classics, but then came the real fall, summed up succinctly by Jack Brickhouse: "Any team can have a bad century."

As that wise diamond philosopher, perfesser Casey Stengel noted, "You could look it up." In 10 playoff series scattered throughout the rest of the 20th century, the Cubs played 50 games and lost 38 of them. And since their last World Series in 1945, they're 3-10 in three postseason mismatches—actually 1-10 after winning the first two in that 1984 debacle in San Diego.

But reality never stopped Cub fans from enjoying the struggle to get there, as long as it lasted, May madness through September sadness, year after year. That was especially true in 1989, when Zimmer's go-for-broke style captivated the North Side. Zim and the Cubs who played his daring brand of Z-ball, deserved this season-ending tribute:

Zim Shows Cubs 'Z' Way to Win
(Daily Herald, Oct. 4, 1989)

The way the Cubs won the National League East title was certainly different than the 1969 Cubs, who won only the hearts of Chicago fans before their legendary September swoon. And it was refreshingly different from the way the 1984 Cubs captured their first NL East crown.

This time, even diehards were ready to lip-synch their old lament ("Wait Till Next Year") at the first sign of tight collars in the home dugout. When rotund Herman Franks managed the Cubs in the '70s, it was a familiar script. In those years, the inevitable Cubs fold would blow away the smoke of pennant dreams like a brisk breeze off Lake Michigan cuts the fog shrouding Wrigley Field.

The yearly self-destruction derby was taken in stride by their fans, who have a remarkably high tolerance for pain. Bitter experience had taught them that the Mets, the Braves or an expansion team from Ashtabula, Ohio, would snatch the prize away.

It didn't happen at all in the summer of '89. No pain. No strain.

Even so, manager Don Zimmer's brand of baseball would have been enough by itself to make that season a revelation. Here were the slow, lethargic Cubs, transformed overnight into a bunch of rambling, gambling baserunning bandits.

For generations of Cub fans used to seeing their team shuffle aimlessly from sack to sack, Z-ball was a dazzling sight. He had them stealing, squeezing, pulling off both the hit-and-run and an equally daring variation, the run-and-hit. They took chances and manufactured runs by keeping pressure on the defense.

A buzz of anticipation in the Friendly Confines proved the fans were tuning in and turning on to a new wave of hustling kids, who transformed their manager's brainstorms into tallies. It was an NL clone of Billyball, the way the Oakland A's stole games for volatile Billy Martin. Regardless of the label, the word was excitement.

"Lots of people keep telling me the Cubs play different now," Zimmer said while standing around the batting cage on a sunny afternoon. "All I'm doing is taking advantage of what this team can do."

"We couldn't run or take chances on the bases with the guys we had last year. This isn't a homer-hitting team, so we have to find runs anywhere and everywhere."

The Cubs took Z-word from Zim, usually eking out enough to take a narrow lead into the ninth inning. Instead of watching it vanish, as Cub managers did for decades, Zimmer waved to the bullpen, summoning Mitch Williams. When the left-handed Wild Thing did his thing, Cub fans went wild. The fireballing, free-thinking southpaw put the perfect finishing touch on an astonishing season with a strikeout in Montreal to clinch the division title on Sept. 26.

Those Cubs had as much fun as the fans, even catcher Damon Berryhill, not exactly a clubhouse cut-up. But after sweating off seven pounds while collecting four RBIs on a sweltering July afternoon, Berryhill was a postgame quote machine, wearing a towel and a wide grin in the clubhouse.

"I'll trade the weight for them ribbies anytime," he said. "At this rate, I'll be thinner than Greg Maddux."

Mr. Cub Comes Through

I covered the Cubs on a gorgeous May weekend in 1970. Waiting, along with the rest of jam-packed Wrigley Field, the city of Chicago and suburbs, plus the entire baseball world, for just one thing—actually, one swing.

Ernie Banks didn't hit his 500th homer until a few days later, but I recall the festival feeling every time No. 14 settled into the batter's box. The Bleacher Bums, still glum from the gigantic collapse of '69, were rooting so hard their yellow hard hats almost imploded with tension. Likewise, everywhere else in the ivy-adorned museum Ernie labeled the Friendly Confines. Wrigley will flaunt that label until the wrecking ball slams into the bleachers where so many of his homers nestled.

Now, in my 32nd year of trudging up and down Wrigley ramps, from the old pressbox on the mezzanine to the new one up in the rafters, I still recall the sights and sounds of that weekend. Waiting for Banks to unload No. 500, along with the fans' belief that this—1970, that is—finally would be that great come-and-get-it "Next Year" made it seem like Christmas Eve.

Well, Ernie made it, but the Cubs didn't. Randy Hundley's knee already had been wrecked when the Cards' Carl Warwick slid into him at the plate. Without the Rebel's fiery leadership, both behind the plate and at bat, the Cubs couldn't erase the trauma of 1969, even with a club I looked at as stronger. They finished second again, this time to Pittsburgh, and the Durocher era kept unraveling.

But Banks was still Mr. Cub, then and even now, three decades later. There was a charm and grace about this black man, who did much to erase racial stereotypes, except among a few morons. So, even when Banks didn't join the 500-homer club on that weekend, Cub fans figured it wouldn't be long coming.

They were right. I flipped on my black and white TV on Tuesday, May 12, to watch an inning before heading to my assigned shift on the *Tribune*'s sports copy desk. Up stepped Banks in the second inning, running the count to 1-1 on Atlanta's Pat Jarvis.

The Braves' right-hander then served up a letter-high fast ball, and I started reaching for my coat.

Boom! Even before Barks' historic homer bounced in and out of the left-field bleachers, I was on the phone with my editor, Dave Moylan. "I'm on my way to Wrigley Field," I told him. Dave, a sharp cookie, needed no explanation.

When I walked into the pressbox, Chuck Shriver, the Cubs' capable PR guy, already was knee-deep in phone messages and postgame plans, with a media horde descending on the Cubs clubhouse. Figuring it was time to lighten the load, I asked, "Anything happen yet?" Chuck chuckled appreciatively. Despite leaden skies and chilly temperatures, it was party time in Wrigleyville. When the game ended, I went to work producing this story, known in the newspaper business as a sidebar, although the *Tribune's* indelicate term for such stories was "sniff," as in dressing room odors.

Take No. 500 to the Banks
(Chicago Tribune, May 13, 1970)

"When he, hit it, I didn't think it was going in," Phil Regan said.

He was talking, of course, about the shot heard around Wrigley Field, Chicago, the National League, the United States and the whole beautiful universe inhabited by that beautiful man, Ernie Banks, the 500th home run of Ernie's illustrious career.

Regan, the eventual winning pitcher, had a good seat in the Cubs' bullpen when Ernie connected. His estimate that the liner would hit the left field wall was wrong, to the immense relief of the reliever.

Billy Williams, the left-handed Sweet Swinger who teamed with Banks to give the Cubs a 1-2 punch from both sides of the plate for 17 years, couldn't conceal his awe at the feat. "You have to remember that Ernie got most of his homers when the Cubs didn't have many hitters," Williams said. "In those days, he only got one pitch to hit."

Banks was pinned in a corner by microphones, cameras and hordes of people, asking the same questions over and over.

"We should have had some champagne to pour on him," said Ron Santo.

A familiar, favorite Wrigley Field scene. Billy Williams trots plateward after a 1970 homer against those villainous Mets, with Ernie Banks (14) and Glenn Beckert waiting to glad-hand the Sweet Swinger.

Fergie Jenkins won 20 games for six straight seasons (1967-72). Yet, because his team saw no postseason action, the Cubs right-hander got overlooked, so author Bob Logan dubbed him "The Unknown Winner." Jenkins finally earned his reward, a berth in the Hall of Fame.

Manager Leo Durocher, who played with Babe Ruth in the 1920s, managed to conceal the envy he felt about the fans' affection for Banks.

"I'm glad that was a shot," quoth Leo the Lip. "I didn't want him to get No. 500 on a ball the wind took out of the park."

How did Durocher, a New York kind of guy, adjust to managing a Chicago institution like Banks?

"You just put him at first base every day," he replied. "I first retired him in 1966, when I played everybody in sight. Ernie got tired of it and took over again.

"I thought for sure he'd get the 500th for the big Mother's Day crowd. It's Ernie's day, too—he always homers on Sunday."

The waiting game ended when Banks drilled Jarvis' pitch. The historic homer bounced back onto the field, so Braves left fielder Rico Carty tossed it to the home bullpen, where Fergie Jenkins took protective custody.

"I touched a milestone," Jenkins chuckled. "Ernie's swing is back in the groove."

It took relief pitcher Regan to put Banks' blast in perspective.

"He's an inspiration to the rookies and the older guys, too," Regan said. "We complain about the travel conditions, and then we see Ernie lifting everybody up. All he wants to do is play ball.

"What a man."

The sparse crowd of 5,264 got a happy ending when Williams' ninth-inning homer tied the game and Santo's bases-loaded single in the 11th won it for the Cubs, 4-3. Another moment to remember happened in the top of the 11th, when Hank Aaron drew an intentional walk.

"I know where Aaron is when he is on first base," Durocher said of his decision not to let the Braves basher break up the game.

So Aaron trotted to first, extending a congratulatory hand to Banks. There they stood, the owners of a combined 1,068 home runs and 5,528 base hits. Pitchers everywhere shuddered at the sight. I had conversations with Hammerin' Hank and easy-does-it Ernie over the years. A couple of polite gentlemen, they sometimes acted a little skittish when writers they didn't know joined the postgame circle that usually surrounded these superstars. I had no idea that my respect for Banks and Aaron was not shared by everybody, so I sometimes wondered about that.

When Aaron retired and talked about the bags of hate mail he got for breaking Babe Ruth's home run record, I was sickened and disgusted, like most fans. Even Banks, one of Chicago's favorite sons, got his share of death threats. Pondering how they performed so well for so long under that kind of pressure gave me mixed feelings of pride and shame.

Anyway, Banks always called me "Mr. Logan," even when he wrote the foreword for one of my books about the Cubs. I should have been calling him "Mr. Banks."

Can't Anybody Manage This Game?

I finally figured out that the Cubs have gone through 19 managers in my 32 years of writing about them and trying to figure out why anybody would want that thankless job. Even without the two-game tenure of John Vukovich in 1986 and a one-night stand for Joe Altobelli four years later, that's a very short dugout tenure. The list, with thumbnail sketches:

Leo Durocher (some kind of ego); Whitey Lockman (not a lock); Jim Marshall (nice guy finishes last); Herman Franks ("You saw it—you write it"); Joe Amalfitano (the writers' pal); Preston Gomez (Mr. Anonymous); Lee Elia (Mr. Mt. Vesuvius); Charlie Fox (Herman's henchman); Jim Frey (San Diego, 0-3); John Vukovich (a .500 guy—1-1); Gene "Stick" Michael (didn't stick around); Frank Lucchesi (the forgotten man); Don Zimmer (Z-ball's Grade A); Joe Altobelli (with Roy "Hardrock" Johnson, the only Cubs manager never to win a game); Jim Essian (who?); Jim Lefebvre (live wire); Tom Trebelhorn (struck out); Jim Riggleman (nice guy backs into playoffs); Don Baylor (jury still out).

I can't imagine how many times I heard these guys chant the cliche of every coach or manager from Abner Doubleday and on down the years: "That was a big win for us."

Manager Don Baylor survived a rocky debut in 2000, but now has the Cubs climbing back into contention.

Very few of them ever admitted "That was a big loss," but Don Zimmer was an exception to every rule of the managerial fraternity. That's why he was fun to talk with, and especially to watch rolling the dice from the dugout. But fun was not the leadoff hitter for Cub fans in that dreary stretch from Durocher to Jim Frey. At least Frey's Cubs ended a 39-year playoff drought by winning the NL East in 1984, setting ecstatic fans up for that lost weekend in San Diego. Most years, winning 1 of 3 on the road would have been a happy trip for the Cubs.

But in what could be the all-time irony for this quixotic franchise, that's all the 1984 Cubs needed to assure a Wrigley Field World Series against the Detroit Tigers, an emotional rematch from 1945. Personally, I don't believe frustrated fans blamed Leon Durham's Gatorade-soaked glove for that final foldup in Jack Murphy Stadium. The real diehards can't forget the Billy Goat hex that hangs over their heroes. The omen of playoff calamity.

The Cubs should have had the home field advantage in 1984, but because Wrigley Field lights did not turn on until four years later, the weekend games went to San Diego. Would Tim Flannery's routine grounder have eluded Durham's soggy mitt in Wrigley Field? Would ace Rick Sutcliffe have blown a 3-0 lead in the Friendly Confines? Would Frey have been hung in effigy by fans for sticking with the exhausted Sutcliffe too long? Frey not?

Frey could equal anyone's profane tirade. Lee Elia holds the hyphenated-word record among Cubs managers for the way he strung them together and laid them on Cubs fans after his team got a few well-deserved rounds of boos for another dreary Wrigley Field loss. Elia, one of the last four-lettermen—in sports, not epithets— in his Philadelphia-area prep days, outdid even those short-fused Philly fans when he unloaded four-letter phrases in the Cubs clubhouse on April 29, 1983. Using up a six-month supply of the bleeps John McEnroe employed to describe the eyesight of tennis umpires, Elia almost talked himself out of a job on the spot.

Crusty Cub boss Dallas Green was ready to swing the ax when sportscaster (and Chicago's facts champ) Les Grobstein played the Elia tape for him. It was more fun than Nixon's White House tapes, but Elia didn't last out that season. So ended the Green-Elia love-in that began when Green hired his former Phillies' coach after the Cubs wound up a dismal 38-65 in the strike-split 1981 season.

"Dallas and I have the same basic (i.e., tough) approach and we holler at each other a lot," Elia told me. "I can't match him for toughness, because if you beat his logic, he outyells you."

"Lee will get after anybody who deserves it," Green responded. He will change the thinking of this club—not overnight, but it will happen."

It finally did happen on Green's watch, but Frey had replaced Elia when George Orwell's vision of "1984" unfolded to rave reviews on the North Side, with Dallas cast in the role of Big Brother.

Cub fans are sadly aware that back-to-back championships happened for this fragile franchise happened only once—1906–07–08. In the modern era, only a dose of LSD could induce such fantasies as three straight World Series trips for the Cubs. Since they moved into Weeghman Park in 1916 (it's been Wrigley Field since 1926), what few recall is that the pennant-winning Cubs of 1918 played all three Chicago Series games in Comiskey Park. They (what else?) lost to Boston, dropping the opener to a young Red Sox lefty named Babe Ruth, 1-0.

At least the Cubs are consistent. If that's not grim enough for you, consider this:

The 1909 Cubs, who finished second in the NL, a half-game behind pennant-winning Pittsburgh, had a better record (104-49, .680) than the 1910 Cubs (104-50, .675), who finished first, only to get steamrolled in a five-game World Series by Connie Mack's Philadelphia A's. Franklin "Home Run" Baker of the A's propelled two out of the park in that dead-ball season—only 64 less than Sammy Sosa launched in 1998.

As proof positive that time heals all wounds (or is that "time wounds all heels?"), Cub fans no longer lament that winning 104 games in 1909 wasn't enough to extend their run of NL supremacy. One bunch of diehards keeps track of games since the '08 Cubs made Ty Cobb fit to be tied with their last World Series triumph. The total gets updated on a Sheffield Avenue wall, across the street from where right-field bleacherites worship at the shrine of St. Sammy.

That's why true Cub fans know another new manager won't make much difference. Hard-as-nails Elia or soft-as-summer sunshine on the ivy-covered walls Riggleman, it matters not. For every shining moment, a thousand points of gloom arise to jinx, hex or hassle the Cubs to the back of the NL pack.

Few Cub managers are as much fun as Zimmer—certainly not no-nonsense Don Baylor. A fierce competitor, Zimmer's love for the game got through to Cub fans. They feel the same way when the game is played right in Wrigley Field, and even more on the rare occasions when it's played there in the postseason. Wrigley's quixotic blend of sun and wind—especially wind—makes crazy things happen, like on May 17, 1979, when the Cubs trailed, 21-9, rallied to tie, and (guess what) lost 23-22 on (guess who?) Mike Schmidt's 10th-inning homer. It was the highest-scoring game in the majors since Aug. 25, 1922, when those same Cubs almost blew a 25-6 lead before hanging on to outlast those same Phils 26-23 in (guess where?) that same Wrigley wind tunnel.

No matter which giant brain sat in the front office or on the dugout hot seat, the Cubs found a way to fold down the stretch. They did it again in 2001, despite a flurry of moves by Andy MacPhail, after demoting himself to the GM slot, and tough-it-out manager Don Baylor. The backstage bickering, which left popular pitching coach Oscar Acosta jobless at the end was tiresomely familiar, too. Acosta actually induced Cubs pitchers to resemble big-leaguers, but the Cubs' curse or hex or death wish or all of the above made him a marked man.

The whole bewildering business got summed up by ex-manager Jim Frey, soon to become ex-general manager Jim Frey, in these two dispatches from the Cubs' maze of mismanagement:

Frey, Zim on the Griddle
(Baseball Bulletin, April 1988)

Jim Frey and Don Zimmer must cook up a winning recipe.
Zim will be french-Freyed, along with poison-pen ivy from
Wrigley's bleachers if the Jim and Zim Show can't concoct a tasty

Wrigley Field was not sold out for every game in 1982, the first year of Dallas Green's "Building a New Tradition" regime. Still, attendance skyrocketed that season, setting off an attendance boom that built a new generation of Cub fans.

dish of contending Cubs. Barring an influx of White Sox fans, this is the year when lights will shine on the gum tycoon's ballpark, where the Cubs gum it up annually. New Cub GM Frey and his buddy, Don Zimmer, saw how the Dallas Green regime disintegrated after the 1984 playoff fiasco. They need to mollify the fans with something better, and better yet quicker, than those never-ending, mythical 5, 50 or 500-year rebuilding plans.

Who knows? If the Cubs hadn't choked in San Diego, the reign of King Dallas I might have lasted longer than that unholy Roman umpire, Ron Luciano. Frey sat there in the dugout, watching Red Baron Rick Sutcliffe go down in flames in that frightful fifth playoff game. He'll need better judgment as GM than he displayed as manager.

New Faces, Old Results
(Daily Herald, July 12, 1989)

Jim Frey was close to a deal with another National League GM not long ago. Why didn't it happen?

"It always comes down to the same thing," Frey said. "They want Greg Maddux or another young pitcher for whatever they're willing to give up. In this job, there's constant pressure to react to what happened in today's game.

"For me to look at it the way the fans and media do would be a big mistake. When the Cubs lose two in a row, the fans are down and the papers make it read like the end of the world. My No. 1 priority was moving some of the older guys. Then I could start trying to rebuild (ah, there's that word again) the pitching staff with young prospects."

So, one by one, familiar faces Jody Davis, Leon Durham, Keith Moreland and other disappeared. While Frey was a rookie mogul (in 1988), pitchers Rick Sutcliffe and Scott Sanderson were large injury question marks and youngsters Maddux and Jamie Moyer had not yet blossomed.

Frey's notion of "building" was to ship both Moyer and Rafael Palmiero, destined to be one of baseball's most prolific power hitters, to Texas in a deal that produced some transitory bullpen bolstering from another in the endless parade of Cubs characters. Mitch "Wild Thing" Williams, an erratic lefty, helped them win the NL East with 36 saves in 1989, but soon faded to end his checkered career with the Phillies by serving the gopher ball to another ex-Cub, Toronto's Joe Carter (now Chip Caray's TV sidekick), that ended the 1993 World Series.

At least Williams got into one. Like every other Cub GM since Jim Gallagher in 1945, Frey couldn't, so he was replaced in 1991 by Larry Himes, who was to charisma what Michael Jordan is to retirement. Himes batted .000 in the communications league, but close to .500 in the horse-trade arena. With the tacit approval of his tight-fisted Tribune Co. bosses, he let Greg Maddux flee to Atlanta after the budding superstar won 20 games with a 2.18 ERA in 1992.

In fairness to Himes, he stole Sammy Sosa from the White Sox for used-to-be slugger George Bell and never-was pitcher Ken Patterson on March 30, 1992. Sosa's decade of dominance since then stamps that trade as the antithesis of Lou Brock for Ernie Broglio, the infamous 1964 Cub giveaway. Still, the Good Guys I've dealt with for three-plus years of trying to sort through Cub confusion are mostly good men or good kids, in the case of Lou Boudreau and his broadcast partner, Vince Lloyd, two of the best.

Sorry, Joe, You're No Ryno

This won't sit well with Joe Morgan fans, and especially with Joe Morgan, but he's only the second-best second baseman I ever saw. My No. 1 keystone sacker? Who else could it Dee, but Ryne Dee Sandberg? Sure, the Morgan–Sandberg career numbers give one or the other a clear edge, according to fans swayed by stats, but I've never been one of those. I saw Ryno do what he did so smoothly and so well for so long that I'll make him a first-ballot Hall of Fame pick when he's eligible.

I take my yearly vote from the Baseball Writers Association of America for a berth in Cooperstown very seriously. Sandberg's credentials deserve a plaque on his first try. For example:

Ryno's Fine
(Daily Herald, Aug. 21, 1993)

Ryne Sandberg's flying feet performed quite a feat.

That's because they were getting messages Friday from the brain of one of the few Cubs who could respond affirmatively to Casey Stengel's plaintive wail: "Can't anybody here play this game?"

Sandberg can and still does, even though he's less than a month away from his 34th birthday. The Cubs' peerless second baseman paused en route to the Hall of Fame to show the young whippersnappers how it's done.

Ryno's 3 for 5 at the plate was window dressing for a comeback 6-5 victory over Atlanta. What the canny veteran did after reaching base—charging like an enraged rhino to steal a pair of runs from the startled Braves—made the difference.

For openers, Sandberg scored all the way from first on Mark Grace's fifth-inning single to put the Cubs up 2-1. Left fielder Ron Gant slipped to one knee, so heads-up baserunning on the hit converted a stolen base into a pilfered run. For his featured act, Sandberg scored from third base on a pop fly to Atlanta second baseman Mark Lemke, beating the throw home with a nifty hook side.

"When Lemke didn't throw right away, I put my head down and went for it," Sandberg said after turning Derrick May's wind-blown pop into a sacrifice fly.

That's Hall of Fame stuff, but Sandberg did such things for years without being noticed, because he played for what *Tribune* columnist Bob Verdi used to call the "Little Blue Bicycle," instead of Morgan's "Big Red Machine."

In 1989, the next California playoff collapse saw a different scenario—San Francisco this time. The Cubs left their hits in the city by the bay, while their fans drowned disappointment by riding a cable car to Fisherman's Wharf and scarfing down stone crabs and Anchor Steam beer at DiMaggio's restaurant.

Resilient as always, those true blue believers didn't chase the blues by cannonballing into San Francisco Bay. The 2001 fade will not induce them to jump off the Michigan Avenue bridge, either, despite the realization that frustration is their lot in life.

The Cubs being the Cubs, it happened as regularly as either Mayor Daley's annual real-estate tax hike. They backed out of the 1998 NL playoffs almost as fast as they backed in, an appropriate epitaph for a century that opened with two world championships in the first decade and zero since then.

Regardless, Cub fans keep returning like swallows to Capistrano, swallowing their hunger for at least one World Series triumph in the 21st century. They'd prefer it over the White Sox in centennial overdue revenge for a 1906 humiliation by those Hitless Wonders.

In all honesty, the Cubs haven't always been pitchlesss—or punchless—wonders themselves. Since I came on the scene, sluggers Ernie Banks and Billy Williams, along with perennial 20-game winner Fergie Jenkins, have gone into the Hall of Fame. Ryne Sandberg and Sammy Sosa are on the fast track to Cooperstown, and so is Kerry Wood—if his ailing arm lets him fulfill that bright promise.

One day the Cubs will win it all. I hope it happens while they're still playing at Wrigley Field.

Kerry Wood be the Greatest, If Only . . .

Yes, he Wood. But it's not Kerry Wood's ferocious fast ball that I root for (silently, of course; after all, *No Cheering in the Press Box* was the title of a book by Jerome Joltzman, dean of Chicago baseball writers.) I'm impressed by the way this young right-hander won't give in to adversity, despite racking up more misfortune that strikeouts in his brief, brilliant career. I wasn't working the day of his 20-K spectacular, but I've seen Kerry pitch well on days when his arm, elbow and shoulder throb almost visibly.

Even so, Wood won't admit to feeling sorry for himself. In an age when whining over petty misfortune was becoming the new national pastime, at least until the shock of September 11, 2001, restored our perspective, Wood is a role model. Like millions of us with mundane jobs, he does his quietly and well.

He's Still Special K
(Daily Herald, July 27, 1998)

For a while Sunday, it looked like Kerry Wood wouldn't.

But even when Wood isn't at his best, he's still The Best. And even when Sammy Sosa is mired in somewhat of a slump, he's still The Beast, whether the Wrigley Field whirlwind blows in or out.

So an almost-mortal Wood and still-struggling Sosa gave the Cubs a vital 3-1 victory over the New York Mets, reopening their NL wild-card gap.

(Daily Herald, July 22, 2000)

This outing wasn't exactly a walk in the park for Kerry Wood.

That's because the Comeback Kid walked the ballpark. The flamethrowing right-hander was all over the place, missing the plate with 55 of his 113 pitches while issuing five walks in six struggling innings. Still recovering from elbow surgery, Wood got some unexpected help from Brewers batters lunging at pitches in spots when he couldn't find the plate with a compass.

"Wood was uncomfortable, but he still has the explosive fast ball," said Cubs manager Don Baylor. "Every start, he might strike out 15."

No wonder Wood ranks right behind Sosa in Cub fans' all-hero lineups.

2001: Another One of Those "Next Years"

The Cubs made things exciting, before exiting the NL play-off race. This is a recording. But a team that wasn't supposed to contend proved it wasn't a contender. Despite finishing 30—count 'em—30 games behind the Cards' cakewalk to the NL Central crown in a dismal 63-99 managerial debut for Baylor, the groundwork for '01 actually happened in '00. Here's how:

Baylor-ing Out the Cubs?
(Daily Herald, April 13, 2000)

Don Baylor never worked for those Wall Street stock hucksters who tried to tell us that everybody listens when they talk. But when Baylor talks, it seems the Cubs are listening hard, and playing the same way.

The Cubs limped home this week after a horrendous 2-6 start, with even their most rabid fans resigned to a new season that looks suspiciously like their old half-century of futility. Even so, new manager Baylor didn't don the frustrated frown worn so often by Jim Riggleman, his deposed predecessor.

"Cub fans think differently," Baylor said. "They expect to lose, and they come out to Wrigley Field asking each other, 'What's going to go wrong today?' I'm trying to get away from that."

A year later, Baylor did. Wrigley hysteria bloomed in June, 2001, when front-runners jammed the bandwagon to fantasize over weekends like this:

Elation, Then Frustration
(Daily Herald, June 8, 2001)

This has to be 1969, only rewritten with a happy ending. Or perhaps 1945, when the Cubs—honest, they did—played in the World Series.

Maybe supreme optimists, meaning virtually all Cubs fans, can create a time warp back to 1908 when they not only got into the World Series, but won it. Any flight of fancy will suffice, after the way the Cubs wrapped up Thursday's Wrigley Field sweep over the St. Louis Cards. For those who believe in destiny, fate or just plain witchcraft, this 4-3 comeback victory in the 10th inning was the Cubs' 15th in their last 16 games.

The last time the Cubs went on a 15-1 tear was July 3-16, 1945. Can it be that the law of averages, null and void on the North Side for 56 years, finally sprang back to life in 2001, just like the Cubs?

"A team of destiny?" manager Don Baylor pondered, rolling the question across his mind like one of those snap dugout decisions he has to make with a game on the line. "I don't jump that far ahead."

It's a good thing Baylor didn't see the onrushing September swoon in his crystal ball. Another rocky road, one more Cub cave-in to add to the pile and an injury-riddled trail of what-ifs for Cub fans to spend the lonely winter with. It's time for a new Cub outlook, so I cheerfully although far from confidently, propose this one:

"Wait till this year."

Like lots of longtime Cubwatchers, I was not surprised by the season-ending turmoil that became the big story in 2001. It's all part of this endless diamond opera on the North Side. The firing of Acosta and the near-revolt by the pitchers he helped to make the Cubs overnight contenders is just the latest chapter. Will manager Don Baylor ride out the storm? Will anxious Cub fans pack Wrigley Field again, hoping against history? Will the Cubs ever play another World Series in the Friendly Confines?

You betchum, Red Ryder. If this generation of Cub fans doesn't see it, the next one will. Or the one after that. Or . . .

2

Sox Appeal:
The White Stuff

White Sox fans are hard-edged realists, in sharp contrast to the dewy-eyed optimism Cub fans refuse to lose, even though the diehard team refuses to win. They've seen their unfair share of losing on the South Side, too, but supporters don't suffer in silence. They loved the real Comiskey Park, dislike—and often stay away from—its replacement:

Their reputation as grouchy brawlers, a hangover (pun intended) that still hangs over since McCuddy's saloon, just across 35th Street, always had a between-innings brew for Babe Ruth. The Bambino reportedly trotted over to quench his gargantuan thirst, and Sox fans appreciated that. Then, as now, they know baseball as few others do and love the game, minus Wrigley Field frills, as much as Cub fans. That's why it's been with us since the Civil War, through World War I and a lot of smaller ones, still providing some needed diversion from new threats to our way of life.

Those who love this American game that spread around the world understand why. Baseball is a bridge, binding generations together. Besides, it's fun. Writing and reading should be, too. The game will survive owners and players screeching at each other, and even the media, boring us to death with excruciating details of every $100 million-plus contract. Ogden Nash, a wonderful, whimsical poet, and fan, told us what baseball is in a few unforgettable lines. When Bill Veeck's St. Louis Browns shifted to Baltimore in 1953, the Orioles, a broken link in the chain of tradition, got mended. Nash spoke for Baltimore and fans everywhere:

> Wee Willie Keeler runs through the town
> All along Charles Street in his nightgown
> Belling like a hound dog gathering the pack
> "Hey, Wilbert Robinson, the Orioles are back!!"

For those unaware who Willie ("I hit 'em where they ain't") Keeler was, or ditto for Wilbert Robinson, beloved manager of the Daffy Dodgers in the 1920s, I feel sorry. When I realize how many of those priceless memories have been blotted out by junk TV, rap and rock, raunchy movies, video games and other modern marvels. I feel sorry for myself.

Thankfully, an unbroken tradition of American League baseball on the south side of Chicago is into its second century. I'm glad, because that kind of permanence ended for me when the real Athletics—not the Oakland mopes in the softball suits—left Philadelphia in 1954. Those pin-striped finks, the Yankees, wanted their own farm team in Kansas City, so they yanked Connie Mack's team from its roots—Shibe Park.

Fortunately, that didn't happen in Chicago. The Sox still operate semi-successfully in what we all know is a Cubs and Bears town. Too bad some old-line Sox fans can't stop yearning for the bygone era of Bill Veeck's Go-Go guys.

Personally, I'm a Veeck fan—always will be. I also believe that if Sox chairman Jerry Reinsdorf wanted to move the Sox to some Florida dome or elsewhere, the franchise would have been gone. But the Sox are still here.

That treasure of good memories, mostly about bad teams, gets passed along from mom and dad and grandparents to kids who will grow up to be lifelong White Sox fans. Even the adults, sitting at home and sulking, still root for them as much as Cub fans do for their adorable also-rans.

Sure, the upper deck at Comiskey Park II is too steep, and it lacks the broken-down charm of Comiskey Park I. Regardless, some of my most enjoyable moments, like the ones in this chapter happened in both Comiskey Parks since I started covering the Sox in 1970.

Babe Yanks Our Sox Off

So what if—as legend has it—that Babe Ruth had a brewski or twoski at McCuddy's, in the shadow of old Comiskey Park? T(R)uth is, all of the Yankees have driven White Sox fans to drink lots more over the years.

They found many ways to torment, torture, terrorize, topple and just plain slug the Sox silly than any other AL foe. On the South Side, contenders become pretenders when the Yankees came to town, despite the managerial savvy Senor Al Lopez could employ, or how many well-pitched games Billy Pierce could muster.

I came to Chicago fully aware of these sad facts of AL life, because the Yankees did it to my team, the A's, blighting my otherwise cheerful boyhood in Philadelphia. So I wrote this story from reality, based on many maddening memories. It rang a bell with a lot of Chicagoans, too. Among the people who sent notes after they read it, all saying, "Yes, we remember it well," were alderman Bernie Epton, who later gave the original Mayor Daley a good run for the job, and Tommy King, then president of the Merchandise Mart:

Pinstripes Lack Sox Appeal
(Chicago Tribune, May 5, 1973)

In case you were yearning for the Bad Old Days, they made a comeback of sorts here last night.

You remember the Bad Old Days. The White Sox would be frisking around the American League, giving a convincing imitation of pennant contenders. Then the Yankees came to town for a weekend series and the bubble burst like a punctured balloon.

Their names didn't matter, starting with Ruth and running through Mantle. They left Comiskey Park a shambles, the pennant dream a nightmare and Sox fans sobbing softly into their suds. A lot has happened to the Bad Guys since their mid-'60s glory era ended, most of it depressing enough to satisfy the most rabid Yankee-hater. Imagine the haughty Bronx Bombers, not only finishing last, but playing second fiddle to Charlie Tuna commercials on the TV network that owned them. Sweet revenge for those years of humiliation by a bunch that beat you and crushed your spirit with the same insolent ease.

A whole generation of kids in Chicago and other AL cities has since grown up without the catharsis of blaming the Yankees for all their troubles, real or imaginary. The new order arising from the demise of the Big Apple's baseball bullies has a more colorful look.

There's Oakland Green and Gold, Kansas City Black and Chicago White and Green. The White Sox are beginning to rake in some of that green money they used to get as a consolation prize for losing to the Yanks before a packed house.

The mob started gathering early last night. Even without the accordion solo offered by the collapsible Dan Ryan Expressway, the pregame traffic jam was bad. With it, the crush around the park was a Yankee Doodle Dandy, some fans filing into their seats too late to see the Sox send a two-run greeting to their ex-tormentors in the first inning.

As long-suffering survivors of Yankee clippings recall, however, that meant nothing. Ted Lyons or Dick Donovan or somebody would go into the ninth inning nursing a 2-1 lead, with Comiskey fans dreaming of a Pale Hose October.

Then one of those finks in the gray suits would steal first base, and up would step Ruth or Gehrig or Dickey or DiMag or Keller or Henrich or Lindell or Howard or Bauer or Tresh or Berra or Mantle or somebody. It didn't matter, because you knew what was going to happen.

Boom!

Charlie Brown said it for all of us while trudging wearily off the mound after serving up the fatal tomato ball: "Some seasons, it doesn't pay to get up at all."

Well, that's the way it used to be. This is the way it is now—the all-conquering Big White Machine brushing aside the lowly Yankees, rumbling toward its rendezvous with destiny and/or the Cubs in the World Series.

Right, Sox fans? So how come you guys were hiding under the bed during the ninth inning?

For Sox fans, at least since 1959, they've had few happy endings. Their team gave away a pennant in 1968, welcomed back Bill Veeck to prove losing can be fun, jammed creaking old Comiskey to salute the South Side Hit Men in 1977 and faded from the AL playoffs fast in 1983, 1993 and again in 2000.

Still, the decades between those brief, shining moments had their high spots, too. Lots of intriguing characters strutted and fretted on the South Side stage, providing more Shakespearean drama, and comedy, fun and frustration than Sox fans could shake a spear at. More than once, the franchise was in danger of fleeing to Seattle, Denver, Milwaukee or St. Petersburg, only to get pulled bark from the precipice just in time.

For me, Chicago sports without the White Sox would be like Dec. 25 dinner without a traditional side dish—that Christmas potato, the Ida-Ho-Ho-Ho. The first year I was on the beat, 1970, the Sox lost 106 games, and almost became a rumor instead of a reality.

But the tough, blue-collar bungalow belters who became the backbone of Sox fandom never lost their affection for them, even though they had nowhere near the tolerance for losers that's the trademark of Cub fans. Like their rooters, the Sox somehow hung in there, beating the odds, if not most opponents, to lurch into the 21st Century with a wait-and-see attitude.

It's always been fascinating for me to watch baseball teams reflect the attitudes and personalities of their managers. Don Gutteridge, the nice guy who finished last in 1970 but couldn't finish out that calamitous campaign, was succeeded by my favorite Sox skipper, and one of the best people in any sport. That's Charles William Tanner, who had to go back to his native Pennsylvania to manage a World Series winner in Pittsburgh, after proving to be a big winner in Chicago.

They could have cast Chuck Tanner as the lead in "Hondo." A tough guy who could—and did—pin recalcitrant players up against clubhouse walls, he also was a good guy. The way be brought the Sox back from that 1970 abyss would have been enough by itself, but he did it with style and a media-friendly approach. Tanner's cheerful outlook, mental toughness and managerial skill brought reluctant fans back to Comiskey Park, although signing slugger Dick/Richie Allen in 1972 certainly didn't hurt.

The Sox made an astonishing 23-game turnabout, from 56-106 in 1970 to 79-83 in '71, Tanner's first full year at the helm, and to 20 games over .500 at 87-67 in '73. Though they could get no closer, the Tanner regime was a resounding success, especially with quixotic crowd-pleaser Allen around. Booed out of Philadelphia, temperamental Richie/Dick could be a charmer when he chose. Or not.

When Allen was with the Cards, I once walked up to him in the Wrigley Field visitors' clubhouse to ask about the game-winning hit he had just stroked against the Cubs. Allen said not a word. He just spun on his heel and stalked away.

But things were different when the Sox gave him a chance to salvage his career. Besides electrifying Comiskey crowds, with monster shots like the liner Allen rocketed into the centerfield bleachers, almost knocking broadcaster Harry Caray into the shower he was giving Sox fans, he brought a near-dead franchise back to life.

So did Tanner, somehow turning a nondescript, error-prone team into a winner. Sox fans responded, with attendance zooming from less than 500,000 in 1970 to well over a million for three straight years.

That Tanner blend of charm and combative spirit did the trick. For instance:

(Chicago Tribune, June 11, 1971)

CLEVELAND—Manager Chuck Tanner's watchword ever since he took over the No-Go Sox late last season has been patience. After the proverbial truck backed up to haul away most of last year's roster, he's letting the kids learn the hard way.

"We traded away 50 years of experience for young players," Tanner repeats at every White Sox stop around the American League. "We're making mistakes, but as long as they hustle, I'll stick with them.

Mistakes are not in short supply, with mental miscues outnumbering physical fumbles. That's saying a lot. Through their first 50 games, Tanner's troops had been charged with a staggering (pun intended) total of 65 errors against 26 for the opposition. Nobody seems to be listening to a voice from the past despite his impressive credentials. Coach Luke Appling, the Hall of Famer who batted .310 in 20 seasons for the Sox, led the AL at .388 in 1936, the highest average ever for a shortstop.

"They get too much batting practice," Appling replied when asked if extra swings might cure the Sox habit of leaving runners on base in clutch situations.

"Everybody's trying to hit home runs," Old Aches and Pains added, warming to his subject. "The main thing is to make the pitcher throw strikes. Tanner took them through the fundamentals this spring, from the plate all the way around the bases. When I was a rookie, you were only told once."

Luke was not a media creature, no doubt because TV cameras were unknown in his day. Even postgame quotes in the newspapers didn't take hold until the 1940s, because baseball writers painted the picture with only their trusty typewriters. But if you wanted to know how to foul off a pitch—Appling's speciality; he once did it 16 straight times—or anything else about baseball, he could, and would, enlighten you. I was traveling with the White Sox when they went to Cooperstown in 1970, to play as part of the salute to Lou Boudreau's Hall of Fame inaugural. When the team plane landed in Utica, after a day game in Detroit, we headed to

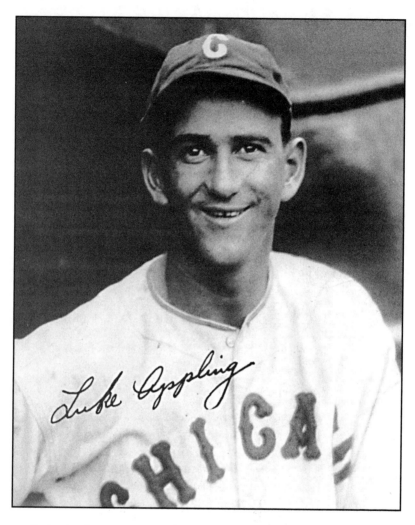

*Luke Appling was a Sox fixture at shortstop from 1930 to 1950.
Along the way, despite daily aches and pain, plus a knack for driving pitchers crazy by fouling off their best stuff, Appling became a
walking diamond museum. He could talk baseball all day—and
often did.*

Cooperstown by bus, a 50-mile jaunt. Appling sat next to me and talked baseball all the way. I've been kicking myself for not having a tape recorder ever since, because his stories about Ty Cobb, Babe Ruth, Zeke Bonura and dozens of other characters were a riot.

All Luke lacked was Tanner's charisma. The South Side's Good Humor Man scored more than his team on this visit to the North Side:

Chuck's Lip Not Zipped; Leo's Is
(Chicago Tribune, June 25, 1971)

Charlie Bustle, Chicago's answer to Cincinnati's Charlie Hustle, was working harder than Pete Rose, and having lots more fun, before his White Sox tackled the Cubs yesterday in Wrigley Field. "I'm enjoying every minute of it," said manager Chuck Tanner, the beaming boss of the suddenly-sizzling South Siders. He obviously enjoyed being in the middle, surrounded by a mob of reporters, TV and radio types, Cub players and coaches, fans and assorted hangers-on.

Impressive, especially in contrast to his opposite number. Cubs manager Leo Durocher was spotted on the left field bullpen bench two hours before game time, talking with a TV newsman. Otherwise, the Lip was zipped, taking no part in pregame socializing between Chicago players. Tanner held court along the first base line, chuckling at boos from early-arriving Cub fans.

In between the tempestuous Allen's antics, including a brief "retirement," Tanner lacked enough talent on his roster to get far in the AL. He did have portly knuckleballer Wilbur Wood, a durable lefty with wall-to-wall class. In my first year on the Sox beat, Wood lost both ends of a double header, pitching in relief. I was young and dumb enough to walk up to Wood in the Sox clubhouse after the nightcap and ask, with what I hoped was a light touch, "Wilbur, ever lose two in one day before?"

I learned later that tough guys like Doug "Red Rooster" Rader and Jim Fregosi took a friendly smile as a personal affront after a loss. Woodie, thankfully, seldom had mayhem on his mind, even under such adverse conditions.

"Not that I can remember," he replied.

It's easy to see why Wil-bah (what Red Sox fans called him in Fenway Park, right across the Charles River from his Bah-ston suburb, near Hah-vad Yard) was a media favorite. He won 20 games for the lowly Sox four straight years (1971-74), a feat as remarkable as Ferguson Jenkins' six-pack of 20-game years (1967-72) for the Cubs. So it was fun to see Woodie's knuckler tie batters in knots, like this:

Wood Wilbur? Yes, 1-0
(Chicago Tribune, Aug. 6, 1971)

ANAHEIM Cal., Aug. 5—They snickered when the White Sox started throwing the ball around earlier this season like it was radioactive. They snorted with derision while Chuck Tanner's athletes made errors at a frantic clip, giving away games in the process.

But the Sox wiped the butter off their fingers tonight, backing Wilbur Wood's pitching with first-rate defense. Wood did the rest, outdueling Clyde Wright to blank the California Angels 1-0. This was a throwback classic between southpaws, recalling the times before moon rockets and tape-measure homers.

"You just pitch a game like that hitter by hitter, inning by inning, and hope for the best," Wood said.

Hope wasn't enough for Sox fans, and especially Sox managers, until Tony La Russa came along in 1979. After generations of seat-of-the-pants managers like Kid Gleason, Jimmy Dykes and Paul Richards, he was the first New Age, button-down, computer-oriented, briefcase-toting CEO to run the club. Because La Russa was not one of those Old Age pilots, he had a hard time surviving constant carping by suspicious Sox supporters.

But the South Side bungalow belt was undergoing a tough transformation, with much of its blue-collar base fleeing to the suburbs. For a strange variety of reasons, the Sox still haven't lured many of them back to new Comiskey Park. They flocked to Old Comiskey though, when La Russa masterminded that wonderful "Winnin' Ugly" 1983 season. The Sox cracked the 2 million barrier for the first time, drawing 2,132,821.

Jeff Torborg was a popular manager while the Sox moved across 35th Street to open a new era in the '90s. To a lesser extent, so was Gene Lamont, who couldn't get a loaded Sox lineup past the first round of the 1993 playoffs. The franchise still hasn't recovered from the public relations blackout—and black eye—during Terry Bevington's tenure (1993-97). A man with few communications skills, Bevington was perceived by the media as Sox chairman Jerry Reinsdorf's revenge for their constant criticism of him.

In a situation where they need all the ink they can get to compete with the Cubs, the Sox hurt only themselves with this undeclared warfare. What they got was a barrage of unflattering comparisons between Comiskey Park and old, undeniably beautiful Wrigley Field. For the shrinking hardcore of Sox faithful, it was a lose-lose scenario.

Fighting is an acceptable option on the South Side, though, so it seems unlikely a truce will be declared soon. Sox fans have been known to duke it out in the stands when the scoreboard or the ever-available beer vendors brewed up enough mood-altering problems. As for the Pale Hose themselves, they've seldom been reluctant to take a few swings, even when not at bat. Some of those battles were real doozies:

Scold That Tiger
Daily Herald, April 23, 2000)

Not all the bad blood was spilled Saturday on Comiskey Park's trampled turf. Plenty remained in both clubhouses after one of the nastiest basebrawls in years erupted, matching the White Sox and Detroit Tigers in a double windup.

White Sox Manager Tony La Russa is NOT telling the South Side fans "You're No. 1." During his tenure (1979-86), Comiskey Park rooters often flashed digital signals to him but Tony silenced some of his critics by steering the 1983 "Winnin Ugly" Sox into the AL playoffs.

Not once, but twice, both teams cleared benches and even clubhouses to punch, kick, claw, wrestle and pile on each other. "If they want to do it again, we'll fight tomorrow," said Tigers welterweight pitcher Todd Jones. Sox pitcher Bill Simas made it clear some scores remain to be settled.

"I saw Bobby Higginson and Karim Garcia ganging up on Keith Foulke, so I went out to help," Simas said. "Garcia sucker-punched Keith, and a bunch of them knocked me down. I told (Tigers coach) Juan Samuel, 'You're supposed to be a peacemaker.'"

Peace struck out in this melee. Frustrated by early-season futility, including Saturday's 14-6 loss, the Tigers blew their tops in an ugly scene that went far beyond most baseball shoving and jawing matches. When warden Sandy Alderson gets the split-lip decision from the referees—oops, umpires—fat fines will follow. "It'll be tough to forget," said Sox manager Jerry Manuel. "You can use the word 'vicious' to describe this."

Crew chief Jerry Crawford's unofficial scorecard listed Manuel, coach Joe Nossek, Simas, Magglio Ordonez, Tanyon Sturtze and Bob Howry as the ejectees, along with Detroit's Dean Palmer, Jeff Weaver, Robert Fick and Denny Patterson. Crawford let other culprits off the hook to get the game over before World War III erupted. Foulke looked like the loser in those nightly slugfests peace-loving Sox fans used to stage at McCuddy's Saloon. The Sox closer needed five stitches to close the gash that sent blood streaming down his face.

The melee erupted when Sox starter Jim Parque hit Palmer with a pitch in the seventh inning. Palmer charged the mound and it went on and on.

"That was kind of retarded," Parques said. "The rest of the Tigers went crazy, and six of them jumped me."

Parque's pitch was retaliation for Weaver's nailing Sox batter Carlos Lee an inning earlier.

"It's a natural process in baseball," Manuel said. "If they pitch inside, you pitch inside, A manager doesn't have to say anything. The team has to be able to take care of the team."

This script has been rewritten thousands of times since Abner Doubleday first said, "Let's play one today" to his Cooperstown chums back in 1839. Usually, it brings players on the warring clubs close together.

That certainly was the effect on the Sox, springboarding them from lightweight contenders to AL Central champs in 2000. It was as exciting, though not nearly as much fun, as the South Side Hit Men, who won nothing except the hearts of Sox fans by bashing baseballs instead of opponents. That season, Comiskey Park was a mini-replay of the wonder summer the Cubs staged in Wrigley Field in 1969.

The difference was that the whole city of Chicago got caught up in the Leo Durocher lunacy, incited by flaky reliever Dick Selma's towel-waving antics to arouse the Bleacher Bums. The Sox surge of '77 was more of a local phenomenon, although homer-hitting heroes Richie Zisk and Oscar Gamble lured a record 1,657,135 customers through Comiskey's rusty turnstiles. Both the Cubs and the Sox faded at the end (what else?), but South Side stalwarts still speak fondly of that serendipitous summer.

So do I. Those "Pitch at Risk to Richie Zisk" bedsheets draped over the bleacher walls were a fitting tribute to him and Afro-coifed Gamble, Veeck's Rent-A-Player daily double. Always quick with a quip, Zisk got off a world class one-liner in the Sox dugout after tapping Veeck's wooden leg with his bat.

"Bill you have better wood than we do," Zisk deadpanned.

Hey, Hey, Na, Na, Bye-Bye Old Comiskey

I wasn't alone in my affection for old Comiskey Park. Bill Veeck loved it, too, even though he was raised at Wrigley Field, where his Dad, William Sr., was president of the Cubs. So did generations of South Side fans, supporting losing Sox teams with part of their meager paychecks during the Depression.

For me, it was Comiskey's lights, exact duplicates of the ones in Philadelphia's Shibe Park, that grew increasingly visible while I walked down Lehigh Avenue, while No.54 trolley cars clattered past. My destination was rooting (usually in vain) for the A's, managed by Connie Mack. That that sense of anticipation is still with me, all too many years later.

I see the same excitement on the faces of kids outside the gates of Comiskey and Wrigley when I walk past on the way to the pressbox. For me, it's a job. For them, it's an adventure.

I don't know how much longer major-league baseball can survive the greed of both owners and players. Along with that boring flood of TV statistics (like, "How many called balls thrown last month by left-handed relievers" as if anybody cared), they're turning the game into a dull, dry affair.

It wasn't like that in Comiskey Park. The smell of green grass and cheap cigars (it wasn't a crime to puff on one when broadcaster Bob Elson extolled "A White Owl wallop" by a Sox hitter) blended in an unforgettable aroma. It was the smell of baseball. Of excitement. And fun.

So, before the real Comiskey Park disappeared, it was fun to write this salute:

Farewell to Field of Dreams
(Chicago Tribune, June 30, 1985)

When Comiskey Park opened in 1910, Art Wheeler already had been a White Sox fan for years. He remembers elation on the South Side when their Hitless Wonders stunned the mighty Cubs in the 1906 World Series. Wheeler was 16 then, reveling in the humiliation of Cub manager Frank Chance's supposedly unbeatable team.

Still a rabid Sox fan at 95, Wheeler will be there Monday night for Comiskey Park's 75th birthday party, just as he was at that historic 1910 opening day. The details of that 2-0 loss to the St. Louis Browns are forgotten, but the first look at Charles A. Comiskey's "Base Ball Palace of the World" is sharply etched in his memory.

"All I could see was the ballpark," Wheeler said. "It was really something. Still is."

Wherever they've dispersed, mainly to the suburbs, Sox faithful return to their home at 35th Street and Shields Avenue.

A new stadium might go to where the fans are, but while Comiskey Park remains, it still reigns in their hearts.

"In Yankee Stadium, they have 54 percent box seats," Sox Chairman Jerry Reinsdorf said. "Here we have 23 percent. People would rather pay the price for a better seat. This park won't last forever. We've got to have a new one."

Just as the Sox have been under the shadow of the 1919 AL champs turned World Series fixers—the infamous Black Sox—so has Comiskey Park. It's been subjected to constant, unfavorable comparisons with small, cozy Wrigley. But spanking new Comiskey Park was something to see on July 1, 1910, when "Old Roman" Charles A. Comiskey flung open the gates for 25, 000 fans to glimpse his dream come true. Chicago's elite got engraved invitations, followed by a lavish banquet. Canny Comiskey brought the South Side Irish into the fold by laying a green cornerstone on St. Patrick's Day, 1910. Noted for his tight grasp on a dime, Commie pared down architect Zachary Davis' plan for an ornate facade.

Still, the 35,000-seat steel and concrete stadium, except for wooden bleachers, cost more than $500,000, a staggering sum in those days. When Davis built Weeghman Park four years later for the Chicago Whales of the short-lived Federal League, it cost only half that much. It soon became Wrigley Field, proving along with Comiskey Park that Davis' structures could pass the test of time.

Few of Comiskey's years have been free of competition from the Cubs and their beguiling North Side home.

"I used to cringe when I heard that 'beautiful Wrigley Field' routine," Bill Veeck recalled of his uphill battle to stay solvent when he owned the Sox in 1959-60 and again from 1975-80. "It is beautiful, but the unspoken inference was that Comiskey Park therefore had to be a dirty, dangerous place in a bad neighborhood.

"None of that is true," Veeck insisted, flashing the streak of common sense that usually, though not always, tempered the wilder side of his maverick nature. "There is a marvelous baseball tradition an both sides of Chicago, with two splendid ballparks to carry it on. Comiskey Park and its fans should not have to play second fiddle."

Too bad Comiskey couldn't return to see Veeck's innovations, notably the exploding scoreboard, the ball popper behind home plate, picnic areas under the stands and Nancy Faust, the organist who belted out, 'Na, Na, Goodbye," turning it into a Sox trademark. Hard times lingered, despite all that, so it's something of a miracle that the White Sox still belong to Chicago. Maybe the loyalty of fans like Ed Carlson, who saw his first Comiskey Park game in 1917, the year the Sox last won a World Series, was the saving grace.

"I saw Babe Ruth homer at the first All-Star game in 1933," Carlson said. "And I was there when Bob Feller pitched a no-hitter against the Sox on Opening Day (1940). How can you forget memories like these?

But "progress" intervened, as it always does. Comiskey Park lived to the ripe old age of 80, although many Sox fans, along with not-so-neutral observers like me, felt it died before its time. Even so, thousands of magic moments came tumbling down when the wrecking ball finally smashed into Comiskey bricks. The death sentence of the old park and new life for Chicago's AL franchise were assured on the same turbulent day—July 1, 1988. That's when the Illinois legislature, in a rare burst of rationality, stopped the state-house clock to push through funding for new Comiskey Park.

I was unaware that the turmoil surrounding the Sox would have to take a temporary back seat for my own problems. For both them and me, things turned out well. When the 1988 football season opened, I was covering Notre Dame's last national championship team for the Daily Herald in the booming Northwest suburbs. It was a seamless switch from 28-plus years of sportswriting for the Chicago Tribune, because I've been fortunate enough to keep covering the things I enjoy most—White Sox and Cubs in the summer, college and pro football in the fall and those fun-filled treks around the Big Ten basketball circuit amid bracing wintry blasts on ice-slicked roads.

I've enjoyed it all, fair weather or foul. Best of all, baseball, the game I grew up with, did not flee the South Side. For me, new Comiskey Park is not "Taxpayer Stadium." Those who stay away, for whatever reason, are missing a chance to recharge their batteries. Root, root, rooting for the home team is just plain fun.

So was saying so long to old Comiskey. It was like wishing an old friend bon voyage when he tottered off into retirement. The change was put in perspective for me by an old Comiskey hand:

Veeck's Park a Wreck
(Daily Herald, Sept. 30, 1990)

In 1978, Bill Veeck had to sell a minor league player for $40,000, just to come up with some cold cash to keep crumbling Comiskey Park from falling apart. That was only a year after the South Side Hit Men kept the Comiskey turnstiles spinning and the scoreboard exploding throughout a fun-filled summer. But the explosion of salaries was much louder, blowing away Veeck's bid to hang on as White Sox owner. He couldn't match offers for Richie Zisk and Oscar Gamble, the major maulers in Veeck's ingenious rent-a-player scheme.

The nature of baseball finally reflected the new age of television and mass marketing that had revolutionized American society. The Cubs, run like a mom-and-pop grocery store by gum tycoon Philip K. Wrigley, and the Sox, barely hanging on with owner Arthur C. Allyn, resisted change as long as they could.

But when Veeck repurchased the Sox on a shoestring in 1976, the first million-dollar player contracts were being signed. Comiskey Park was a wreck, as in Veeck, plaguing him with big bills for emergency repairs. Barnum Bill never ran short of ideas, promotions, or love for baseball. All he lacked was money. Bottomless bank accounts and unlimited egos spurred owners like George Steinbrenner, the latter-day Simon Legree of the Yankees, to buy pennants. Veeck bowed to the inevitable, selling the franchise to the Jerry Reinsdorf-Eddie Einhorn group for $19 million on Jan. 29, 1981. They soon found out it came with astronomical costs to shore up a sagging ballpark.

"The situation was worse than desperate," said Comiskey Park superintendent David Schaffer, son of Veeck's long-time associate, Rudy Schaffer. "This old park is on its knees. Since 1981, $25 million has been spent on structural reinforcement and essential maintenance, just to keep Comiskey in one piece and make it presentable.

"When you can poke your hand through a steel girder, things are in bad shape. We did a major structural review in 1977, showing how dangerous things were getting, but repair money wasn't there.

Critics still complain that Comiskey could have been re-habbed.

"Some people will always believe Reinsdorf wanted to take the White Sox to St. Petersburg," Schaffer said. "My dad was one of Veeck's best friends, but he knows that's not true. Jerry is an integral part of the South Side."

That tradition began in 1901, when Charles A. Comiskey brought a new Chicago team into the upstart American League. Comiskey had his own army of detractors, but he built a living monument in 1910. The shell, Comiskey Park's bricks and mortar, will disappear quickly. The real substance of his baseball palace thankfully will be with us a lot longer.

Daley Life Goes On

A new Mayor Daley, Richard M., was there when they broke ground for Comiskey Park II on May 8, 1989. His father, Richard J. Daley, the original "Da Mare," a lifelong Sox fan, was there in spirit. Big   Jim Thompson, also known as The Guv, was there, too, admitting he twisted arms to get the bill for a 2 percent hotel-motel tax to finance stadium bonds.

"Chicago is the only city to get a baseball stadium from the pockets of out-of-towners," Thompson gloated.

Jack Brickhouse, play-by-play man for the game-ending twin kill that gave the Sox their 1959 AL flag, recalled how the air-raid sirens saluting that triumph unwittingly touched off fears that the Russians, or perhaps their ICBMs, were coming.

"Let's get the stadium built, so the Sox can play the 1991 World Series right here," said Brick, an optimist to the end.

The final chapter was sad, but it's all right to shed a few tears at the end. Other writers shared their own memories before we sat down to write one last story in the Comiskey press box. This was mine:

Wring Out the Old
(Daily Herald, Oct. 1, 1990)

It's over. The gates are shut. The lights are out. The grand-stands are empty.

Comiskey Park is dead. At 80 years and 3 months, the majors' oldest ballpark gave up the ghost Sunday afternoon with 42,849 close friends on hand for the wake. In Comiskey's hey-day, just about every star in baseball's galaxy had a shining mo-ment here, from the opening game on July 1, 1910, to this Sept. 30, 1990, finale. A sense of regret, spelled out on a "Goodbye, Old Friend" bedsheet hung out in leftfield, ran rampant.

Along with a million memories, fans recalled Art "Wottaman" Shires, Fat Pat Seerey, Turk Lown and Bee Bee Ri-chard in the place where these former Sox players entertained us. At 4:23 p.m., Comiskey Park joined the Polo Grounds, Sportsman's Park, Crosley Field and other places where big-league baseball used to be played.

In a way, this pitching duel between winner Jack McDowell of the Sox and loser Rich DeLucia of the Mariners was a fitting epitaph. Such low-scoring affairs as this 2-1 last gasp took place here with monotonous regularity over the years.

Sox fans being Sox fans, new Comiskey Park would have taken plenty of heat, even if it had been an exact replica of old Comiskey. It wasn't, so the roars of outrage got redoubled—in many cases, retripled.

A peculiar, hardy breed, these South Siders. They came from strong roots, like Jacob Rifkin, a Russian immigrant, who came to Elgin in 1914. A skilled tailor, Jacob and son Ben soon were riding the interburban train to Comiskey Park, joining a new tradition for new Americans.

Their story, multiplied a million times, explains why baseball flourished despite scandals, strikes and the Great Depression of the 1930s. Wherever they settled, immigrants passed loyalty for a team along to their families. Working-class people, lured by 25-cent bleacher seats, became Sox fans. But the fierce, independent spirit that led them from the old world to a better life also produced generations of critical, aware fans, unhappy with anything short of maximum effort. Old-time, hard-line Sox loyalists rejoiced when the Go-Go Sox of Nellie Fox, Little Looie Aparicio and Jungle Jim Rivera stormed to the 1959 AL pennant. They finally warmed to the Winnin' Ugly 1983 team, although not to the steel-trap mind of manager Tony La Russa.

Everybody came together to share the misery of the first-round playoff loss to Baltimore in '83, especially that heartbreaking 3-0 clincher to end it in Game 4. Ironically, that moment in the old park in a losing cause brought the Sox fan clan closer together than either of their two division-winning seasons in the new park. Baseball fans were outraged by the strike that wiped out the 1994 World Series, none more than Sox supporters, because they blamed Jerry Reinsdorf for being the owners' ringleader.

Even before that, they carped about nosebleed alley in the upper deck and the alleged sweetheart deal with Illinois Sports Facilities Authority, the park's rent collectors. The incredibly complicated Sox-SFA pact turned fans off as much as multimillion contracts for .250 hitters. At least the prolonged shutdown gave the Sox time to spruce up the park and eliminate some glitches before the delayed home opener on April 24, 1995.

Because the Oklahoma City federal building bombing a week earlier had stunned the nation, increased security precautions provided a chilling premonition of the horror that changed all our lives on September 11, 2001.

"The Comiskey Park staff is trained in emergency procedures," David Schaffer said. "The scariest thing is, somebody could walk up with one of those (explosive devices) strapped to him."

That warning, issues in the mid-90s, sounded unbelievable then. Now we have learned, to our sorrow, that even ballparks can become battlefields in America's war on terror.

2000 Reasons to Root For a Sox Century

Jerry Manuel kept talking about wining with pitching and defense, from the day he became Sox manager in 1998. His first two years, they finished second without much of either. Suddenly, it didn't matter much when the third time proved to be the charm.

That was 2000, a year when the White Sox surprised everybody, probably including Manuel, by ending Cleveland's stranglehold on the AL Central Division. Well, at least temporarily. It sure was fun while it lasted.

Not just the Sox, but all Chicago teams have an unhappy habit of fizzling a year after sizzling. Repeating is harder than winning the first time anywhere. Around here, it's just about impossible. Maybe that famous Billy Goat hex (dating from the 1945 World Series) on the Cubs has an all-franchise clause.

Since hope is the emotion of choice for Chicago fans, they forget about history as soon as their team comes out on top just once. The Michael Jordan-Bulls dynasty proved to be an ecstatic exception, though now that they're lousy again, hope—or in this case, hoop—springs eternal for Bull followers. Unfortunately, the once-bulging base of Sox faithful keeps shrinking. Mary Frances Veeck saw that happening even before Bill died in 1986.

"Bill disliked labels, but he knew the franchise historically has been rooted in support from working people," she told me. "I saw changes in the pattern when we bought the team (in 1975) for the second time. Part of that tradition still holds, but I think it's dying out."

The proof is not in the pudding; rather, in the patronage. In 2000, the Cubs lost 97 games and drew 2,734,511 paying customers to the North Side bandbox. In 2000 the Sox won 95 games and drew 1,947,799 to their bigger South Side playpen.

Regardless, 2000's Sox-cess didn't go unnoticed. TV ratings rose with their ascent in the standings, probably validating vice chairman Eddie Einhorn's long-cherished notion that baseball could be as much a pay-TV sport as a live spectator game. In 2000, though, you really had to be there for happenings like this:

Valentin's Day
(Daily Herald, May 28, 2000)

The Jaime Navarro factor took its toll again Saturday night in Comiskey Park, this time on the Cleveland Indians. When the White Sox unloaded the bombs-away pitcher to the unsuspecting Milwaukee Brewers for pitcher Cal Eldred and shortstop Jose Valentin, it was the biggest steal since the Louisiana Purchase.

Eldred and Valentin have been making everybody else in the American League rue that Brew boo-boo, so now it's Cleveland's turn. After getting strong-armed into submission Friday by Eldred, the visitors got the kind of treatment from Valentin that's reserved for rowdy drunks in South Side saloons. A big band of Indians fans in the stands felt like singing "Jose, can you flee?" when Valentin tomahawked their reeling AL Central dynasty with a homer, triple and double in his first three trips. His career-high 6 RBIs turned Round 2 of this showdown for division supremacy into a rerun of the Fort Dearborn massacre. The first-place Sox romped 14-3 with a 16-hit assault, hiking their lead over the Indians to 2 1/2 games. Valentin had two more chances to become the only AL player ever to hit for the cycle twice in the same season. The switch hitter, 3-for-3 from the left side, batted right when he walked in the fifth inning and grounded sharply to third in the seventh. He already had hit for the cycle here April 27 in a 13-4 bashing of Baltimore, so a feat pulled off only by Babe Herman of the NL's then-Brooklyn Dodgers in 1931 still stands.

I don't want to dwell on the 2000 playoff debacle. The same Sox who couldn't lose before the first round couldn't avoid a first-round knockout by Seattle. Mariners pitchers manacled the Pale Hose, turning them into a pale shadow of the sluggers who slapped the AL silly all summer. Crusty Lou Piniella outmanaged mellow Jerry Manuel, too.

So I elect to recall that good season, not for its bad ending, but for the fun that got the Sox that far. They have to outscore, outhustle and outwin the Cubs to get much coverage in Chicago.

Fortunately for them, doing all of that was easy in 2000, a banner year in all respects. I prefer to credit Manuel for patiently crafting a clubhouse climate that brought back winning ways on the South Side.

It wasn't easy. Before he became 2000 Manager of the Year in the AL, Manuel had to sow the seeds when he took over in 1998 and watch them grow erratically, haphazardly, but steadily. Growing pains eventually began turning slipshod starts into bad finishes, like this one:

Sox Still Winning Ugly
(Daily Herald, June 6, 1999)

Jerry Manuel is 45 years old, going on 95. The reason? He has a very stressful job. Even when the White Sox win, the way they did by slogging from behind to beat the Pittsburgh Pirates 6-5, it's as nerve-wracking for their manager as a summons from an IRS auditor.

Manuel has restored stability and civility in the Sox clubhouse, a couple of conditions sorely lacking during the Albert Belle era. His calm style sets the tam for a roster full of eager youngsters, all trying to grow up overnight.

Then the game begins, and Manuel's rules of order no longer apply. Take Saturday's first inning. Please.

The Sox staged another of those all-thumbs fielding displays that add a few more gray hairs to Manuel's head with each comedy caper. They committed three errors right off the bat, no pun intended, presenting the Pirates with four unearned runs. First, Magglio Ordonez dropped Ed Sprague's windblown fly. Then third baseman Greg Norton threw low to the plate on Kevin Young's grounder. When Warren Morris lifted a fly ball, catcher Brook Fordyce elected to play Carlos Lee's throw home like a hockey goalie, saddling Lee with error number three.

At that point, starter Jim Parque probably figured the Sox were a trifle late with today's promotion, a free fielder's glove to 10,000 Comiskey kids. The youngsters behind him could have used them, especially the kind without holes in the pocket.

You get the idea. I have high hopes that Manuel will stick around long enough to become the managerial icon that Sparky Anderson was in Cincinnati and Detroit. Sparky added a spark of class to every ballpark he entered, including new Comiskey, where he only had to push buttons from the bench while his Tigers clawed the Sox 16-0 on the South Side playpen's first day. As always, when Sparky speaks, as he did before that not-so-festive affair, people listen:

Sparky Lights Up Sox Park
(Daily Herald, April 19, 1991)

Just like it surely would have in Florida, if the White Sox had been crated and shipped there, the sun was shining for them Thursday in Chicago—until the game started.

Long before the first pitch hurtled plateward in new Comiskey Park, politicians and assorted name-droppers waded into the media mob on the field, making pitches of their own. It required nimble sidesteps through the throng of back-slappers beaming into TV cameras to squeeze into the Detroit Tigers' dugout and along the tunnel to the visiting manager's office.

There sat George "Sparky" Anderson, the man Hollywood would have cast in the role of kindly, venerable Sox manager. But instead of Tinseltown fantasy, this was real, just like the brand-new ballpark, and Tigers manager Anderson was prepared to deal with reality.

"People think I have a lot of nostalgia for the old parks like Tiger Stadium and Shibe Park," he said. "The truth is, we have to move on. This place is great for Chicago. It's not gaudy. Everything is so well laid out, you can tell it's a real baseball park. The fans want to come and see games where they're comfortable. This is so much better for the players, the writers and everybody else, even old guys like me."

The 57-year-old Anderson should know. He's in his 22nd season as a big-league manager, surviving the long, hard trail through the minors and one season (1959) as the Phillies' second baseman.

"I rode the buses and dressed in the crummy minor-league parks with no hot water," Anderson recalled. "I lived through it and never imagined a place like this. Now you see new parks all around the country. Most baseball players came from poor or middle-class backgrounds, so I watched them enjoy this big, carpeted clubhouse."

Never mind that nowadays, even mediocre players match in one season what many working people earn in a lifetime. Sparky's point was that the tradition of old Comiskey Park was not an acceptable substitute for new Comiskey's creature comforts.

"The history and tradition of the old park won't die just because the walls are coming down," Anderson said. "History lives on in people's memories and in books. Blood and Guts Patton and Joan of Arc are history. What would have happened without Thomas Edison and Henry Ford coming along to give us something new?"

For the record, Tigers slugger Cecil Fielder christened new Comiskey Park with its first homer, off Sox starter Jack McDowell.

"I was thinking of giving us a boost, not hitting the first one here," Fielder shrugged off his 3-run shot in the third inning.

Ballplayers tend to have that kind of tunnel vision. Not so the men who run the show, especially Tony La Russa, still the thinking man's manager. I talked baseball with Tony before and after many Sox wins and losses during his 1,035-game tenure as resident genius. Tony has an analytic mind, totally unlike such seat-of-the-pants bench bosses as Leo Durocher, but he analyzed things better than almost any manager or coach I've known.

That covers a lot of territory over 40 years of covering games and the people who play them from coast to coast. It's a pretty exclusive club—La Russa and Sparky Anderson in baseball, Bud Grant and Neill Armstrong (not the astronaut—the ex-Bears coach) in football, Red Holzman and Bob Cousy in basketball. They were able to get past the emotion that makes competition a drug, turning us all into junkies, so swept up in the emotion of frantic finishes that we lose track of everything else.

Very few of the Chicago managers and coaches I've known and written about over the years could step back, separate the cold facts from the hot passions of the moment and operate consistently on that level. I'll have more to say about emotion-driven guys like Mike Ditka later. For now, this visit with La Russa, just before the 1990 All-Star game in Wrigley Field illustrates my point:

(Daily Herald, July 7, 1990)

When Tony La Russa strides out of the dugout to manage the American League All-Stars Tuesday night in Wrigley Field, he will close the circle of a long journey that began 13 years ago in Comiskey Park.

It's only a few miles from the South Side to the Cubs' legendary den at Clark and Addison Streets.

But for Anthony La Russa Jr., it was an enormous trip, spanning the spectrum from defeat and despair to fame and fortune.

So here's La Russa, at 45, the field boss of the world champion Oakland Athletics. He's the prototype of a new generation of college-trained, computer-oriented baseball managers. Handsome, articulate, well-groomed, in command of himself and his team, La Russa is the hottest ticket around, the manager who helped lift his craft out of the tobacco-chawin', hunch-playing mold and into the space age. In Gilbert and Sullivan's world, La Russa would have been the very model of a modern manager.

"A manager has to work with the players available to him at that time," La Russa said. "He can't win by wishing they were different or better. If the ones he has don't get it done, the responsibility is his. The A's aren't the same team without Rickey Henderson and Jose Canseco in the lineup. That doesn't mean we can't win without them, but it calls for a different set of options. I enjoy trying to put together a combination that best fits the situation."

La Russa was lucky to become the White Sox manager, just 34 years old when he was promoted from the Iowa farm club on Aug. 2, 1979. Ex-Cubs shortstop Don Kessinger had just proved once again by going 40-64 in his short stint at the Sox helm, that Leo Durocher's "Nice guys finish last" line included him. La Russa had the ability to say "No more Mr. Nice Guy" in the clubhouse.

Bill Veeck, still the Sox owner then, took time to give his novice skipper a crash course in handling the media covering Chicago's second-fiddle baseball team. But La Russa had the will and the skill to convert fate's bases on balls into winning runs. Adversity on the Sox sharpened his desire to compete and succeed.

"There are ways to improve the odds, such as computer analysis, that weren't used much when I first came to the majors," La Russa said. "Now everybody's doing it."

La Russa earned his law degree in 1979, and for a few years it seemed his legal career was only a pink slip away. Few managers have had to break through barriers like the hostility toward his newfangled methods that sometimes bordered on paranoia. That's all over with.

"When I was learning my job with the White Sox, being an All-Star manager never entered my mind," La Russa said. "Right now, I would put my level of excitement up there with Connie Mack or anybody who's managed in one of these games."

Hurt Helps Sox Survive, If Not Thrive

I was sitting in the visitors' dugout in Milwaukee's County Stadium before trekking up the old park's ramps to cover a Sox-Brewers twi-night doubleheader on Aug. 3, 1990, when a new face came out of the clubhouse for his first glimpse of life in the majors.

It was Frank Thomas, just called up from Birmingham to become an instant starter at first base for the Sox. I shook hands with the sweat-soaked rookie, still savoring his rips in the batting cage. His first words to me were prophetic.

"It's my time, I guess," Thomas said. "Coming up with a contender just makes it more exciting."

Well, Thomas' bat proved to be plenty exciting, even if he wasn't. I can't think of another right-handed hitter who matched the Big Hurt's average and RBI totals in the decade of the '90s, and just two with his consistent power—Sammy Sosa and Mark McGwire. Unfortunately, the slugger's talent far outweighed —pun intended—his ability to handle stardom. If Thomas also got a charisma transplant when his torn shoulder muscle was repaired while he sat out the disastrous 2001 season, he still could become the newly popular Big Bopper of some 21st Century Sox squads. (He vowed to hit harder in the charisma league while toning up for 2002).

Almost as an afterthought to Thomas, the Sox also called up a chunky right-hander. He was Alex Fernandez, who stuck around long enough to match Jack McDowell's pair of losses to Toronto in the 1993 AL playoff, when the Blue Jays booted out the Sox in six games. Another personality kid, Sox general manager Larry Himes, provided insight into the way these decisions are made.

"I talked to Jerry Reinsdorf yesterday and we thought, 'What the hell, we need Frank,'" Hines said. "We're not asking him to turn around the club all by himself."

Ironically, Thomas turned out to be the once-in-25-years superstar who could rank with Lou Gehrig, Hank Aaron, Willie Mays on the all-time list of consistent hitters. In another strange development, David Wells, seemingly springing right from the pages of Ring Lardner's baseball classic *You Know Me, Al*, unwittingly helped Thomas to salvage his sagging reputation with Sox fans. Wells accused him of "jaking," the players' word for declining to play with pain, after the April 27 triceps injury. Wells' blend of a bad back and boorish behavior ended his Sox sojourn as a total bust.

Some other superstars drifted through the old and new Comiskey clubhouses since I strolled onto the scene three decades ago. One who fared much better in the old setting was Harold Baines. His struggling finale in 2001 was embarrassing, both to him and the Sox fans who rooted for him.

When I picked my all-time Sox team as part of the new Comiskey festivities, I put it this way:

Harold Baines couldn't catch this homer in old Comiskey Park. The South Side favorite hit his share here.

"If these guys had ever come together in the same lineup in the same season, the White Sox might have made the mighty 1927 Yankees look like a bunch of batboys. Besides Baines (1980-89; '96-97; 2002-01) in left field, Thomas displaces slugging Dick Allen (1972-74) at first base; Eddie Collins (1915-26) is all alone at second base, untainted by the Black Sox scandal; Luis Aparacio (1956-62, 1968-70) gets the shortstop nod over Luke Appling; third base— Robin Ventura (1989-98) had the softest, surest hands of anybody I ever saw at the Hot Corner; center field—Jim Landis (1957-64), a truly great glove man; right field—Magglio Ordonez has a long way to go, probably too long, to replace Shoeless Joe Jackson (1915-20); catcher—Many Sox fans will disagree, but I prefer Ray Schalk (1912-28) over Carlton Fisk (1981-93); designated hitters—Appling and Fisk; pitchers—Big Ed Walsh (1904-16); Grandpappy Ted Lyons (1923-42, 1946), Billy Pierce (1949-61). Utilityman—Jacob Nelson Fox (1950-63). Just like the ways he found to get on base, you, I, nor anyone else could find a way to keep Nellie off this team.

There were some other unforgettable guys. For instance, Bo Jackson, who had a knack for dramatic home runs. Everybody remembers the Bo blast that clinched the 1993 AL West title for the Sox, and his mammoth shot in the first turn at bat since hip replacement surgery that would have ended most careers. Not Bo's. He played in severe pain to hit other homers, like my personal favorite:

Bo Bashes Cubs
(Daily Herald, May 7, 1993)

Bo knows frustration, too.

Bo Jackson sent Cub fans home going "Bo-Hoo" Thursday night with a classic moment in a Comiskey Park Crosstown Classic that until then had been anything but classical. His 2-run, eighth-inning home off Frank Castillo pulled the White Sox into a 3-3 tie, and Chicago's neighborhood feud followed a similar script from there.

A pair of South Side heroes, Minnie Minoso and Bill Veeck, flash their Comiskey chuckles.

Steve Sax greeted Cubs reliever Heathcliffe Slocumb with a leadoff single in the last of the ninth. Frank Thomas rammed the next pitch into the left-center alley and Sax, off with the pitch, scored easily for a 4-3 victory. It was their eighth straight marred only by a 6-6 tie in 1988, over the North Siders.

"I just stuck my bat out, and the ball jumped off it," said Jackson of his 414-foot blast over the right-center fence.

For sheer power, this one fell a trifle short of the Bionic Basher's home-opening pinch homer in his Sox debut.

"It feels good to give something back to the fans," Bo said. "This is a day off for the players, but we came out to perform for them."

Another Sox hero who reveled in the fans' affection for him was Saturnio Orestes Arrieta Armas "Minnie" Minoso. The only five-decade player in big-league history, Minnie homered in his first Sox at-bat in 1951, and still is a big hit on the South Side, more than a half-century later.

Then there's Ron Kittle, a good hitter and good guy, who got to the White Sox only because Bill Veeck invited him for a Comiskey Park tryout. Kittle's array of quips and one-liners (as in, "I hope I'm wearing rubber pants when I walk out there,"—Kittle's response to the news that he'd be on the AL All-Star squad for the 50th Anniversary game at Comiskey in 1983), endeared him to the media, too.

I saw Kitty hit his first Sox homer in the Minneapolis Metrodome, under unusual circumstances on Oct. 2, 1982. The Sox played the Twins in the morning, and the ugly rug on the field was converted for the Illinois-Minnesota football game that night, while I stuck around to cover both games.

If the Sox had more fun guys like Kittle, Comiskey crowds would warm up to them. Better yet, a Cubs-Sox World Series.

3

Surviva-Bull in a Bear Market

The Michael Jordan dynasty was unheard of and undreamed of in 1966, when my I unloaded my first load of Bull prose on unsuspecting Chicago fans. A quarter-century streaked past before it came true.

I got to know His Airness during this rookie season in the league. That was before he was surrounded by a howling, out-of-control mob, pushing, shoving, and shrieking for a word or a glance from MJ. And that was just the media. Fans were more polite.

I don't regret passing up a chance to cover all of those six NBA championship years that Jordan brought to Chicago. It would have been fun to write a story after rotund Bulls mogul Jerry Krause uttered his ultimate pomposity: "Players don't win championships. Organizations win championships."

Well, the Bulls didn't win any championships in the 16 years when I was on the beat for the *Chicago Tribune*. They should have in 1975, when I wrote the first book about their struggles to compete on the court, and to survive in the cut-throat jungle of NBA off-court intrigue. The backstage backstabbing was a lot more bizarre, but watching the Bulls battle the world when that mighty midget, Dick Motta, became their coach in 1968, was just plain fun.

Dealing with him daily throughout his stormy eight-year reign was not always a barrel of laughs, but I learned to respect Motta then, and I still do. His players always knew who was boss. More about that later, because this two-decade trip down memory lane has triggered far too many memories for me to describe in a single chapter.

The Wild Guys, The Good Guys, the Bad Boys, and the Dandy Dudes keep parading through my mind in a disorderly jumble. That's about the only way to cope with the mixture of agony and ecstasy that made up every one of my NBA years. Lots of people think sports writing is a glamorous way to make a living. One trip around the league, coast-to-coast, playing one game and out of town would change their fantasy into reality, especially the two-week See America Fast grind that always happened around Thanksgiving, because an ice show was booked into Chicago Stadium.

Merely surviving the travel would be tough enough—blizzards in Cleveland, fog in Seattle, lost baggage in Atlanta, endless delays everywhere—in between trudging down miles of airport corridors, laden like a beast of burden with crammed suitcase, typewriter (now it's a PC) and tons of statistics. Toss in 10 p.m. starts for road games, unrelenting deadlines, unsympathetic editors (just like the fans, they're convinced a road trip is an undeserved vacation for the writers), fatigue and general bewilderment about what day it is and which city you're in. I haven't even mentioned what all this does to home and family life. While you're gone, your kids are growing.

In case this sounds like a complaint and/or lament, it's neither. In many ways, those NBA years were the time of my life. I wouldn't trade the good times and above all the friendships I made while wandering around the NBA wilderness.

We huddled together, not for warmth, but for survival. Too many of those Good Guys are gone, especially lifetime pals Dick Mackey of the *Kansas City Star* and George Cunningham of the

Atlanta Constitution. But I still get together with Joe Gilmertin in Phoenix, Bill Halls in Detroit, and Bill Livingston in Cleveland to laugh about those Bad Old Days.

Trying to figure out what made NBA coaches and players tick was fun, too. This was before million-dollar contracts became the standard reward for mediocrity, but when the American Basketball Association arose to challenge the NBA in the late '60s, things got even more schizophrenic. Coaches were The Boss before then. Now they're reduced to roles like Phil Jackson of the Lakers, trying to referee kid-stuff squabbles between child-man superstars who could have bought the Bulls' franchise (it cost them $1.5 million to join the NBA in 1966) with one week's pay.

And then there were the owners. The overinflated egos of today's overpaid players would seem almost humble in comparison with the hands-on guys who ran NBA franchises back then. Sam Schulman of the Seattle SuperSonics once called my hotel room at a league meeting to babble something about death threats from his fellow NBA owners. "Knowing Sam, he might have been right," one of those owners told me.

He was just kidding—I think. Anyway, the shouting matches that passed for NBA meetings always made for good stories. Entertaining guys like Dick O. Klein of the Bulls and that wonderful whacko, Franklin Mieuli of the then-San Francisco Warriors, would emerge from smoke-filled rooms to regale us with their spin on these strange goings-on. For a sportswriter, it was Christmas morning.

Those were the days, my friends. Here's my take on the way the Bulls somehow lasted until Jordan arrived in 1984 to become their Moses.

There Goes Mr. Jordan

It's never been easy for the Bulls, even when they were on Easy Street with Michael Jordan. The best basketball player in the known universe stopped popping jumpers in 1993 to start popping up baseballs, under the delusion that he could hit .300 as easily as he hit three-pointers. When Jordan tired of riding his own luxury bus through the bushes and returned to terrorizing the NBA, the Bulls' championship six-pack started flowing again.

Bulls brass bungled by allowing this dynasty to disintegrate, meaning that today's fans had to discover what life was like in the BJ (Before Jordan) era. It was wild from the day they got the franchise in 1966 until the Jordanaires finally got to wave the NBA title trophy—which I once described as a bowling ball perched on the edge of a wastebasket—for magically making Magic and the rest of the Lakers vanish in the 1991 final playoff.

It only took a quarter-century to get there, a lot faster than the Cubs, streaking toward 100 years without a World Series triumph. What most front-runners, bandwagon jumpers and just plain Jordan worshippers don't realize is that Chicago's NBA franchise hung by a thin thread for years. It took heroic effort, a little bit of luck and the ferocious, canny coaching of Dick Motta to save the Bulls from following the Stags (1946-50) and Paclkers/Zephyrs (1961-63) to the toxic waste dump of sports history.

Another gutsy guy, Dick O. Klein, sold the idea to some fat cat backers, despite the smart money's belief that Chicago was a pro basketball graveyard. If not for this truly odd couple, Klein and Motta, the wise guys would have been right. Even so, the customers stayed away for two years, amid rumors that the franchise would be shipped, horns, hoofs and all, to Memphis, Omaha, Cincinnati or who knew where. Almost from the start, Klein and Motta fought like, well, like egotistical owner and headstrong coach, unaware they'd found the formula to save the Bulls from the slaughterhouse.

Fight.

Just like that, vanished fans resurfaced, and the Bad News Bulls were a hot ticket. With the Klein-Motta bout offstage and the Bulls brawling nightly on the court, Chicago Stadium was the place to be.

So their survival saga entered new phases fast. Motta, labeled "the unknown coach" when he came to town in 1968 from even lesser-known Weber State, in far-off Ogden, Utah, took an increasingly dominant role. I liked both of these complex people, even though Motta's moods made some conversations with him the ver-

Coach Dick Motta (left) and this array of battle-tested Bulls are ready for NBA fireworks before fired-up Chicago Stadium crowds in the early '70s. Left to right: Jerry Sloan, Tom Boerwinkle, Chet Walker, Norm Van Lier, Bob Weiss.

bal equivalent of strolling through a minefield. But he would take on anybody or anything—especially the NBA hierarchy—a trait that made him a favorite in Chicago.

Anyway, the Bulls battled and bullied their way through eight years under Motta, winning a lot of skirmishes, but ultimately losing the war. They set Chicago on fire in 1974-75, clawing to the doorstep of the NBA finals, only to fall agonizingly short. From my front-row seat to witness this nightly mayhem, I sought the riot stuff, writing deadline-defying scribbles in a vain attempt to explain whatever the heck had happened in the ensuing mugfest.

At the center of all that flailing, gouging, kicking and occasional fisticuffs was No. 2 in your scorecard, but No. 1 in your heart. Stormin' Norman Van Lier was—and still is—Chicago's kind of player and man, ready to take on all comers, the bigger the better. At 6 feet 1 and 170 pounds, with five or more melting off nightly via his nonstop defense, Norm's heart weighed a ton. It was vintage Van Lier when he went after 6-8 Sidney Wicks of the Portland Trail Blazers, delighting a Chicago Stadium crowd.

Norm Goes on Chair Tear
(Chicago Tribute, March 21, 1973)

As happens frequently in NBA games, the shadow outweighed the substance.

A brief, explosive flareup between Portland's Sidney Wicks and the Bulls' Norm Van Lier sent the fans home buzzing after the home team romped 123-109.

The main event unfolded in the first minute of the third quarter, when Wicks and Van Lier tangled under the basket. Their wrestling match took a turn for the worse when Stormin' Norman headed for the sidelines, grabbing a chair from his bench.

"Van Lier didn't go get that chair for exercise," Coach Dick Motta underscored the obvious. "He wasn't going to sit down on it."

Fortunately, the Bulls' trainer, Dr. Bob Biel, tackled the incensed Van Lier before he could renew hostilities, while Chet

Walker reasoned with the equally unhappy Wicks. Both combatants got ejected by Referee Ed Rush, though it took a few minutes to calm some boisterous spectators before play resumed.

"The last game in Portland, Wicks hit me on the head," Van Lier related later. "I was just protecting myself. I was coming across a pick when he nailed me with an elbow and I reacted.

"Nobody is going to run over me. I might have got a broken jaw, but his career would have been over, because I tried to plant that chair on his head."

Wicks, after a period of stomping around the Trail Blazers' bathhouse declared, "Van Lier is gonna get his butt kicked," then calmed down.

That was the script for dozens of Norm's storms. With his backcourt partner, Jerry Sloan, he gave the Bulls a brand of defense as impenetrable as Fort Knox. But Van Lier wasn't the only Bull unafraid to stick a snout into the fray.

Even Nate Thurmond, normally the most affable of men, had a boiling point. I remember him trading punches with Tom Boerwinkle of the Bulls when the big men bounced off each other once too often. Sadly, Nate the Great didn't live up to his nickname when he came to the Bulls in 1974 for Center Cliff Ray.

"They told me I'd be in San Francisco as long as the Golden Gate Bridge," said Thurmond, unhappy about trading his comfortable lifestyle in cable car country for those icy winter winds howling off Lake Michigan. "Well, the bridge is still there, but I'm gone."

And so was the notion that Thurmond's hard rebounding and soft shooting touch would help the Bulls to their first NBA championship. He was totally ineffective in Motta's system, lacking Bowerwinkle's deft passing touch, so the big deal flopped. Ironically, Cliff Ray played a major part in helping the Warriors to stun —you guessed it—the Bulls in the 1975 Western Conference finals.

Later that year, I stuck my neck out by writing that Thurmond was on the trading block, with the Cleveland Cavaliers making a strong pitch for him. The Bulls' angry denial went coast-to-coast on the *AP* sports wire, just ahead of the word that Thurmond had been traded to—guess where—Cleveland. My NBA spy network was right, but writers don't hear apologies—nor should they— when they break a story. It's all part of the job, and so is handling the guff that comes with it.

Anyway, Chicago fans were anxious to welcome Thurmond into the fold. They were a frustrated as the Bulls themselves after four straight 50-plus win seasons, followed by playoff exits. So when Nate served notice that he would play Motta's rock-and-sock game in 1974-75, it was mistakenly taken as proof that he was the answer. No such luck, even though Thurmond's battle with Sonics rookie Tom Burleson raised this sort of false hope:

Bulls Get New Ali for NBA Bouts
(Chicago Tribune Nov. 24, 1974)

"Well, I guess the first thing to do when I get home is to take my phone off the hook," Nate Thurmond said.

A tower of unruffled nonchalance in a tasteful green suit, he was the center of attention in more ways than one when the Bulls got back to Chicago at last. Fans and teammates swirled around him at O'Hare Airport while the veteran center waited for his baggage.

"Hey, Nate," bellowed an onlooker, shattering the early-morning stillness and waving a fist aloft in triumph. "I dig it, man! Muhammad Ali!"

Not that there was any kind of organized welcome for the Bulls, returning from an 11-city tour of the NBA. The noteworthy thing about the long flight from Seattle was the apparent effect of Thurmond's one-punch TKO victory over the Sonics' Tom Burleson Friday night. It sparked the Bulls from behind to a 93-89 victory.

Fatigue seemed to ooze from the road-weary wanderers in the NBA wilderness. The rookies provided an enthusiastic audience while the veterans laughingly recounted their roles in the brief bout.

"No, I didn't hurt my hand,' the 6-foot, 11-inch pivotman said of the looping right he employed to convince Burleson that NBA rookies should not try to bully the Bulls. "My elbows hurt from the way he was pounding on me all night, though. Burleson better learn you don't step right in and intimidate people in this league."

It was a high note (or is that Nate?) on which to wrap up a voyage with its share of low points.

That's the way it went for Moving Van's Bulls throughout his career. He was suspended for laying a block the Bears would envy on NBA referee Darrell Garretson, one of his favorite targets, and least favorite whistle tooters. Norm's frustrations eventually spilled out on Motta and others ("My own coach won't back me up, the way he does for Sloan," Norm grumbled, but he made his feelings clear after this altercation:

Van Lier Can Block and Tackle Block
(Chicago Tribune, Dec. 9, 1972)

PHILADELPHIA—Even in a town where losing is right behind the Liberty Bell and Italian hoagies, heavy on the mozza-rella, as a local tradition, the 76ers stand out. This team is so bad, intra-squad games probably end up 0-0.

So it wasn't a surprise that the Bulls deep-sixed the Sixers 118-102 tonight, despite the absence of Jerry Sloan, out with a pulled hamstring. And probably not, either, that Sloan's fellow backcourt bouncer, Norm Van Lier, boiled over at frustration from his sloppy showing. In the City of Brotherly Love, even Bob Love's peacemaking effort couldn't stop Van Lier, the NBA's bantamweight champ, from going after the 76ers' 6-10 John Block and normal-sized referee Jake O'Donnell.

When Block missed a free throw, his elbow didn't miss Van Lier. It unleashed the load of rancor gnawing at the fiery Bulls guard. He went after Block, throwing punches from all angles. O'Donnell stepped in, almost getting nailed by a haymaker and later displaying welts on his arm. Block didn't miss, though. Van Lier calmly discussed the incident, sporting a taped cut over his left eye and a swollen cheekbone. He's been stewing since Atlanta's Walt Bellamy clothes-lined him.

"I'm tired and frustrated," Van Lier said. "Anybody does that to me, he'll get the same thing. I'm an aggressive player, and I expect to take my lumps, but nobody in this league can ever say I played dirty basketball. Check how many times I drive, handle the ball and still don't get to shoot free throws.

"If it hurts the Bulls, I should shut down, but I'm human. How much can I put up with?"

According to O'Donnel, that was not the question.

"He took a deliberate swing at me," the Ref said. "Van Lier went wild, swinging like hell. It was the most flagrant fight I've ever seen."

That was Norm, in a nutshell. He took guff from no one, not even Motta. Bitter feelings between coach and player surfaced when Moving Van accused Motta of not backing him up the way he did for Sloan.

"I fear for Norm," Motta told me. "The consequences of his actions hurt his teammates, and I'd hate to trade him to a good friend."

That was life on the Bulls in the Motta era. Forward Chet Walker, one of the NBA's most respected players, summed it up in a single sentence:

"The Bulls are the Oakland A's of basketball."

Throughout Motta's eight-year moving festival of ferocious emotion, there was a stabilizing influence. Ironically, he was—and still is—a man who thrives on totally emotional basketball. He poured his guts onto the floor every night, along with a lot of his skin, while diving for every loose ball, snapping down rebounds with a hawk-like, one-armed swoop.

That was Jerry Sloan. Defense was his game, although he could score, and did. Because he was so relentless on defense, that one-dimensional label stuck.

It was unfair, just like the names they called him in the heat of hand-to-hand NBA combat. Most of those epithets were hyphenated, starting with the letter "m". Some called him "The Butcher," as though Sloan's all-out effort could be blunted by such kid stuff.

The names hurt, but couldn't stop Sloan from doing it his way—all-out, all the time. He willingly paid the price, just like Van Lier, wading into the middle, where the big men with sharp elbows and short tempers ruled.

"Jerry sets up on defense and dares people to run over him," Motta said. "Those long, bony arms are like telephone poles and he sticks his knee out, refusing to let them drive around him.

"Nobody in this league takes more punishment than Sloan. They beat on him all night under the boards, but he won't quit."

I know that's true, because I saw Sloan outhustle Pete Rose during his 11-year war with the NBA. The sight I can't forget was Sloan, stretched out on a rubbing table in the Bulls' dressing room while a foot-long cortisone needle got jabbed into his torn groin muscle. He got up, hobbled onto the court and played, while his teammates shook their heads in amazement.

Not Motta. The tough little coach knew this 6-foot-6 guard was even tougher than him; something few of the hulking athletes he dealt with could claim. They were more like brothers than coach and player. Both of them, the man who taught aggressive basketball and the man who made it happen on the floor, got accused of dirty tactics, a charge that stuck and stung.

In a signature episode, Elvin Hayes stood on the Chicago Stadium sideline one night, close enough to the press table for us to hear the stream of profanity he aimed at Sloan. None of the Big E's epithets began with the letter "E".

Sloan stood his ground, as always, replying to Hayes' threat of mayhem with a quiet, "Well, you better come on, then." The Big E backed down.

But the word was out. Phil Jackson, a rough customer in his playing days for the Knicks, enraged Motta by likening the Bulls to the Capone mob when they came to Madison Square Garden, with the New York writers lapping up every line. That sort of putdown from his peers probably caused Sloan more pain than all the injuries he kept playing through. Motta never failed to react.

A one-shot history of the way Jerry Sloan (top) and Norm Van Lier (bottom) played defense for the Bulls. They're making a sandwich of Elvin "Big E" Hayes in all-out pursuit of the basketball. It's under Stormin' Norman here, but Sloan and Van Lier were all over the court, leading the NBA in floorburns to pounce on every opponent with equal-opportunity ferocity.

"We work harder than anybody else, playing basketball the way it should be played," Motta told me repeatedly. You wouldn't be reading that 'dirty player' stuff if Sloan was on the Knicks." So there was some merit in Van Lier's notion that Motta spoke out in Sloan's defense a lot more than he did so after another stack-blowing eruption from Mt. Van Lier, a live volcano. When Sloan became an NBA coach, he and Motta competed just as ferociously against each other, but it never dampened their lifelong bond.

The Sloan-Van Lier backcourt duo needs no defense from Motta or anybody else. In their prime, during the early '70s, they were the best defensive guard tandem I've ever seen, in any era, on any level. Van Lier's explosive temper and Sloan's controlled fury blended like Abbott and Costello—Lou, not Larry.

Now, 35 years after he came to Chicago as an obscure selection in the expansion pool to stock the Bulls' roster for their inaugural season of 1966-67, Sloan still seeks his first NBA championship as a player or a coach. That had no impact on the way Chicago fandom elevated Sloan and Van Lier to their top-shelf blue-collar favorites. So did I.

Professional objectivity is fine, but I rooted for the Evansville Hustler and Moving Van, albeit a lot more quietly than the wild bunch that made the old Stadium rafters reverberate as though World War 6 7/8 was unfolding in the Madison Street Madhouse. Blackhawk fans aren't the only ones who remember the roar.

So when Sloan's aching knees and battered body finally wore out from a decade of unrelenting NBA effort, it was the end of a golden era in Chicago. If Sloan, Van Lier, Chet Walker, Bob Love, Tom Boerwinkle, and above all, Motta had failed to pull the Bulls back from the brink of oblivion, Michael Jordan would have won all those NBA championships somewhere else, because the Bulls would have been somewhere else.

When the last of the original Bulls retired, Motta moved out to win the 1978 NBA title as coach of the Washington Bullets. In Chicago, not even Sloan, in his first head coaching gig, could do what Motta did with them. No wonder, without a Sloan or Van Lier on the roster—so the Bulls sank back into the doldrums.

Nobody knew that it would take 13 years for the Bulls to get back to a conference final after the heartbreak of 1975. MJ led the way and the championship drought was over, with that tear-jerking scene of a sobbing Jordan embracing the 1991 NBA trophy. I was assigned to write a lot of playoff dressing room stories, "sidebars," in newspaper jargon, during the unprecedented era when the Bulls ruled not only the NBA, but also the sports scene across America and around the world.

Jordan's blend of charisma and incredible ability to make the play, hit the shot or do what had to be done in the clutch, kept the string of titles growing, the excitement mounting and the money rolling in. Everybody was happy, except the Bulls' final playoff victims—the Lakers, Portland, Phoenix, Seattle and the Utah Jazz twice. With good times up and unemployment down, scalpers got fat because people would pay almost any price to see Jordan make miraculous moves. His supporting cast contained some intriguing role players, especially moody Scottie Pippen, enigmatic Toni Kukoc and totally balmy Dennis Rodman.

I had dealings with the new breed of Bulls through most of the nifty '90s. It didn't take me long to discover what the beat writers already knew—Rodman was the all-time NBA flake, possibly the strangest character in Chicago sports history. That covers a lot of territory, but Dennis the Menace was a far-out case.

Oddly enough, pun intended, he was a very likeable man, despite the array of tattoos, nose ring, earring, metallic implants and self-inflicted punctures to various parts of his body. Rodman, to me, was a walking, talking cry of pain, bent on destroying himself. Instead of getting him the help he needed, the sports establishment cashed in on Rodman's unique rebounding skill and flamboyant crowd appeal.

But athletes always have been willing to sell their bodies, and even their souls, for the ultimate high—adulation from their fans, groupies and assorted hangers-on. I got an intriguing glimpse of how sports had changed when Isaiah Thomas, a Chicago native, came to play for Indiana against Northwestern. Already a superstar as a college sophomore, Thomas carried all the trappings, includ-

*With that trademark tongue hanging out, Michael Jordan drives
for another Bulls basket early in his illustrious career.*

ing a huge NBA-style retinue to provide a barrier between him and the media.

It was an amazing sight, especially for an Indiana player, the last team anyone figured to develop a personality cult rivaling the one that already existed. Bobby Knight always submerged individual talent and identities into the team concept. There was plenty of adulation from Hoosier fans, though it mostly went in one direction—straight to the coach.

So the Thomas traveling troupe was a revelation for Knight, although it already was happening elsewhere, with less-dominant coaches learning that putting up with super athletes' super egos was the only way to win games and save their own jobs. Knight never believed that, so it was no surprise to me that Thomas departed for NBA fame and fortune after leading IU to the 1981 NCAA tourney title. Although Knight would rather be boiled in oil than admit it, I'm convinced he did not go into mourning when Isaiah became the Detroit Pistons' newest multi-millionaire.

But the glorification of players and the downgrading of coaches' authority already was in vogue, especially among pro teams. NBA All-Star games suddenly turned into fashion shows, with an array of fur and jewelry—bedecked players strutting through hotel lobbies past goggle-eyed fans.

With that sort of anything-goes approach, pro basketball might have turned into a branch of the WWF. Fortunately, the ferocious competition between Larry Bird and Magic Johnson, followed by Jordan's incredible feats, kept the focus on the game instead of the off-court circus that threatened to engulf it. Rodman was caught between these conflicting forces. He was a natural, instinctive rebounder with a nose for the ball. That kept him in the league, despite a constant spate of outrageous antics in defiance of anything and everything that attempted to restrain his out-of-control lifestyle.

Luckily for Rodman, he found staunch allies when the Bulls dealt their fans' favorite punching bag, Will Perdue, to San Antonio for him on October 1, 1995. Those same fans promptly became rabid Rodman rooters, mainly because his rebounding helped lift the Bulls to another three-pack of NBA crowns. Jordan put up with Rodman's wild ways, because His Airness, unlike Bulls' boss Jerry Krause, was smart enough not to break up a winning combination.

Regardless, controversy surrounded Rodman like the tutti-frutti hair-do he wore in psychedelic colors. On the same day that Pat Kennedy took the reins at De Paul, vowing to restore the Blue Demons to college basketball's elite, the flower child of the Bulls was issuing an apology for insulting Mormons and getting slapped with a $50,000 NBA fine:

I'm No Mormon Menace—Dennis
(Daily Herald, June 13, 1997)

Dennis Rodman apologized Thursday for slurs made in Utah about the Mormon religion.

Too late and too little to prevent a big $50,000 fine, imposed by the NBA.

"I had no business saying that, so I take it back," Rodman said at a Bulls' workout before they tried to wrap up this final playoff with Utah. "If I had known it was one of those religious-type statements I never would have made it.

"But it was just a joke. I should have called them the Utah polygamists, because I was speaking about some of the people in Salt Lake City, the ones who cursed at me."

The fine marked the third time the league has come down on Rodman this season. He was suspended for 11 games and fined a then-record $25,000 in January for kicking a courtside photographer. Then Rodman coughed up $7,500 more in March for an altercation with Milwaukee's Joe Wolf. The suspension cost him more than $1 million in salary.

Bulls coach Phil Jackson, who's known to dabble in mysticism, came up with an outer-space explanation for Rodman's behavior.

"To Dennis, a Mormon may be just a person from Utah, Jackson said. "He might not even know the Mormons are a cult or a sect."

A few days later the Bulls were champs again and all was forgiven:

Bulls, Rodman Fine and Dandy
(Daily Herald, June 14, 1997)

Dennis Rodman was fine.

Not the $50,000 fine that had been slapped on him a day earlier, but fine and dandy, nonetheless. The NBA firebrand, now just a fizzling firecracker, scored one point but grabbed 11 rebounds Friday night while the Bulls' Drive for Five got the checkered flag, wheeling past the Utah Jazz 90-86. Fortunately, the man with the technicolor hair and matching vocabulary was speechless after the Bulls won NBA title V in Game VI of this final playoff.

Dodging the champagne-soaked media mob that got crammed into the Bulls' dressing room, victory cigar-puffing King Dennis held court in a United Center hallway. It was a spellbinding sight, especially his adoring claque of hangers-on from somewhere in the solar system.

"I didn't get involved in any incidents (well, not many), and I wasn't looking to get hit with technical fouls," Rodman purred. "All I can do is be what I am. I'm an entertainer, putting on a show for the crowd. You media guys wouldn't have a job without me.

"I have the bad reputation, but I've done a lot of good for this city. The fans won't give up on me, so I hope the Bulls don't. It's time to rally around and stop throwing darts at me. I give everything I've got on the floor and the real people appreciate me.

"David Stern (NBA commissioner) knows I'm an attraction," Rodman said, cutting loose at one of his favorite sparring partners. "They don't like something about me, but I make money for them and put fans in the seats."

True enough, although the unreal people appreciated him most. Rodman's NBA career was a springboard, catapulting him into the mainstream of the former underground society that now operates freely under the full glare of nationwide tabloid and TV coverage. It wasn't until the Magic-Bird-Jordan phenomenon of the '80s that pro basketball became really big news, spilling over onto Madison Avenue and rap-rock celebrity status. I had more fun dealing with only slightly flaky Bulls like Erwin Mueller.

A pleasant surprise in the Bulls' 1966-67 NBA debut, Mueller was "Wolfgang" to the other players. The gangly 6-foot-8 rookie became the starting center, largely by default, but playmaker Guy Rodgers, a tough, street-wise veteran, took Mueller under his wing.

John "Red" Kerr, the Bulls' first coach, should have been named NBA Coach of the Century, instead of just that first year, for somehow nudging his expansion team into the playoffs without a center. In those days, the paint was ruled by behemoths like Wilt Chamberlain. Mueller found that out in a hurry, although the 6-8 neophyte astonished lots of people, including himself, by scoring 18 points in one memorable first quarter against towering Warriors' veteran Nate Thurmond.

Then came the rude awakening, when Chamberlain used Mueller and Jim Washington as footstools for his last 60-plus NBA game, pouring in 68 points to bury the Bulls. No wonder Mueller soon learned to ward off anxiety attacks by stuffing a couple of six-packs into his traveling bag, Even though the fans jeered Wolfgang's ungainly appearance, he fit in better than the roly-poly Bill Buntin or Nate "The Great" Bowman, who later became a sort of cult figure with the New York Knicks.

"I can teach Buntin to play center, but I can't teach him to grow,"quipped Kerr, in another of his inexhaustible one-liners.

Mueller was no Rodman, but he served as the house character for a while. With so few spectators in the International Amphitheater, the boos for Wolfgang weren't too loud to prevent this easygoing guy from enjoying himself. He deserves to be a footnote in Bulls' history, along such other forgettables as Izzy Schmissing, Dave Schellhase, Lonnie Klutz, Zvonimir Petrocevic (the only thing major-league about him was his appetite, Kerr lamented about the seven-foot Yugoslavian reject), Cliff Pondexter, "Andy Collier" (actually, sportswriter Bob Billings) and more. Lots more.

My nomination for the most forgettable signee in franchise history was Howard Porter, who might have made it if the NBA played the way girls' basketball teams used to in Iowa: one team on offense, another on defense, with neither allowed past halfcourt. An All-American at Villanova and an early pawn in the costly ABA-NBA bidding war, Porter simply could not play defense.

He was a costly mistake by Dick Motta, who demanded that the Bulls sign him away from the other league's Pittsburgh franchise. "He can be the next Gus Johnson," Motta said, somehow confusing the raw youngster with a real basketball player. So the Bulls forked over $1.6 million for Porter, more than it had cost them to get the Chicago franchise five years earlier.

The Bulls finally junked their failed Porter venture, palming him off on the Knicks. It gave Phoenix columnist Joe Gilmartin, master of the one-liner, an opening. Accosting Knicks coach Red Holzman in a New York hotel lobby, he inquired, "Red, where you gonna put the Howard Porter statue?"

Fortunately for me, the statue of limitations hasn't expired on crummy puns. I still trade them with my fellow NBA hoop scribes, who respond by recalling my trademark pressbox line (Honest, it was quoted verbatim by Bill Nichols of the *Cleveland Plain Dealer* in a Bulls-Cavaliers game story): "I predict a hard-fought contest between two evenly matched squads."

But not all of the NBA's daily doings were pure fun and games. In an increasingly complex world, the actions of pro athletes are looked at all the time, not just when they're performing. With millions showered on them, a sizeable percentage of players play harder off the court. The sports page increasingly resembles the police blotter. It's a dilemma for the beat writers, but everything gets covered now, especially when the participants are uncovered.

Such was the case of Quintin Daily, the Bulls' first-round draft choice in 1982. He came to Chicago with some baggage, acquired at the University of San Francisco, and it turned into a gigantic public relations fiasco.

The three-year probation Daily got for allegedly assaulting a woman student at USF was known to the Bulls, who put incentives in his $1.5 million contract that would reward him for staying out of trouble. What they didn't take into account was that the ERA had been voted down by the Illinois legislature a few days before they drafted the 6-3 guard. That added feminist fuel to the firestorm of abuse heaped on the franchise.

For new coach Paul Westhead and General Manager Rod Thorn, it was a bad dream that wouldn't go away. Dailey, under a cloud from Day 1, lasted only slightly longer than Westhead, who stepped down after a dismal 28-54 record in 1982-83. Trying to defuse the issue, the Bulls moved their training camp to Peoria, only to be greeted by this word from the National Organization for Women:

"Peoria NOW is dismayed at Dailey's lack of repentance and the Bulls' callous lack of respect...".

It also listed plans to picket practices with such attention-grabbing signs as "Neuter the Bull". No wonder season-ticket sales, already low, dropped by 10 percent.

Weird goings-on seemed to go on often around the Bulls. Such stuff happened in games, on planes (where Bob Love delighted in bankrupting low-budget writers in an exotic card game were the lone rule often turned out to be "You lose"), in the locker rooms, deep in the bowels of ancient Chicago Stadium and especially in the Bulls' front office. A random sample:

Time Stands Still for Baffled Bulls
(Chicago Tribune, Nov. 7, 1969)

The Atlanta Hawks owe this weird victory to the fact that another team named the Hawks plays in Chicago Stadium.

If that sounds strange, it figures. Lots of strange things happened, including the final score: Atlanta 125, Bulls 122. Time-keeper Jim Seri, who controls the huge, 20-minute hockey clock hanging over mid-court, got into the act as the end, along with both coaches.

The Bulls blew a nine-point lead in the second half, so two Lou Hudson free throws put the visitors on top with five seconds on the clock. Clem Haskins (Later the Minnesota coach forced out by charges of illegal classroom aid for Gophers players) took a desperation shot from 30 feet, and Tom Boerwinkle grabbed the rebound, soaring to slap it in for the tying basket. With the crowd of 9,087 in a frenzy, referee Jack Madden, bounded out, waving his arms in the "wipeout" signal. Meanwhile, the other official, Bob Rakel, indicated the basket was good.

No wonder Hawks player-coach Richie Guerin started haranguing both referees and Seri. Coach Dick Motta of the Bulls promptly got into the act, with players from both teams forming a Greek chorus to add their lamentations to the pandemonium. The clock was stopped, two ticks away from the straight-up position signaling the end of play.

"The buzzer went off a split second before Boerwinkle touched the ball," Madden said, abruptly declaring the game over and sensibly fleeing the premises. Enraged, Motta had to be restrained from charging after him.

"Hell, no, there's not a chance of our protest to the league standing up," Motta said.

This time, the Mighty Mite was wrong. The Bulls' beef was legit, so after a hassle that stopped just short of the Supreme Court, the refs ruling got reffed up, Boerwinkle's bucket counted and the final-second tie was ordered to be finished seconds before the teams next met in Chicago. The second time around, the Hawks won in overtime.

Weird games? The Bulls were bullish on them. My all-time favorite was the Super Shay Halimon spectacular—three baskets in the last eight seconds of the fourth quarter—enabling the Bulls to pull a bigger heist than a Brinks job. And if I had to pick one zany scene from the thousands I saw all over the NBA, it might be the sight of mild-mannered Bucks General Manager John Erickson, lunging across the courtside press table in blind fury. Erickson later ran for the U.S. Senate from Wisconsin, but maybe he would have lost even bigger if this opponent had circulated a photo of

Aside from Artis Gilmore, the two best centers ever to play for the Bulls, Tom Boerwinkle (left) and Clifford Ray (44) are pitted against each other in Chicago Stadium. Sadly, they were on opposite sides when Boerwinkle and the Bulls lost a heartbreaking 1975 Western Conference NBA playoff to Ray and the Golden State Warriors.

Erickson's hands clutching the official timer's throat. He didn't make it, but the Bulls did in this insane affair:

Super Shay a 1-Second Sensation
(Chicago Tribune, Jan. 18, 1970)

Milwaukee, Jan. 17—Six points by one player in eight seconds? Pick your word to describe it.

Some suggestions from a tourist who, like the rest of today's 10,746 Milwaukee Arena witnesses, still finds it hard to believe:

(A) Fantastic, (B) Unbelievable, (C) Take two tarot cards and call your friendly neighborhood soothsayer in the morning. It should take the city of beer and bratwurst a few burps to digest the 132-130 overtime decision the battling Bulls swiped from the baffled Bucks.

It took a little bit of luck and a lot of dead-eye shooting by Shaler Halimon, a throw-in on the trade with Philadelphia that brought Chet Walker to Chicago. All Super Shay did was throw in three straight baskets in the last eight seconds of regulation time, nailing a 15-footer on the final tick for a 122-122 deadlock.

Tom Boerwinkle fouled out early in the extra session, but reserve Bob Kauffman somehow stopped 7-foot-2 Bucks rookie Lew Alcindor from bullying the Bulls into submission. Milwaukee led 115-100 less than four minutes before Halimon's third clutch shot. He got the chance because an inbound pass hit a wire supporting the basket with one second on the clock.

Erickson's ire was understandable, because a quick trigger on the final horn would have saved the staggering Bucks.

"I asked if I should pass," said Halimon, who shot the tying prayer from behind a double screen in the left corner. "The coach (Motta) told me, 'There's no time. Get it up.'"

He did.

The Bulls didn't always get the better of it from officials, opponents and out-of-town reporters, who called them the NBA's dirtiest team and other high-octane epithets. It ate at all of them, none

Bob Boozer, the Bulls' big gun in their early years, gets shadowed by legendary Philadelphia 76ers. Left to right, they are Chet Walker, Billy Cunningham and Wilt Chamberlain.

more than Chet Walker, one of the NBA's best players and best people. Used to the spotlight as a member of the mid-60s Philadelphia 76ers, one of the top basketball teams in any era or any league Chet, the Jet, felt overlooked and underappreciated in Chicago.

He had too much class to whine, but when Walker went wild, he let loose of a lot of pent-up bile. Such was the case after the Bulls lost a 106-105 crusher to the Los Angeles Lakers in Chicago Stadium on December 12, 1972. Walker's last-second basket was tossed out by referees Paul Mihalik and Mark Mano, although Bob Blaha, the official timer, told them the shot had beaten the final horn. Mad as hell, Chet wouldn't take it any more.

"Nobody respects this club," Walker roared. Any superstar in the league would never have been questioned on the shot. All I want is a fair shake. It's easy to make a call against us. Who are we? What kind of a name is the Bulls? Bulls-bullshit."

At that time, there was some merit to Walker's lament. Not until 15 years later did "Bulls" become the most famous team nickname in the wide world of sports, because it was linked inseparably with the greatest athlete in the known—and quite possibly, the unknown-universe, mercurial Michael Jordan. That was too late for Walker and the rest of the original Bulls, who never got the one world championship ring they deserved, let alone the half-dozen weighing down Jordan's dexterous digits. The Motta-fired Bulls were Motta-fied by their loss to Golden State in the 1975 Western Conference final playoff, an experience traumatic enough to rank up there with the 1969 Cub collapse.

The way I look at it, they were winners, none more than former Bradley All-American Walker. An intense competitor, the 6-7 forward fretted so much when playoff time rolled around that he sometimes had to perform with hives, a rash that causes intense itching. That itch to excel drove Walker to a 56-point barrage against the Cincinnati Royals in a Sunday Stadium matinee on February 6, 1972. He's in the Bulls' record book as the only man—besides Jordan, of course—to crack the 50-point barrier.

Nobody who knew Chester at Bradley or in Philadelphia, where he was even a favorite of those flint-hearted Philly fans, or in

Chicago was surprised that he went to Hollywood when he retired from the Bulls to become a successful movie producer. One of the best things about my NBA years was dealing with the original Bulls— Walker, Sloan, Van Lier, Love, Boerwinkle, Bob Weiss— the king of dressing room one-liners—and a lot of other good people. Walker had innate class and dignity that earned respect even though he didn't believe the officials felt that way. The Bulls were a lively bunch, turned into a mean, though not always lean, fighting machine by Motta's intense coaching style.

And Jim Durham—"Just call me J.D."—was the right radio and TV voice for this charismatic crew. He had the ability to keep things under control on the air, even when they gyrated wildly on the court. Amid all the flying oaths, bodies, elbows, knees, fists and occasional chairs, his voice cut through the pandemonium.

But basketball teams, great and small, need coaches. In Motta, they had one of the best, although nobody—except Motta himself —knew that on the day Bulls boss Dick O. Klein pulled a rabbit out of his hat. Thanks to the little man from the Big Sky country, this was the start of something big in Chicago sports.

What's the Motta with the Bulls?
(Chicago Tribune, May 28, 1968)

Baseball has its unknown soldier in Commissioner William D. Eckert and the Chicago Bulls now have their unknown coach.

It became official yesterday when the Bulls admitted that Dick Motta had signed a two-year contract as head coach of the NBA team. The word had leaked out, so unveiling the Weber (Utah) State coach was no surprise.

Ironically, a new face on the Chicago scene made his debut on the day that one of the great names, George Halas of the Bears, stepped down. Things have been going that way lately for the Bulls.

Motta, a winner in college, is climbing into a difficult situation. He has seen only 12 NBA games as a spectator, but added, "If I didn't think I could coach in the NBA, I wouldn't be here." As successor to the easy-going John (Red) Kerr, Motta served notice that he would run a tighter ship.

"I don't like to be taken advantage of," he said of his coaching philosophy. "My job is teaching and selling myself to the players. I'm not a good loser and I don't intend to be a loser in the NBA."

Motta's rubber-stamp reference was an admission that he knew of the friction between Kerr and Dick Klein, the Bulls' general manager. Their acrimony resulted in Kerr's resignation to become coach of the new Phoenix NBA franchise.

Klein shrugged off a suggestion that Motta was hired to serve as a yes man.

"My job is to get Motta the ballplayers he thinks he needs," Klein said. "He'll have the same authority Kerr did—total and complete—in running the team."

If any of we dim-witted hoop scribes had been able to read between the lines of that exchange, it really was battle lines being drawn between these strong-willed men. Because he knew how to make pros win most of their battles on the court, Motta eventually won that behind-the-scenes war with Klein. Both wanted the same thing badly—an NBA championship—but because they had different ideas of how to make it happen, clashes were inevitable. It didn't take long for bitter personal enmity to emerge.

When Klein dealt holdout Keith Erickson to the Lakers for recycled Erwin "Wolfgang" Mueller, the honeymoon was over in a hurry. Motta's outraged gesture, throwing a dollar bill on the court "to see if it could play," touched off a struggle for survival with Klein. It escalated so fast that Motta issued an ultimatum to Klein just hours before a Chicago Stadium game on November 23, 1968, only his 20th as coach of the Bulls.

"If Flynn Robinson shows up to play for the Bulls tonight, I quit," Motta told his dumbfounded GM.

That would have put Klein on thin ice with the money men who held shares of the Bulls, so he was forced to trade Robinson, a sharpshooting showboat, to the Milwaukee Bucks for a couple of fringe players named Bob Love and Bob Weiss. Motta's description of the panic-driven transaction as one of the NBA's best ever wasn't totally inaccurate.

Besides landing two players who turned out to be more productive than anyone could imagine on that dark and stormy night, Motta also gained the upper hand for the rest of his volatile eight seasons as the Bullmaster. The skids were greased for Klein, but when the owners hired Bill Veeck protegee Pat Williams as general manager, Pat suffered the same fate in a one-sided power push by Motta.

It wasn't that easy to unload players, so Motta had long-playing disputes with some of them. There was no love lost between Motta and Love, even though they played major roles in the Bulls' sudden switch from a DOA franchise, wearing a toe tag that read, "Ship to Memphis, Cincinnati, Omaha or wherever." Sadly, twin holdouts by Love and Norm Van Lier, in a bid to copy the Sandy Koufax-Don Drysdale salary squeeze on the Dodgers, came back to torment the Bulls and their fans, probably costing them the 1975 NBA crown Chicago was so anxious to wear.

But Love's success story was too important to be ignored. Eventually, his No. 10 jersey got retired, to hang in the arena rafters alongside Sloan's No. 4, plus a No. 23 that, by some wizardry, later resurfaced in Washington. All was forgiven, because the fans preferred to remember Love's blend of slick scoring, plus his dogged— at times, even Bullish defense:

Bulls Join Fans' Love Affair
(Daily Herald, Jan. 14, 1994)

It's about time the Bulls got around to retiring Bob Love's No. 10.

Few, if any, NBA defenders had Love's number during the first half of the 1970s, when the stringbean forward they called "Butterbean" was canning points and jarring opponents. Soon after the 6-8 forward with the automatic 15-foot jump shot proved he belonged in the big time, the tag got shortened to

"Butter". His friends still call them that as a token of affection and respect.

Love has earned it, along with the honor of watching his jersey hoisted to the ceiling. His ability to spot up around the lane for that money-from-home jumper fit into Coach Dick Motta's disciplined offensive patterns. Although he and Motta clashed frequently, usually about salary, neither would have been as successful in the NBA without the other man. Love matched up with pro basketball's top-scoring forwards, usually holding them under their average.

Because the rip-snorting backcourt of Jerry Sloan and Norm Van Lier symbolized the Bulls' defense, Love's contribution sometimes got overlooked. But NBA peers respected his work on both ends of the court.

And today's fans know of Love's battle against a speech defect that had plagued him throughout his career, preventing the stuttering star from cashing in on his success. Sometimes, as in one TV spot with Jack Brickhouse, attempts to speak became a futile struggle. But Love overcame that with the grit that turned him from an unknown to an All-Star. Cut by the Cincinnati Royals, Love rode buses for $25 a game in the semi-pro Eastern League to earn a second NBA chance.

With the Bulls, that effort paid off. Love and Chet Walker gave the Bulls one of the best front lines of their era. With the offense rotating smoothly around center Tom Boerwinkle's passes, they kept the Stadium rocking for a frantic, fantastic time in Chicago sports. It all came crashing down in the 1975 Western Conference finals. Leading the Golden State Warriors 3-2 in that unforgettable series, the Bulls fell one agonizing game short.

The bitterness triggered by that painful failure has faded with time. What Bulls fans will recall tonight is the sheer pleasure of watching the Bulls' bread get buttered by Butter in those wonderful years.

But the Bulls wouldn't be a Chicago team without more thorns (not Rod Thorn, of course) than rose petals strewn in their stormy existence. After Motta left, the Bad Old Days of the lost games and empty seats returned. For instance:

New Year's Hangover Starts Early
(Chicago Tribune, Jan. 3, 1979)

Landover, Md.—Happy New Year, Bull fans.

You can crawl out from under the bed or wherever you fled to escape that apparition on the TV screen. No, it was not a horror flick entitled "The Merciless Mottamen's Revenge." Merely the Bulls, starting 1979 with a dull thud Tuesday night in the Capital Centre. The Washington Bullets chopped them into Bullburgers 109-86. So remorseless were they that even the massive electronic scoreboard couldn't bear to watch.

Frazzled by the strain of toting up points faster than a speeding Bullet, the king-sized Nintendo game blew a fuse in the third quarter. Since the Bulls had done the same much earlier, it seemed pointless. Instead, the ensuing 22-minute delay gave the crowd of 7,578 time to ponder if the Bullets are that good or the Bulls that bad.

"A little bit of both tonight," said Dick Motta, coach of the defending NBA champs, after thoughtfully inserting the Washington waterboys to get it over with. Until then, the onslaught was so balanced that the Bulls went down in a hail of Bullets.

"The next time we play them, it'll be a different story," said Reggie Theus, the lone bit of flash and dazzle in a Chicago lineup overloaded with dismal dribblers.

Rapid Reggie didn't mean the Bulls would be worse. That might prove impossible.

My parting shot to the Bulls, I hope, will turn out to be a line I wrote almost 30 years ago. A team owner told me it had influenced their vote to reject Canadian millionaire Peter Graham's $3.5 million offer to buy the Bulls. If the vote had gone the other way chances are Michael Jordan would have won six NBA titles for the San Diego Bulls, with thousands of laid-back California types sipping Chablis and yawning their approval. In setting up the scenario, with some pivotal votes still on the fence, I asked the musical question:

"Are you a Graham backer or a Graham cracker?"

It's not up there with "I shall return", or "This was their finest hour," but for better or worse, that line was read by the men who held the franchise's fate in their hands.

Three decades later, the Bulls are still in Chicago. Even if I didn't have anything to do with that, I'm glad they stuck around.

4

Bear Downs—And Ups

Neill Armstrong was my idea of a Bears coach. There were only 11 1/2 Bruin tamers, George Halas to Dick Jauron, from 1920 through 2001 counting co-coaches Hunk Anderson and Luke Johnsos (1942-45), an amazing statistic.

The Cubs seem to go through that many every other season, especially in their golden age of comedy (1962-65) when seven—not the lucky Seven Dwarfs, but the unlucky seven Mental Midgets—flunked out of their ill-conceived College of Coaches.

But in the NFL, where they keep statistics about the number of statistics, a dozen coaches in 81 years is a paltry sum, indeed. I got to schmooze with the Grandpappy of them all, George Stanley Halas, while he tooled around the old practice field at Lake Forest College in his golf cart. Once in a while, Papa Bear would invite us ink-stained wretches into his den, an office on Madison Street. If those picture-laden walls could talk, the history of football, from the flying wedge to the Champaign Bears, would spring to life. Whatever tall tales they told, Halas could—and would—top them all.

Armstrong, a true Southern gentleman, shied away from the free-flowing ribaldry that's as much a part of the locker room as sweat-soaked jock straps. He was a gentle, genial guy, a former end on Greasy Neale's powerhouse Philadelphia Eagles. Not many of us are liked by everybody, but he was one of the rare exceptions.

Unfortunately, Armstrong's charm did not translate into coaching prowess. He lasted only four years (1978-81), with a 30-35 record, right in the middle of the all-time Bear list. But he was my first NFL coach, so I stupidly assumed they were much more of a genteel breed than the Bulls' Dick Motta, a small man with a large temper, who could terrify strapping 6-10 NBA goons with one merciless glare.

A five-letter word proved my NFL-coach-as-good-guy theory was (a) Goofy, (b) Wrong. That word was spelled D-I-T-K-A. When the Bears went to their Platteville, Wisconsin, training camp for the first time in the summer of 1984, I went with them because Don Pierson, the *Chicago Tribune*'s Bear beat man, and one of the best pro football writers anywhere, got packed off to cover the summer Olympics.

So there I was, right in the middle of a wilderness I described in print as "Miles and miles of nothing but miles and miles," surrounded by hulking bodies with gargantuan appetites and a couple of charismatic characters—Ditka and Jim McMahon. I soon discovered it was too bad Jungle Jim Rivera of the 1959 White Sox— the last pennant-winner on either side of Chicago—already had dibs on that nickname.

For Madman McMahon, the moniker would have fit like the straitjacket that should have been worn by some of his fiercely protective linemen. The punky QB was so fearless, disregarding the danger to his fragile body amid swarms of burly pursuers, that he willed the Bears to win. If McMahon had been in command of a rival army, he would have given Blood and Guts Patton a snootful of dust while roaring past him on the fastest route to Berlin.

Even a pro football babe in the woods could see that, while standing on the sidelines for those murderous two-a-day workouts under Platteville's sweltering sun and stifling humidity. McMahon stuck his nose in there, daring Bears bruisers to hit him, while Ditka screamed from the sidelines, loud enough to be heard in Dubuque, Iowa.

It's fortunate that Ditka and McMahon sometimes saw eye to eye, and probably inevitable. Each of these reckless, devil-may-care men recognized the same craving for combat in the other, so there was mutual respect. Between them, they were the driving force that whipped the Bears into a frenzy, and into their 1986 Super Bowl XX triumph.

Buddy Ryan, boss of the fearsome 46 defense that bullied Bears' opponents, disputed that fact then, and still does. Ryan always stood up for his guys, forging a personal bond with them that Ditka's rigid personality couldn't match. No wonder there was constant conflict between the head coach and his defensive coordinator, sometimes stopping just short of a broken jaw—which doubtless would have been Ryan's.

For that, and countless other reasons, this 1984 maiden voyage aboard the S.S. Platteville was plenty stormy, the sort of scene writers delight in covering and fans revel in reading about. The whole place was a Freudian theory in living color, with the clash of ids, egos, bodies and minds reverberating through Southwest Wisconsin. There were lots of other moments to remember, both before and after that eventful summer of 1984, but it was what some ponderous pundits in my profession would label a defining moment in the modern era of the Bears.

Besides that, Harry Caray was inciting Cub fans into orgiastic frenzies by bellowing "Cubs Win! Cubs Win!" at least until the playoff scene shifted from rapturous Wrigleyville to sushi-sampling San Diego. With the Cubs going down and the Bears on the way up, I figured George Orwell knew it all the time when he wrote a frightening glimpse of the future. For the Bears, almost every year has been Orwell's *1984*. Like this, for instance:

Miracle on McFetridge Drive

Yes, I left Solder Field in the fourth quarter on November 4, 2001. So did thousands of others, convinced the Bears had run out

*Quarterback Jim McMahon (left) and running back Walter Payton
stood taller than the Sears Tower and the Wrigley Building while
sparking the Bears and their Shufflin' Crew to a 1986 Super Bowl
triumph. Yet, coach Mike Ditka's decision to let William "Refrigerator" Perry score instead of Payton in that 46-10 romp over New
England struck a sour note with Sweetness.*

of miracle finishes, rabbit's feet, voodoo or whatever had been trans-
forming this sad-sack bunch of losers to a band of vandals (no, not
Vikings), intent on sacking and burning the NFL. Even the most
beered-up of Bearaholics knew it was too late.

With the Bears down 21-7 and mere minutes left, no chance
to Bear up on this sunny Chicago Sunday. The shades of night
were falling fast, but the Cleveland Browns fell faster. Before the
baffled Brownies could blink, they were deader than the St. Louis
Browns. The last-minute blitz that took the Browns downtown
was a rerun of the way the Bears tore the heart from San Francisco
a week before.

So the Monsters of the Midway are back. Well . . . almost.
Beer-guzzling Bear boosters must switch to Champaign until their
Soldier Field den, stuffed into a strange sort of saucer, reopens for
business in 2003. If they can afford the ransom for a seat license in
the refurbished lakeside fumble factory, those fanatics will sit through
"Halas weather"—that's bitter cold—to see an NFL Central contender.

These selfsame Monsters had been in hibernation for far too
many frosty Chicago winters. Those icy winds that cut you in half
when they blow straight off Lake Michigan felt no colder than
Despairbear fans waiting in vain since 1985 for Da Bears to hold
on to da football. Chances are Mike Ditka could have brought them
back to their Super Bowl pinnacle, instead of playing pinochle,
after a long-simmering dispute with Mike McCaskey got him fired
on January 5, 1993.

McCaskey held the dual titles of Bears president and role model
for those Supernerd flicks of the '90s without distinction in either
case. McCaskey himself was demoted to executive in charge of
flipping cards into a hat, or some such similar innocuous task in
the Bears hierarchy after his incredible goof-up in the abortive hiring of Dave McGiniss as coach in 1999. Not surprisingly, Madison
Avenue Mike McCaskey, unlike Iron Mike Ditka, sank into obscurity without his public persona.

No such thing happened to Ditka, nor ever will. He was—
and is—the kind of man who will not go quietly into that dark
night, or sunlight or anywhere else. Controversy gets wrapped

around this complex man like his own skin, and he barreled through it as a coach the same way he did it as a football player—straight ahead, all-out.

Ditka would have been an exceptional man in any era or any profession. Unlike a lot of his contemporary NFL Hall of Famers who were largely forgotten except for rehashes of their on-the-field feats, Ditka remains larger than life. He still is one of the most popular Chicago sports figures and front-runners in what passes for Chicago's unique version of upper-crust society, welcome at every black-tie charity event.

Quite a turn of evens for a rough, tough son of first-generation Ukranian-Americans who settled in Western Pennsylvania and earned a living by sweating in the steel mills. Ditka knew how to survive before he became the Bears' first-round draft pick in 1961. Once he got to Chicago, it seemed like destiny. Instead of Sinatra warbling "My Kind of Town," it should have been Ditka.

His blend of brains and brawn was a winning Windy City combination. Ditka knocked off some of the rough edges by bashing into beefy, burly NFL types until his body was so battered, he had to quit taking more punishment than he dished out. By then it was 1973, and Ditka wore a Super Bowl ring from the Dallas Cowboys, where he became an assistant coach under legendary coach Tom Landry. It's hard to imagine how the poles-apart styles of taciturn Landry and volatile Ditka meshed, but that apprenticeship furnished the tools for Iron Mike's reunion with Halas, the coach—and the man—he respected above all others.

They had been clashing ever since the brash All-American rookie from Pittsburgh burst onto the NFL pigskin parade with the Bears. Ditka soon was the leader here, as he had been ever since high-school days in Alaquippa, Pennsylvania. People there still fondly recall the mixture of awe and fear he created among not only opponents, but his own teammates and coaches. Clearly, this was a guy you didn't want to mess with.

It was true then, although Ditka shows signs of mellowing in his 60s. But the steel is still there, right under that iron hide. Radio station WSCR still rekindles the spark in Ditka diehards by replaying the classic tape of Da Coach telling a belligerent listener

Mike Ditka, with that traditional victory cigar in his mouth, was the center of attention wherever he went. The charismatic coach of the Bears knew how to charm even hostile fans, but it was his popularity in Chicago, bordering on adulation, that kept "Da Coach" in power.

to meet him later, "and I'll whip your ass." A coat of big-city polish couldn't conceal the competitor who could talk, or brawl, or both with the biggest or baddest, one at a time or all at once.

Verbal and/or physical free-for-alls were Ditka's trademark. That was true during the conversation I had with him at the Bears 1984 training camp. It was their first season in Platteville, Wisconsin, and after 3-6 (in his strike-shortened 1982 debut) and 8-8 records in Years I and II of the Ditka Dynasty, the coach was wrangling with Mike McCaskey about a new contract. Bears' fans already were swearing by Ditka and swearing at McCaskey, who was trying to fill shoes much too big for him. Papa Bear, George Stanley Halas, had died at 88 on October 31, 1983, leaving a gaping void in the league he brought to life in 1920.

In fairness to McCaskey, very few men could have followed George Halas. He was the man who warmed up right field for Babe Ruth before the Yankees brought the Bambino to New York to bash gargantuan home runs that made fans run home and spread the word. Babe brought everybody rushing to the box office, anxious to kick off the Golden Age of sport. For the record, Halas played the outfield in just six games for the Yankees, collecting a pair of singles and striking out eight times in 22 at-bats, a feeble .091 average. Released, Halas played out the season in the minors and then got back to the game where he belonged, to be in the eye of the NFL whirlwind for 63 eventful years.

But 1919 was an exciting year all over America. While Halas and his cronies prepared to sit around and dole out pro football franchises to each other at $100 a throw in that Canton, Ohio, auto showroom scene that's probably more familiar to lots of us than the Declaration of Independence signing, the roaring Twenties were dawning. Bootleg booze, hip flasks, flappers, Stutz Bearcats, raccoon coats and Al Capone shared headlines with Ruth, Rockne, the Four Horsemen, Dempsey-Tunney, Bobby Jones—and Harold "Red" Grange. The Wheaton Iceman was the hottest thing ever to come out of the University of Illinois, including Halas himself.

When Grange electrified the country in 1925 by scoring four first-quarter touchdowns against Michigan to inaugurate Memorial Stadium on the sprawling Illini campus, he became an instant immortal. Halas was smart enough to cash in on Grange's fame, giving the struggling NFL enough visibility to survive and eventually flourish. He paid the '20s version of Michael Jordan enough money to parade him around the country, whetting fans' appetites for the post-collegiate game.

Halas needed his business acumen and his fierce competitive nature to keep the Bears afloat in a sea of red ink during the Depression. He came through it all, handing down a sports legacy to Chicago that's worth lots more than money. What Halas built is what made Ditka turn down a far bigger offer from Houston of the rival American Football League. Ditka needed the tradition and work ethic Halas personified. In a real sense, he was the son that Halas wanted to entrust with the franchise.

I realize much of this tale is ancient history to young fans. Some of them gave up on the Bears during the Dave Wannstedt stage of frustrated hopes, from 1993 through '98. Even some hardline Bears fans were ready to wave the white flag in Dick Jauron's first two years as Wannie's successor. In all sports, though, the pendulum swings sooner or later—as post-Jordan Bulls fans discovered to their dismay.

I believe the Halas legacy is alive and well. Ditka kept it going at a time when traditionalists were looked on as not-quite-with-it people. Now the skeptics are on the wane, true-blue believers are feasting on those miracle finishes, and fans of the Champaign-bound Bears are ready for another sip of Super Bowl champagne.

Whether any or all of this will happen before Soldier Field's long-overdue facelift gets finished is a good question. For me, it's not the most important one. I keep reflecting on the talk Ditka and I had in Platteville. He seldom opens up with the media, so I didn't know what to expect when we sat down and I asked where he intended to go with the Bears, and how he expected to get there.

"There are some guys on this team who like to question everything I try to do," Ditka said. "They won't be around long. I'm not looking for a bunch of robot yes men. Jim McMahon goes his own way, but when it comes to winning, we're on the same page.

"He's a leader, because apathetic people get him ticked off. Apathy kills a football team more than turnovers. If a guy turns it over trying to make something happen, I can't fault him. But if anybody's out there playing for a paycheck, he won't last."

The Bear defense was ahead of the offense at that stage of the Ditka regime. Cantankerous Buddy Ryan, the defensive coordinator, missed no opportunity to gloat about it. With all-out hitters like Danimal Hampton and Gary Fencik in Ryan's corner, Ditka had to swallow much of his dislike for the defensive dictator, rather than torpedo the team. It was a shrewd move. Ryan's bunch of bashers proved they would go to war for him, and Ditka had to make sure it wouldn't turn into a civil war.

"We kicked their ass," Ryan chortled gleefully to me after the defense dominated the 1984 intra-squad scrimmage. The personal enmity between Ryan and Ditka kept growing, but so did the Bear victory totals—10-6 in '84, 15-1 in '85, plus a three-game playoff sweep, capped by their colossal 46-10 pounding of the overmatched New England Patriots in Super Bowl XX, on January 26, 1986.

The final score was widely noted as a tribute to the notorious 46 defense, Ryan's pride and joy. He stopped short of claiming he invented that alignment, using four down linemen and six defensive backs, leaving middle linebacker Mike Singletary free to roam and pursue with wide-eyed abandon. When I visited with ex-Bears head coach, Neill Armstrong, later an assistant with Ditka, on Landry's crackerjack Dallas staff, he reminded me that variations of the 46 defense had been used around the NFL for years.

Gleeful fans and writers, keeping score on the hate-in between Ryan and Ditka, recall that Buddy played the one-upmanship game with fiendish skill to enrage his boss. Ditka always insisted he didn't care if players like or loathed him—and all shades of emotion between those extremes existed on his teams—although Ryan's popularity among the players had to be irritating. Not as much, in all probability, as the way Buddy and his defensive buddies flaunted their mutual admiration society.

Amid the jubilation of the Bears' Super Bowl rout, the clash of super egos raged on. While Ditka was being carried off the field by Refrigerator Perry and Mongo McMichael, a couple of defensive stalwarts, it seemed like at least 46 other Bears defenders were vying for the chance to hoist Ryan on their shoulders as well. They knew their best Buddy was being wooed by the Philadelphia Eagles, and some of the emotion at finding the Bears on football's summit for the first time got tempered by the gloom of his impending departure.

The night before the Superdome slaughter, Ryan met with his defense for the last time. It was a scene straight out of "Knute Rockne, All-American", with Pat O'Brien, as Ryan, delivering the tear-jerking pep talk.

"You guys are my heroes," Ryan blubbered.

Cornball, colossal hoke? In Damon Runyan terms, the old phonus bolonus? Probably a little of each, mixed with the awkward affection men show for each other, especially when they try to verbalize instead of the standard fanny pats. What mattered to Ryan's heroes is that they believed in him.

Few Bears have been more respected than Mike Singletary, on and off the field. I trudged to the Bears' den in Lake Forest to write a story about USC offensive tackle Keith Van Horne, the 1981 top draft pick, when grunts of disbelief and grimaces of dismay arose. The No. 2 Bears choice turned out to be an undersized, unheralded Baylor linebacker. Mike Singletary? Sure, he was known to be a heavy hitter for the Baylor Bears, but this was the Chicago Bears.

Asking Singletary to handle middle linebacking chores seemed silly to those who recalled the way Dick Butkus dominated that position, rewriting the concept of NFL defense from 1966 through '73. True, Butkus played on some bad Bears teams, especially in 1969, when their 1-13 catastrophe made the Cubs' September swoon in that same year seem like a stretch drive, if only by comparison. Those Midgets of the Midway made Butkus loom even more fearsome, again by contrast.

But Singletary was the mainstay for a dandy dozen years, especially the five straight smash-and-crash seasons from 1984 through 1988, when the Bears reclaimed their Monsters of the Midway identity, recalling the glory days of Halas-coached bruisers and brawlers. Such legends as Ed Sprinkle and Doug Atkins, two of the meanest maulers in NFL history, had to move over and make room for Samurai Mike Singletary and his wrecking crew, with Dan Hampton and Gary Fencik sharing co-ferocity laurels.

Bear traditionalists still rank the linebacking crew of Bill George, Larry Morris and Joe Fortunato, the blocks of granite who splattered enemy ball carriers to lay the foundation for George Halas' last NFL championship team in 1963, as their top all-time linebacking trio. Even so, those '85 Super Bowl shufflers—Singletary, Otis Wilson and Wilbur Marshall—took a back seat to no unit.

So when Singletary singled out Buddy Ryan as the architect of the fabulous 46 defense, his words carried lots of weight. It was clear that he respected Iron Mike Ditka, but credited Ryan for lining the Bears' defensive backbones with steel. Above and beyond the 46 scheme, or any comparable alignment, the feeling of togetherness on that unit made it even more formidable.

"Buddy did that," Singletary told me when I called the future Hall of Famer to write a story about his selection as 1988 NFL defensive Player of the Year. "He welded us into a cohesive unit, and we still miss him. I don't believe we could have won the Super Bowl without him. He's a defensive genius."

Coming from a man who played with the same kind of relentless fury for 172 starts, ever since the eighth game of his rookie season, it was quite an accolade. Unfortunately, the same qualities that made Ryan tick and click as a defensive coordinator proved his undoing when he tried wearing the head coach's headphones. To begin with, defensive people are crazy, by definition.

"Sure we are," Dan Hampton concurred with a malevolent grin while we sat at a long training table, littered with the scraps of what had been prime steaks only moments before. "You know how coaches find the guys who want to play defense back home in Arkansas. They shake a big old tree until everybody falls out. The ones that get up and walk away go on defense."

Hampton fit his own mold, plummeting from a tree when he was a kid. Those who had to contend with him in the NFL a few years later wouldn't have been surprised if Danimal got up and went back to practice without waiting for someone to set his broken arm. Hampton played in pain, with pain and through pain for the Bears, inflicting lots more punishment on foes intrepid—or dumb

—enough to get in his way of this defensive end's one-man war on the NFL, stretching over three decades, from 1979 though 1990, finally getting a berth in pro football's Hall of Fame.

"It's tough enough to practice against this Bear defense every day," said fullback Matt Suhey, better known for his blocking and pass-catching prowess. "When it matters, and they show up to play, nobody can beat them."

But Suhey got a reward that eluded his close pal, Walter Payton, blasting 11 yards for the Bears' first-ever touchdown in a Super Bowl. By then, the Pats already were patsies, becoming New England calamity chowder in a 21-0 third-period blitz that turned them into Boston baked has-beans. It got extra embarrassing—and not just for the Patriots—when defensive tackle Refrigerator Perry found a resting house in the end zone. Fridge rumbled over from a yard out to match the TD that made him a national pinup among the stylishly stout set when he crashed through the Packers' bratwurst brigade on Monday night football.

Ditka took a perverse sort of pleasure in doing things like letting the 300-pound-plus Perry (estimates ranged up to 390 at various stages of Fridge's career) play both ways. That, plus his gap-toothed smile and a sort of rustic charm, acquired naturally in Aiken, S.C., growing up with 11 brothers and sisters, added to the Fridge Frenzy.

"I made you a national hero," Ditka told Perry. That's debatable, because Perry already was something of an icon in college, with his Clemson growth chart, an astute move by the college publicist, quickly becoming a collector's item.

What's beyond dispute is that Perry's overnight celebrity was bitterly resented by Bears veterans, who figured the fat rookie hadn't paid enough NFL dues to get paid big bucks by sponsors clamoring for him to pitch their products on TV. Just like loyalty, jealousy is a powerful emotion. Still, whatever disdain they felt for Perry, was overshadowed by protectiveness toward quarterback Jim McMahon among the close-knit ranks of the Bears' inner circle.

When Hampton slapped the derisive label of "Bambi" on quarterback Doug Flutie, he was saying less about his dislike for Flutie than he was about his admiration for McMahon's James Dean

Bear fans enjoyed watching Jim McMahon (9) and Doug Flutie (2) vie for quarterback status at their former Platteville, Wisconsin, training camp. They soon discovered Bear veterans preferred punky QB McMahon to "Bambi" Flutie.

attitude. No wonder. McMahon's rebellious spirit made him a magnet for anybody with a healthy distrust of authority. For instance, pro football linemen in general and Bears' linemen in particular. Living up to his persona as the Punky QB, McMahon palled around with these hulking slabs of beef instead of the upper crust, high-salaried skill position stars. Together, McMahon and his trademark dark shades, along with a muscular posse, cut a swath through what was laughingly known as Platteville's nightlife. They'd have a few beers in one joint on the main drag, with the townsfolk politely pretending not to gawk. Then a game of pool and a nightcap down the street, studiously avoiding the bar where the assistant coaches would gather to gab and guzzle after a hard day's workout. Nobody could mistake this bucolic setting for Chicago's Rush Street, but McMahon seemed more comfortable there than he did in the glare of TV spotlights and incessant pestering from nosy newspaper types. That training camp was his last chance to avoid paying the price of fame, because the Bears, driven by Ditka's hunger for perfection, clearly were an NFL force to be reckoned with.

Sure enough, the 10-6 Bears made the playoffs in 1984, chopped down the Washington Redskins in the first round, then got whitewashed by the San Francisco 49ers in the NFC title game, one step short of the ultimate goal. Hungry Bears fans, denied a championship since 1963, were convinced the overdue next year finally would be this year. The year was 1985, and they were right.

The debate will rage forever, but I'm convinced McMahon was the main reason, though far from the only one, for that magical 15-1 season. A 3-0 playoff sweep capped it by a combined 91-10 margin. That number should rank right up there with the still-unbelievable 73-0 stampede over the Redskins in the NFL championship game on December 8, 1940. When the minority of Bears fans who can remember the words start warbling, "We'll never forget the way you thrilled the nation, with your T-formation," that's what they've been celebrating for seven decades.

History does not record any Bears mooning the media before that 1940 massacre, the way McMahon did to an intrusive TV helicopter crew on the eve of super Bowl XX. McMahon had gotten to the point by then where he didn't reveal much of himself, either verbally or in the flesh. He didn't have to. The legend of the punky QB was indelibly engraved on Chicago, the way injured McMahon came in to hit Willie Gault with laser-guided TD passes before a mesmerized Monday night audience in the Metrodome on November 11, 1991.

It wasn't as dramatic as Joe Namath's called-shot upset of haughty Baltimore Colts in Super Bowl IV, but for Bears fans, the final proof. They knew he was right and the media wrong in that never-ending war of words (by the writers) and no-comments from McMahon. One trick McMahon failed to master was the art of using the media to his own advantage. He could have learned how from Ditka, a master of alternately charming and cowing swarms of people covering him daily. Da Coach played them like an accordion. He lectured and cajoled, ranted and raved, flattered and flummoxed his band of pursuers. He picked his spots at times, and tried in vain to control his overflowing emotions in other situations—especially after the Bears lost —although Ditka couldn't help unloading on fans unwise enough to jaw at him.

Ditka's "Get your mouth shut!" advice to a postgame heckler was captured on tape, becoming part of the legend of Iron Mike. At that, the intruder into the postgame media area, in the bowels of Soldier Field, was fortunate Ditka wasn't close enough to end the debate his way. As a Bears player, he didn't waste words on a Philly lush who invaded the field, turning him into mincemeat with a block audible in the press box.

Ditka always got his message across to the writers. One of the few times he lost a confrontation was to a worthy opponent, *Peoria Journal-Star* columnist Phil Theobald, who told Ditka off for calling the working press "a bunch of S.O.B's," then stomped out of the room. Iron Mike promptly got the lead out, to his credit, following Theobald to apologize for his illegal use of adjective. The fact that Ditka professed to regret such an outburst no doubt provided boatloads of belly laughs for NFL referees.

As for McMahon, this rebel with—or without—a cause was capable of driving everyone crazy, especially Bears fans, sometimes his teammates and occasionally Ditka. Both parts of this matched, driven player-coach duo willed themselves to play through pain, even though the Mac attack was unpredictable enough to rattle his coach, a creature of habit, who needs to be in control. With McMahon out of control so often, and sidelined often by the injuries his reckless style sometimes triggered, the harmony of 1985 faded fast.

So the Super Bowl shuffle was a one-trick pony for the Ditka-McMahon Bears. When Walter Payton took a truckload of NFL records with him into retirement, after 13 years and 22,134 total yards—16,726 rushing, 4,538 receiving, 539 on kickoff returns, and 331 as a passer—plus 125 touchdowns, the Bears offense lost lots of Sweetness. With Payton exiting in 1987 and McMahon breaking down physically, the pain of a first-round 1986 playoff knockout by the Redskins had not faded when the Punky QB went out again with a sore right knee.

That didn't cheer up some veterans, notably Hampton, a walking outpatient clinic himself. But the Bears once again found themselves a game away from the Super Bowl. Young Mike Tomczak was getting it done under center, until he joined the walking wounded. With two banged-up starters to choose from, Ditka rolled the dice, and it came up snake eyes:

Ditka Wants Mac, Not Mike
(Daily Herald, January 7, 1989)

McMahon's the McMan.

Coach Mike Ditka ended a week of suspense Friday, naming Jim McMahon as the Bears' starting quarterback for Sunday's NFC championship game against the San Francisco 49ers. Because, in Ditka's words, "This is based on what I know is right," a semi-healthy McMahon will be on the field and a semi-disabled Mike Tomczak will be on the bench when the battle for the Super Bowl begins.

"McMahon will start—period," Ditka said after returning from Suwanee, Ga., where the Bears practiced this week. "Mike wanted to play badly, but I don't know if he can take a hit."

For the second time this season, Tomczak separated his left shoulder during last Sunday's 20-12 playoff victory over the

Philadelphia Eagles. He shrugged it off all week in a determined bid to keep the No. 1 quarterback status that had been his since October 30, when McMahon sprained a knee in the Bears' 30-7 loss at New England.

"We have to go with (Ditka's) decision," said middle linebacker Mike Singletary. "I found out about the same time you did," added running back Neal Anderson added. "Jim knows what it takes to win big games."

Ditka, as always, went with his gut feeling.

"If Tomczak got a good hit on that shoulder, we'd have to take him out," he growled.

How about the controversy McMahon started by declaring his right knee was too bad to play on? Defensive stalwart Dan Hampton labeled him "not concerned with the team." Since, then, the embattled quarterback has been speaking only through pay-per-quote media outlets.

"Jim's pretty healthy, " Ditka said "He might be a little rusty, but he can sprint out close to full efficiency. I hope he doesn't have to run for his life out there."

What happens if McMahon goes down again?

"Then it's Tomczak, and if he can't go, it's Jim Harbaugh," Ditka said of his top 1987 draft pick. "Realistically, that would mean things aren't going too well for us."

Ditka insisted he had not reacted to the clamor from fans, fearing T-zak's lack of playoff experience might lead to fatal turnovers. "Nothing political about this decision," he said. "I waited until this morning's workout to see and feel in my heart what had to be done. It wasn't because one of them was a Polack."

If Ditka is right, the Bears will go to the Super Bowl, January 22, in Miami.

"This is a decision you guys can really second-guess," he said.

Ditka was wrong—49ers 28, Bears 3. The McMahon era was over, and with him went some high times for Chicago's charter NFL franchise. It also ended a stretch of Bearmania which enriched lots of the Punky QB's supporting cast, though none more than him.

Lots of things were changing during the McMahon's '80s hey-heyday, as Jack Brickhouse would put it. For instance, Ditka found out that descriptive terms like "Polack" for any ethnic group no longer flew, well-intentioned or not.

Political correctness was in. Da Bears, in like the Cook County machine, were soon were to be out, along with Da Coach, making way for a new sports dynasty, a Bulls market that was MJ-estic in every way.

Following the law of nature, sports run in cycles. Suddenly the Bears are back, making a 21st Century Dick Jauron jolt, unheard of during the dreary Dave Wannstedt stewardship. So are Bears fans. Some of them left in body during the post-Ditka debacle, but few, if any, left in spirit. They long for the happy days of Grange, Paddy Driscoll, Bronko Nagurski, Bulldog Turner, Sid Luckman, Johnny Lujack, George Connor, Dick Butkus, and Gayle Sayers.

One reason for that fervent loyalty has been the setting. Almost as soon as the Decatur Staleys moved to Chicago in 1921, crafty Papa Bear Halas wangled a way for them to play at Clark and Addison Streets. That pile of bricks had been built seven years earlier for the ill-fated Chicago Whales of the short-lived Federal League. It was known as Cubs Park when the Bears became tenants, changing the name to Wrigley Field in the Babe Ruth-inspired wave of prosperity and expanded ballparks during the 1920s.

So along with the Cubs, the name "Wrigley Field" became synonymous with the Bears for a half-century. But Halas didn't have gum tycoon Phil Wrigley's bottomless bankroll to hang on his bedpost overnight, so their contrasting views about money finally drove the Bears across Madison Street—the ancient dividing line between them and their bitter rivals, the Chicago Cardinals— in 1971. That's when they set up shop in Soldier Field, the imposing array of Greek colonnades that casts a giant shadow on the fringe of Chicago's loop. Actually, Halas and the Bears might not have survived in Chicago without the Cards, because they would have been squeezed into unsuitable home fields and dates, unable to build a Wrigley Field fan base. The Cards played a real death match in 1920, whipping the Chicago Tigers, 6-3.

Loyalty and toughness, two traits prized by George Halas, turned the Bears into the Monsters of the Midway. Both are abundant in this Wrigley Field fracas with the Los Angeles Rams. Halas (back to camera) is ready to ram 'em all while Abe Gibron (67) defends his embattled coach by ramming into Don Burroughs. Meanwhile, crafty Halas hand-checks his top receiver, Harlon Hill, to keep him out of harm's way.

The team owners agreed that the winner of this game would get Chicago franchise rights, with the losers leaving town. That paved the way for the Bears to survive, if not thrive, on the North Side until the NFL hit it big with the riveting Giants-Colts 1958 title game on national TV.

No question, Wrigley Field was a better place to watch football than Soldier Field. Old-timers wax nostalgic about the gigantic center-field bleachers, the end zones ending perilously close to the ivy-covered bricks on the outfield wall or the box seats at the home-plate end of the field. I can recall sitting in the upper deck to watch strong-armed Bear quarterback, Bobby Douglass, unleash a rain-making pass against the Pittsburgh Steelers, higher than the trajectory of some Sammy Sosa homers. It soared diagonally across the field, from the third-base line to the end zone in deep left-center, at least 70 yards in the air.

Memories are the fabric that binds lifelong fans to their teams. So, while the Bears are taking their long-playing fumblefest on the road at Halas' alma mater, the University of Illinois, it's fitting to reflect on the irony of it all. If the Bears had not abandoned their Wrigleyville homestead to start a contentious relationship with the Chicago Park District, they could have been forced to build a suburban stadium meeting the NFL's minimum 60,000-seat requirement.

And if not for Halas' frugal nature—he was raised on the Bohemian easy payment plan, consisting of 100 percent down, nothing else to pay, a staple of Chicago immigrants—the Bears might well have stayed in Wrigley Field. But Phil Wrigley no longer could afford to ignore the need for a new look at this aging ballpark, hang the cost. Part of the renovation was junking the old, green uncomfortable seats in the field boxes for fixed, wider spots to squat. The fat fannies crammed into those cramped quarters for decades could afford more space, and they demanded it.

But removing the folding chairs meant less top-ticket revenue for Halas. When the dispute could not be resolved, he vamoosed. Such trivial incidents change the course of history (as in, "for want of a nail, the horseshoe was lost," etc.), and that rule holds true for sports. I can't imagine kings, generals and prime ministers with bigger egos than owners of big-league franchises, from George Steinbrenner of the Yankees to Lee Stern of the Chicago Sting. So Halas packed up and left in a huff (not including Gary Huff, a Florida State quarterback drafted by the Bears in 1973 as part of the decades-old search for another Luckman), and things haven't been the same since.

Change isn't always for the better, a fact we're all sadly aware of. Halas flirted with the suburbs during his Wrigley impasse, unveiling ambitious plans for grandiose arenas close to places like Woodfield Mall in the booming Northwest boondocks, that somehow faded. He also tossed Dyche Stadium into the pot as a bargaining chip. Northwestern was willing, but Evanston residents weren't, mounting an aggressive anti-Bears campaign, with angry emphasis on their fans' alleged propensity for imbibing bracing beverages, heavy on the malt and hops. So the NFL games played in those Unfriendly Confines hardly qualified as a smashing success:

Bears Barely Beat Bumbling Birds
(Chicago Tribune, September 28, 1970)

The Bears didn't resemble the Monsters of the North Shore when they invaded the bone-day confines of Evanston yesterday.

Fortunately for their thirsty partisans in Dyche Stadium, they were up against the Charlie Brown football team, a/k/a the Philadelphia Eagles. The bewildered Birds found themselves trailing 7-0 before they realized the game had started. After that, the Browns (Philly, not Charlie) matched the Bears mistake for mistake, lost opportunity for lost opportunity. They failed at everything, including a last-ditch effort to prevent the winners from sneaking out of this temperance territory and back to their favorite Chicago watering holes with a 20-16 decision.

It was not a day that Ed Sabol will try to immortalize in his NFL Films collection of classic contests. Inability to break their losing streak here gives the Eagles a fighting chance to go 0-14 in 1970. Surely, nobody will try harder to present them with a victory than the Bears did. They couldn't out-fumble or out-stumble each other, so it came down to the day's premier goof, a field goal snap by Eagles center Mike Evans that might have been finger-tipped by Lew Alcindor, but not anyone under 7 feet tall.

Former NU standout Irv Cross, now the defensive secondary coach for the Eagles, admitted he spent a lot of happier afternoons in Dyche Stadium.

"It was a strange game," Cross conceded.

But if their Evanston reception was chilly, that was to be expected in a place where the Bears were viewed by many upscale denizens as a band of carpetbagging ruffians, attracting a swarm of blue-collar followers with liquid refreshment in their carpetbags that definitely was not sarsaparilla. What the Bears didn't expect—but what they got—was a lot of wrangling and long-simmering disputes with the park district. They fought over lease terms, upkeep of Soldier Field, and general unhappiness about the sod getting torn up by soccer games, rock concerts and other attempts to squeeze revenue from what many of Chicago's upper crust view as a huge white elephant, blocking the view of their pet environmental project, Lake Michigan. Then there was the ongoing skybox wrangle, with Chicago politicians clamoring for more money from those lucrative roosts. Besides that, Soldier Field needed expensive, extensive repairs and maintenance just to stave off a calamitous collapse for the creaking joint, built in 1923 on 10,000 piles, driven 60 feet down through lakefront landfill.

This place staged the Dempsey-Tunney long-count bout and hosted the all-time record crowd of 123,000 to view Knute Rockne-coached Notre Dame's 7-6 victory over USC (both headline-grabbing events happened in 1927, the year that Babe Ruth hit 60 homers). It slowly lurched downhill as the years marched past. A trip underneath the stands sometimes gave the impression you were taking an all-expense tour through a toxic waste dump, replete with dark, drab, dingy dirt, dust and exotic aromas.

Still, the politicos wanted assurances that their prime tenant would not flee to some pristine spot, free of all the grime, and especially from Chicago taxes. The real Mayor Daley, Richard J., angrily declared they no longer could be called "Chicago Bears" if they turned their broad backs on his "wunnerful" city. The prospect of the Schaumburg Bears seeking new aliases, like "The Mall Molesters" or "Tollway Terrors", created a lot of yocks for stand-up comedians packing comedy clubs all over Chicagoland. Meanwhile, lawyers were gleefully rubbing their hands, anticipating the BMW payments sure to start rolling in when the Bears tried to claim in court that the New York Giants and Jets playing home games in New Jersey did not prevent the Bears from keeping the Chicago label while enriching themselves elsewhere in Illinois—or even in Gary, Indiana.

The Bears actually got ejected from Soldier Field, at least temporarily, for illegal use of threats. It turned out to be the classic teapot tempest, but while the controversy raged, I got some rare exposure outside the Fun and Games Dept., with this headline story, splashed across the top of the page one news section: "Bears told to stay out of Soldier Field."

Unbearable Exorcism
(Chicago Tribune, July 12, 1980)

Officials of the Chicago Bears said Friday that the football team has been barred from Soldier Field and canceled Monday's schedule sale of single-game tickets at the stadium box office.

Raymond F. Simon, Chicago Park District president, said the Bears have not been thrown out, but that the district wanted written assurances that permission to sell tickets would not be used in a lawsuit against the district.

It's an outgrowth of stalled negotiations with the Bears over a proposed 20-year lease. Sources indicated the Bears are considering a suit that would force the park district to allow the NFL team to play in Soldier Field until agreement is reached on a new lease. If it got rejected, the Bears might have to play the entire 1980 schedule outside Chicago.

Jim Finks, the Bears general manager, said that stadium manager Pleasant Amick told him Friday the stadium would be closed to the Bears until a lease had been agreed on, and that his orders came from park district superintendent Ed Kelly.

"I can't believe what I just heard," Finks said he told Kelly.

Later, Simon indicated the ticket-sell ban (8,000 for each of eight league games, plus two exhibitions) would be lifted as soon as the Bears sent him a letter with specific assurances.

"Finks told me he got a harsh message, barring the Bears from Soldier Field," Simon said. "In no way did I intend to prevent them from selling tickets for scheduled games. But I've heard they're planning a lawsuit. I'll give Finks a letter Monday outlining conditions for their sale. Jim is obviously irritated because not everybody in the park district says yes to everything the Bears ask."

Finks consulted with attorneys and owner George Halas before issuing a statement claiming, "as operator of the only facility in the city where the Bears can play, the park district is applying coercive tactics." Later, Finks said the Bears stood by that.

"We've canceled the ticket sale, and it's too late to change," he said. "Simon claimed we have to send him a letter, but they knew for months about our plans. My God, it's incredible."

Informed sources indicated that the Bears and Kelly had been 98 percent of the way to agreement on a 20-year lease. They added that Simon's insistence on the Bears paying a larger share of the $32 million Soldier Field renovation deadlocked the negotiations.

More than two decades later, the Bears are still playing in Soldier Field. When they return from a brief exile in Champaign, their fans will restore the roar in 2003. Not all of the roaring came from the Solder Field stands, though. A tidal wave of controversy swept through Chicago when it saw sketches of renovated Soldier Field. Critics blasted it as a stainless steel bowl, perched atop those familiar columns. The uproar did not convince Mayor Richard M. Daley, son of "Da Mare" to back down, because he was committed to keep the Bears, and all the revenue they generated, within the city limits.

No champagne in Soldier Field since 1985, because the Cinderella Bears got bombed 33-19 by the Philadelphia Eagles in the last game at the lakeside landmark as we knew it. The venerable structure, home to the Bears since 1971, is undergoing a radical restructuring, forcing them to become the Monsters of Middle Illinois in 2002, farmed out to Memorial Stadium in Champaign.

So it seems the Bears are here to stay, at least for the next 20-30 years. What might happen after that, or even before then, in our fast-changing society can only be imagined. Regardless of their future, the Bears already have a rich legacy of ferocious competition, a melange of magical and miserable moments, plus lots of physical pain for the Bears and their opponents and mental pain for their fans. Those pictures, pigeonholed in our minds, can be hauled out for a brief rehash or a total nostalgia trip whenever we want.

As a youngster in Philadelphia, I saw Bulldog Turner and the Bears bash Steve Van Buren through the protective bar in his helmet with fists, forearms, elbows, everything except blackjacks, whenever the Eagles' halfback came through the middle. Afterwards, I walked onto the field—security was a lot looser in those days—to see future Hall of Famer Van Buren standing there with a dazed look on his face, blood running from a cut above the eyebrow, dripping on his green jersey and staining his white No. 15. I'm not a blood-and-gore type, but those scenes stick with you.

Even more unforgettable are the Bears coaches and players I've dealt with, starting and ending with a pair of soft-spoken gents, Neill Armstrong and Dick Jauron. Their low-key style could not have been further from Mike Ditka's nuke-'em nature, but they all found a place in the shoestring operation that George S. Halas turned into a football empire.

There were some spectacular moments on the road in my years of Bears coverage. Two that jump right out are the Ice Bowl in the Meadowlands on December 18, 1977, and the Thanksgiving Day spectacular in the Silverdome on November 27, 1980. Bob Thomas' 29-yard field goal, only nine seconds before the end of overtime brought the Bears from behind to a 12-9 victory over the New York Giants in the ice-crusted Meadowlands, propelling the Bears into the playoffs for the first time since that championship season of 1963.

Thomas' slick kick was a Christmas present, ending 14 years of frustration for the Bears and their fans. The scene of jubilation on the Jersey tundra was worthy of the Super Bowl. But that wouldn't happen for eight years, when Da Coach, Da Bears and Da

Fans finally spent a season on the summit. Anyway, the Dallas Grinches stole Christmas joy by ousting the Bears 37-7 in a first-round playoff rout, Jack Pardee's last game as their head coach.

The Turkey Day game in Pontiac, Michigan, looked to end up that way for the Bears until quarterback Vince Evans (no, he wasn't operating from the wishbone) gave fans their filling of holiday fare by scrambling for the tying TD in the closing minutes of the fourth quarter. The writers, including me, were standing by the tunnel leading to the visitors' dressing room in the Silverdome, so I saw vacillating Vince hesitate, elude a couple of lunging Lions, and streak across for a 17-17 deadlock.

Like most of my fellow grid scribes, I had a flight booked to get home in time for a late Thanksgiving dinner. Instead ,we started making dinner plans for rubber chicken and cold shoulder (from spouses grappling with a houseful of relatives by themselves at home) for what looked to be a less-than-rollicking overnight stay in snow-bound Detroit. We huddled glumly behind the same end zone to watch the Bears' Dave Williams field the overtime kickoff at his 5-yard line.

Boom! It took Williams just 21 seconds to hotfoot 95 yards for the 23-17 victory. That was fast, though not quite as swift as the way the world got told about this 21-second overtime, still the NFL record. An amazingly similar array of leads about this hard-fought contest between two evenly matched squads got cranked out and unloaded on various Chicago and Detroit sports desks, followed by a stampede toward rental cars and a series of I-94 drag races to Metro Airport. Some of us even found our front door unlocked, with no sign of high-fashion wardrobes in shopping bags on the lawn when we got home.

But pro football is a tough, grim game, unlike the mystic, glamorous image popularized by those intriguing mini-movies, replete with classical music and John Facenda's booming baritone. I used to hear Facenda's smooth delivery nightly on the Channel 10 news in Philadelphia so I knew how mesmerizing he could be. Few players will talk openly about what they have to go through to make it in the NFL.

Jim Harbaugh was an exception. I saw him take a lot of big hits when he was Michigan's quarterback, so I figured he was tough enough. That was overshadowed by the courage he displayed in talking about the unspoken bane of all sports, not just pro football:

Harbaugh Blitzes Steroids
(Chicago Tribune, June 11, 1987)

Rookies are supposed to keep their mouths shut, no matter what league they're trying to make. NFL veterans, especially those on steroids, don't tolerate criticism of their paycheck-protecting habit.

But Michigan quarterback Jim Harbaugh is not your standard, silent, scared rookie. The Bears' No. 1 draft choice believes steroid use is common, and he's not afraid to speak out about it.

"Steroids are widespread in high school, college and pro football," Harbaugh said after a Halas Hall workout with Bears' strength coach Clyde Emrich. "There are ways to mask the drug test so they can't be detected in the system. I was shocked to find out how many high school kids are on them just to look bigger and faster. Some pro scouts told me, "If you test positive for cocaine or marijuana, you're gone. Then they made it clear taking steroids is a decision left to the players."

Anabolic steroids—readily available to players—are chemical compounds that act like hormones to enlarge muscles and improve blood flow to them. They can add bulk, increase tolerance for pain and trigger aggression. Studies indicate long-term doses can damage the liver, kidney and heart, deform joints, and even induce psychotic behavior.

"I won't take steroids, so some guys have an unfair advantage," Harbaugh said. "What bothers me is the hypocritical attitude that these things somehow aren't as bad as other drugs. Nothing is more important to me than making the Bears. I wonder what I'd do if I were a defensive lineman, and sticking in the NFL depended on my taking steroids."

Chicago was listed last month as one of 16 major steroid distribution points in the United Sates. NFL commissioner Pete

Rozelle has been trying to ban them, but Steve Courson, a former Tampa Bay guard, estimated 95 percent of NFL linemen have tried them.

"You need them to survive," Courson said. "If you can't keep some 280-pound genetic mutation away from the quarterback, you lose your job."

Harbaugh agreed, adding, "Players shouldn't be put in that position. I'll probably get knocked on my butt by some of those monsters."

Sometimes, the bare facts provide a better Bear story. It happened for me a few years ago, when the Bears lost (again) in Green Bay. This was the lead that had to be written:

Packers Green and Bear It
(Daily Herald, December 14, 1998)

GREEN BAY, WIS. – Defense, decent. Offense, abominable.

This is a recording. Unfortunately, it will go on record as the Bears' ninth straight loss to the Green Bay Packers. But there was little else of record-sharing significance in Sunday's 26-20 Lambeau Field squeaker. Aside from stretching the Bears' string of futility against their ancient NFL rivals to an all-time record, it was the same old broken record, another entry in the no-hit parade.

A sad, familiar story, to be sure. Still, out of the futility, a fond farewell for Edgar Bennett, a long-time Packer favorite who played out the string with the Bears, provided a small ray of cheer amid the gloom:

Bennett's Homecoming Hazardous
(Daily Herald, December 14, 1998)

GREEN BAY, WIS.—At least Edgar Bennett had a bittersweet Lambeau Field homecoming.

It was some consolation in a season that long since has been totally bitter for running back Bennett and the rest of the Bears. Another disheartening defeat, this one 26-20, couldn't pile much more dirt on the grave of a 3-11 team that has been buried since midseason.

But Bennett kept hope alive Sunday, if only briefly, breaking loose for a 43-yard gallop around right end on the Bears' first play from scrimmage. It was the veteran's longest career run, but he picked up only 35 more rushing yards on 14 carries the rest of the way.

"My own feeling is we lost," the dejected Bennett said.

The Bears might be finished, but the love affair between Bennett and Packers' fans endures. The soft-spoken Florida State product had been Green Bay's run to daylight guy during their rush to victory in the 1996 super Bowl, bringing a glimpse of Vince Lombardi glory back to Titletown, USA.

"It was phenomenal to come back here and recall good times," Bennett said. "These Green Bay fans are very loyal, but I tried not to get caught up in their (cheers for him)."

When Bennett trotted off the field after the final, futile Bears drive fizzled, home fans interrupted their playoff-clinching celebration to give him a standing ovation. And his ex-Packer buddies, including, Reggie White, chased after Bennett to offer handshakes and hugs.

"They're still my friends, even though this rivalry is fierce," Bennett mused. "Packers and Bears. It's always like two heavyweight fighters trading punches."

The way it was everywhere for the Bears seems to be the way it always has been, with the defense monstrous and the offense minuscule. It was true again in this 20-13 loss to the Atlanta Falcons:

Bears in No-Scoring Zone
(Daily Herald, November 23, 1998)

ATLANTA – Georgia Dome?

As far as the Bears are concerned, they should rename it the Penalty Bowl, or in the interest of accuracy, the No-penalty Zone.

Either way, it was a Dome shame.

If you're keeping score at home, Chicago's defense outscored its offense 7-6. Together, it still wasn't enough. The lone Bears touchdown was sparked by Jim Flanigan, blitzing to strip Atlanta quarterback Chris Chandler, enabling Shawn Lee to grab the ball and run 15 yards to score. Maybe Lee should have brought some arrows along to point the way for the Bears' offense. It still hasn't located the end zone.

Even though the new-look Bears are personified by crunching linebacker Brian Urlacher, a hands-down (actually, hands-on) winner of the Dick Butkus clone contest, their fans figure something good must start happening here. Maybe even on offense.

5

Michael, Mike and Motta-vation

Superstars, by definition, excel at what they do best. Nowhere is it written that they also have to be superior tap dancers, prestidigitators, salespersons, astrologers, grammarians, vegetarians and/or soapbox orators. Social and verbal skills are nice, but definitely not required.

In fact, action is supposed to be a superstar's calling card. No flowery phrases are needed. Sportswriters have been pulling out what's left of their thinning hair after years of trying to interpret the significance of such predictable post-game quotes as these old standbys:

Winning coach—"That was a big win for us."

Winning player—"I don't care about my stats. When the team wins, I'm happy."

Losing players—"Get off my xx00x, you *xxxx000##@#%%##* vultures!"

Losing manager—"My guys busted their butts. As long as the effort's there, you can't fault the mistakes. They happen in (fans, fill in your blank of choice: football, baseball, basketball, hockey, jai alai, croquet, water polo, whist, etc., etc.,)"

There are exceptions, of course. Genuine, classy people like ex-Cubs pitcher Kevin Tapani, Bears quarterback Jim Miller, White Sox first baseman Paul Konerko, and lots more manage to keep the game they play, the big bucks they make, and above all their personal equilibrium from spinning out of control. But conflicting pressures tug at athletes in an era where the big business of sports squeezes the enjoyment out. Often, backstage games played by wheeler-dealer agents, aggressive owners like the Sox' Jerry Reinsdorf and the Yankees' George Steinbrenner and the all-powerful players association predetermine what will happen on the field.

Most of the time, superstars have an entourage to serve as a buffer from such crass realities. They don't have to worry about getting shipped back to the minors on the last day of spring training, or being stalked by The Hawk at NFL cutdown time with the dreaded summons to report to the coach "and bring your playbook." And with an honest agent and a competent advisor, that small, elite band can afford to travel with a crew of flunkies and yes men, eager to assure their benefactor he's the greatest.

Somehow, not many of those egomaniacal types ended up on my superstar list. From Michael Jordan to Ray Meyer, a select few I've dealt with personally over the last four decades turned out to be real human beings. Rich ones, undeniably, but still aware enough of the responsibilities bestowed on them by fame to handle it well—including the media. Some of us print and electronic whiz-bangs can resemble the south end of a northbound horse, but sports lives—or dies—on publicity, so we can't be ignored. None of this band of sporting thoroughbreds—well, maybe a few—was unaware of that.

Here Comes Mr. Jordan

I got to talk with Michael Jordan before he was Michael Jordan.

Sure, everybody knew he was a hotshot North Caroline rookie when the Bulls drafted him in 1984. He'd already made The Shot—

the jumper that lifted the Tar Heels to Dean Smith's first NCAA championship two years earlier. The youngster's poise, charm, good looks and ability to put coherent words together to form meaningful, to-the-point sentences made him a rarity, right from the start.

I hope nobody reads anything derogatory, or even worse, remotely racial, into that assessment. Simply put, Jordan is above and beyond all that stuff, just as he still is the greatest athlete of all time. Forget that New York bastion of sports snobbery (hint: initial *SI*), with its laughable list of the 20th Century's top 50 or however many politically correct athletes. I'll save the obligatory denial that I'm a chauvinist pig until the media chapter of this book, which, appropriately enough, brings up the rear.

The facts are that Jordan stands alone. I suspected he was something spectacular the first time we talked, shortly after he came to the NBA, soon to change the face of not just that league, but of all games all over the world. Hyperbole is not now (I hope) and never has been my style, in print or yakking it up at my friendly neighborhood saloon, the Press Inn, on Chicago's North Side. There's just no way to overstate this case. MJ's impact on Chicago was not diminished by his new role as executive sorcerer for the Washington Wizards, and then, back to his baronial self as the NBA's Crown Points (pardon the pun) Prince in 2001-02 while critics and skeptics kept blustering that it wasn't happening.

Nobody closing in on Jack Benny's favorite age (39, for those of you who missed out on the comedic genius of another American icon) could come back and play like Michael Jordan. True. Nobody except Jordan.

I was covering the Bulls when Jordan came to his first NBA training camp, with a 1984 Olympic gold medal around his neck and a $6 million contract in his pocket. When he talked with me or the other beat writers, it was not rookie to hoop scribe. It was man to man. None of us figured this remarkable newcomer could play better than he communicated. We were wrong:

This Kid Can Play
(Chicago Tribune, October 4, 1984)

PEORIA—Sure, Michael Jordan has wowed 'em all over the world, but will he play in Peoria?

Yes, he will, because the Bulls and their prize rookie open the NBA exhibition slate Friday in the Peoria Civic Center. Jordan has a rendezvous with destiny and the Indiana Pacers, not necessarily in that order.

"I can't wait to get started," Jordan said before the Bulls wrapped up a week of two-a-day workouts in their Angel Guardian gym training camp. "I'm fitting in with the Bulls, and my new teammates have received me very well."

Anyone who didn't soon will be a candidate for unemployment compensation. Jordan is The Franchise in the Bulls' 1984-85 rebuilding campaign. Elsewhere around the NBA, skyscraping centers are foundation stones, but 6-foot-6 Jordan will have to do for them.

So far, he's doing nicely. Camp onlookers are impressed by Jordan's physical potential, along with his court sense, aggressiveness and positive attitude.

"He's great," enthused Bulls' general manager Rod Thorn. "Michael plays in the team setup. It's too early to tell how fast he'll develop, but his potential is unlimited."

Jordan's NBA debut will be a unique experience. Along with the star-is-born buildup, Peoria fans will see the North Carolina All-American in a totally unfamiliar role: coming off the bench.

"Michael will play maybe a half, like everybody else, but he won't start," said coach Kevin Loughery.

After a week of nose-to-nose scrimmages, Jordan shares other Bulls' eagerness for a real game. He realizes a lot will be expected of him from the opening tip.

"New goals will begin for me at that moment," Jordan admitted. "I want to be able to look back with satisfaction at my rookie season. I'll have to contribute to the Bulls in several areas, concentrating on defense, along with helping to run the offense, getting the fast break started, rebounding and scoring."

"I know the Bulls haven't won much (lately), but I've seen a winning attitude here in camp. All I can do is be a part of it, not the reason for it."

"If we prove we can win, our fans will get behind us, the same way everybody in Chicago is pulling for the Cubs now."

Wilt Chamberlain couldn't have said if better. Or Hondo Havlicek or Elgin Baylor or any of the old guard NBA superstars Jordan was soon to eclipse. Years later, I'm pleased that my forecast of his potential turned out to be accurate, if understated:

Here Comes Mr. Jordan
(Basketball Times, October, 1984)

If Michael Jordan is just another rookie, Secretariat was just another horse.

So here comes Mr. Jordan, burdened by a big reputation. At 21, he already has been a NCAA champion, twice college Player of the Year and an Olympic hero. There's only one basketball world left to conquer—the NBA, where an exhausting 82-game schedule means almost nothing, but the playoffs play on into infinity.

"This is not going to be the Michael Jordan show," vowed the 6-6 prize package. "I'm just another rookie, and my job is to fit in."

Instead of press clippings, Jordan brought extra sweat socks to training camp. He soon made believers out of coach Kevin Loughery, his assistants and the other players.

"Michael will help us three ways," said Fred "Mad Dog" Carter, Loughery's morale officer and another of the bright young NBA aides who will be stepping up to the head spot soon. "First, he'll be a big gate attraction. Second, forget the talk about the kid's potential. He's a great player right now. Third, the level of performance on the Bulls has been much higher since he showed up."

That's heavy baggage to lay on any NBA rookie, especially one under seven feet tall. Jordan has handled it. Despite doing more already than most players in a career, Jordan is still hungry. After the procession of overpaid stiffs parading through the NBA in recent years, Jordan knows how good he is, but he has sense enough to keep it in perspective. A bright, articulate young man, he's aware how important his total package of talent is to the Bulls.

In cavernous Chicago Stadium, ranking eighth in NBA seating capacity at 17,473, "crowds," if you'll pardon the expression, under 1,000 were common last season. Step one in Loughery's resurrection program is to keep as much franchise-saving pressure off Jordan, so this extraordinary performer can proceed with saving the franchise.

"I've never seen a kid come into this league and handle the hype as well," Loughery said. "The best part is the way he's fit in with everybody, but when you play for team-oriented coaches like Dean Smith and Bobby Knight ('84 Olympic boss) that's not surprising.

For Jordan-watchers, the intriguing part will be seeing whether his down-to-earth approach can survive the high-rolling NBA scene. Although they're encased in personalized sneakers to mark a $300,000 endorsement, Jordan's feet are planted firmly on the court, evidence of solid upbringing by his parents, James and Delores, in Wilmington, N.C.

"I have to prove myself in the NBA," Jordan insisted.

He had to, and he did. No wonder I took sort of a proprietary interest in the magnificent career that unfolded after Jordan's low-key beginning at Angel Guardian gym. Nobody, probably not even Jordan himself, dreamed that he would become the biggest and best part of the NBA, eventually the personification of the pro game, then the catalyst of a world-wide basketball boom and finally, the most recognizable face and personality on the globe.

Unsuspecting, I used to watch rookie Michael Jordan stay after practice, working relentlessly on his game until there was nobody left in the gym except me and him. Then we'd sit and talk briefly about his next angle of attack on the perfection he never stopped seeking. Finally, still dripping with sweat, Jordan would walk away.

Once he turned and gave me that wink. When I saw him do it after he became master of the basketball cosmos, always picking his spot for maximum effect, I realized Jordan was practicing that move on me. After all, practice makes perfect.

Veeck's Vision: Fun for Fans

Bill Veeck should have been a teacher.

Shirt-sleeved, glasses sliding down his wrinkled face while he read a passage from Plato, he would have mesmerized any classroom of spellbound students, from kindergarten to grade school. Veeck probably couldn't have been kept cooped up all day, more's the pity.

If the object of teaching is transmitting ideas and opening minds to infinite possibilities, Bill Veeck was your man. Not just for all seasons, but all disciplines, all levels of thought, all the untapped, limitless potential for human imagination. That's the effect he had on me.

For those who think I'm over-hyping a man others put down as a glamorized carnival barker, a huckster who specialized in peddling flesh (with his wheeling-dealing general manager, Frank "Trader Horn" Lane) or illusions about the grandeur of baseball, you're entitled to your opinion. Chances are you never sat at Veeck's table in the Bards Room at old Comiskey Park.

That was where the writers dined before games. In reality, it was a field of dreams whenever Veeck held court. It's too bad he never had enough money to run a baseball franchise the way he should have—and he could have—run it, especially the Chicago White Sox. What he did on a shoestring was enough for me and lots of other Veeckophiles.

I tried, without success, to stuff an overflowing life into a single column a few years after Bill died at 71 on January 2, 1986. I was somewhere out West, wrapping up coverage on a bowl game I've long forgotten, although I still remember the shock when I heard the news. Like Larry Doby, I looked at Veeck as sort of a surrogate father. Trying to capsulize him was—and still is—an impossible task. Anyway, I tried:

Veeck as in Heck of a Man
(Daily Herald, April 7, 1991)

When new Comiskey Park opens April 18, Bill Veeck will be there, at least in memory.

Those of us who knew him will sit in the press box and swap stories, recounting the 1976 stunt he pulled on opening day in old Comiskey. Reenacting the Minutemen of 1776, Veeck hobbled out on his wooden leg, accompanied by a fife, drum and flag. None of our rehashes will be half as entertaining as his.

I first met Veeck at a basketball game. That figured. Veeck was liable to pop up wherever people asked for his help. In this case, the request came from Pat Williams, the young general manager who helped turn the Bulls from a failing NBA franchise into Chicago's hottest ticket in the early '70s. When he took over the Phillies' Spartanburg, S.C., farm team a few years earlier, Williams wrote to Veeck, seeking advice on how to put some fannies in the seats. That was like asking Winston Churchill how to write a soul-stirring speech or asking Saddam Hussein how to lose a war.

Veeck was not a genius in the business of baseball, as his failures with the St. Louis Browns and later with the White Sox indicated. When it came down to the fun of baseball, though, he wrote the book. It was a best-seller, *The Hustler's Handbook*. Williams begged, borrowed and stole freely from those pages, and it paid off in his career as an adept promoter for the Bulls (remember Victor, the wrestling bear?), Atlanta Hawks, Philadelphia 76ers and Orlando Magic. The night I met Veeck, Williams had him flown in from his Maryland home to headline Chicago Stadium's "Pack 'em tight for Bill Veeck night."

Bringing Veeck to Chicago seemed as natural as handing a hip flask to W.C. Fields. He planted the ivy on Wrigley Field's outfield walls and later sank roots just as deep on the South Side. If Veeck hadn't made that final comeback in 1975, Chicago's

charter American league franchise might now be known as the
Denver Pale Hose or the Florida Foot Coverings or some such
silly name in some unworthy place.

Veeck loved baseball because he understood it was a reflec-
tion of life. The Good Guys didn't always win. Some towns,
none more than Chicago, had to sip a lot more losing lager than
championship champagne.

That never stopped Barnum Bill from trying instead of
crying. When his long-overdue plaque hangs on the wall in
baseball's Hall of Fame, it will blow some stuffiness out of the
place, replacing it with fun. Thanks, Bill.

If not for Veeck, the baseball tradition that helped glue the
fragmented south Side back together for a century would now be
buried in the hole where Comiskey Park used to be.

I'm aware there are higher priorities than a new stadium or a
major-league team. Veeck knew that, too. He also knew, better than
most of us, that something worth keeping lived in the bricks and
beams of both Chicago baseball parks.

This was no saint. Veeck had a temper, and he would mix it
up with anyone, even after losing a leg in South Pacific combat
with the Marines in World War II. He was sitting in the Comiskey
press box on night, spinning yarns as usual, when a fight broke out
in the upper deck stands just outside. Before I knew it, Veeck was
gone, and my next glimpse at the brawl found Veeck in the middle
of it, grappling with a couple of burly drunks.

This from a man in his mid-60s, with a history of aches, pains
and ailments, including a near-fatal brain tumor. No wonder he
was respected and admired by so many people, including me, despite an occasional wildly misguided promotion, notably the dread-
ful Disco Demolition night on July 12, 1979, when rioting teen-
agers took over Comiskey Park, a situation that teetered on the
brink of disaster. That fiasco was a sign of desperation from an
owner who lacked the money and backers to prevent his team and
his park from falling apart. It was not the measure of the man.

What I'll remember is the last one-on-one conversation we
had. It was in Wrigley Field, with a high school baseball game go-

ing on and Veeck relaxing with me in the empty grandstand instead of his beloved bleachers. We talked about lots of things. Veeck's mind was seldom at rest, but his eyes were just as active that afternoon, taking in the sights and sounds of the ballpark where he grew up, when his dad was president of the Cubs.

"Now you've got people wanting to put lights in here and tear down Comiskey Park," Veeck said. "The two baseball parks have given so much pleasure to us. They deserve to be treated better. So do the fans.'"

Harry Can Still Caray the Cubs

Always larger than life, Harry Caray even proved to be larger than death.

Years after the final inning in 1998, Harry Carabina's vibrant spirit still beats with the pulse of Chicago. It was his Second City, after a quarter-century in St. Louis, but the Windy City became No. 1 to Harry, and he was—and—is one of its top attractions. Caray legend and lore abounds in his Chicago and suburban restaurants and in Wrigleyville, where an enormous pair of his oversized glasses overlooks the ballpark he made even more famous.

Spectacles were not needed to glimpse the sad spectacle of the Cubs when a Harrycane blew into Chicago in 1971. Over three decades later, fans here, there and everywhere still get blown away by memories of Harry's reign. He was larger than life, a phenomenon that's still true. "You can't beat fun at the old ballpark!" Harry used to tell us. We believed it then, because Harry was a fun guy, in the broadcast booth, dazzling the tourists in the lobby on his domain, the Ambassador Hotel, and especially on his legendary Rush Street pub crawls. The crowd kept growing while Harry made the rounds of his favorite watering holes, plunking bucks on every bar, buying everybody in the house a drink and tossing big tips around like confetti. Along the way, a traffic jam developed, especially from cabbies, among the most rabid of his loyal legions.

I never could buy Harry a drink. Not for lack of trying, along with other diamond scribes, when I was traveling with the White

Sox and later the Cubs. He enjoyed bellying up to hotel bars with us after night games, letting it all hang out in gab sessions that lasted until one of two breakup times—late or later. No matter when, the tab was signed by Harry before we tottered off to our rooms.

A few hours later, fresh and frisky, Harry would be regaling a circle of listeners with nuggets from his stash of anecdotes, rivaled only by Jack Brickhouse's in my time around both of these Chicago superstars. Even though he was seated in a lobby chair 100 yards away, we could hear Harry's booming voice as soon as the elevator doors opened: "Tom Egan (Sox catcher in 1971-72) can't hit the ball as far as he throws it past second base when they're stealing on him." And that was just his before-breakfast warmup for a day of such encounters.

Harry could say things about players' shortcomings that we mere mortals had to soft-pedal in our stories, because we had to approach them for quotes, and muttered obscenities are hard to translate into passable prose, especially on deadline. Harry knew they couldn't ignore him, so he let it all hang out to dry. Some White Sox players fumed, and when Harry teamed with Jimmy Piersall to create their own Comiskey Park cult, owners Jerry Reinsdorf and Eddie Einhorn did a not-so-slow burn. Along with fun, every night on the South Side became a raucous party, not quite like the disastrous Disco Demolition Night on July 15, 1979, though plenty loud.

But the Bill Veeck era was winding down, and it was time for Harry to move on. Those who figured his blunt brand of honesty would not appeal to Cub fans badly underestimated the man. Caray had star power, a kind of charisma that worked. His critics couldn't figure it out, but his fans were wild, not mild, about Harry, and they were a huge majority, drowning out the cynics. Later, especially after a 1987 stroke jeopardized his career, Caray knockers amused themselves by aping his slurred speech and tendency to stumble over tongue-twisting names.

That was a staple of his routine before the stroke, something even he kidded about. Afterward, Harry's fans saw little humor in the lampoon, harpooning those who harassed him with angry calls

A lot of writing and talking about Chicago baseball goes on display at Wrigley Field. Old friends Bob Logan (left) and Harry Caray get together during Harry's last season as the nationwide symbol of the Cubs.

and letters. Caray was so touched by this outpouring of affection from all over the country, including a welcome-back phone call from President Ronald Reagan to the Wrigley Field broadcast booth, that he mellowed in his last years as the voice of the Cubs, becoming a sort of a great uncle to the country at large.

It wasn't so much the losing Cubs they were coming to see by the busload from Keokuk, Iowa, Wisconsin Rapids, Wisconsin, and all points on the compass. Harry's seventh-inning rendition of "Take Me Out to the Ball Game" was the main attraction during normal seasons when the Cubs lost, and abnormal ones when they made an occasional playoff entrance, followed by the invariable quick exit.

Elsewhere in the wide, wonderful world of entertainment, things were changing daily, seemingly hourly. Every act, rock band, TV sitcom and standup comic was in direct competition to become louder, raunchier and more no-holds-barred than the day before. The '80s was not a time of big demand for the good old days, with a few notable exceptions.

Wrigley Field was one of them, especially just before the Cubs came to bat in the seventh. Caray's routine never changed. It was as predictable—and comforting—as the Harlem Globetrotters clowning to victory with their sure-fire formula. If Harry had sung duets, brought in a marimba band to accompany him or otherwise fooled around with what Cub fans and the nationwide TV audience anticipated, it wouldn't have worked as well or for as long.

Harry was much too well plugged into his power base to get off a winning horse. That's why Harry's tradition survived and even thrived during the time he missed early in 1987, until the triumphant Wrigley Field return on May 19. The lineup and batting order of designated celebrity warblers, clamoring to pinch sing in Caray's spot was proof positive. The itinerant tonsils ran the gamut, from venerable Ernie Harwell, the second-best baseball pitchman —next to Caray, of course—to show-biz biggie Dennis Franz and the fans' favorite, Bill Murray.

The show went on, even after Harry's death on Valentine's Day, 1989. It's a living tribute to his magnetism, like the Caray statue unveiled outside the gates to Wrigley's right-field bleachers on opening day, 1999. Since then, the seventh-inning tradition proved strong enough to survive even Mike Ditka's rendition, in full bellow and cacophonous croak, of the new Chicago anthem.

I knew something spectacular had hit town when I first met Harry at the 1971 Chicago baseball writers' dinner. It was in the Chicago-Sheraton Hotel, right next door to Tribune Tower, making it easy to pare down copious notes from Caray's voluminous quotes to get a story in the 10 p.m. street sale edition. A few days later, I got a hand-written Caray note, telling me in part, "Wow. Just like I said it. How did you get the story in the paper so fast? We will have a cool (brewski) soon."

The story was vintage Harry, because quotes by him capsuled the whole saga, from the time he first milked "Holy Cow!" on the air to avoid the cow-patty epithets of his tough neighborhood as a St. Louis street kid. He was at his self-deprecating best about getting fired after 25 years as the radio catalyst for rabid fans, with "the Cardinals are coming, tra-la, tra-la" as their battle cry.

"After 25 years, I thought the Cards would give me a gold watch," Harry told me. "They gave me a pink slip. Now I found myself headed for Oakland (to broadcast A's games in 1970), which I thought was Siberia. In all that time with the Cardinals, I hadn't spent two weeks in Oakland.

"But I got just as excited about Reggie Jackson, Bert Campaneris and Sal Bando as I was about Stan Musial and all the Cardinal stars. I learned a good lesson. It's the game that I'm a fan of, and the team just happens to be a casual coincidence."

Very little about Harry's long, boisterous life was casual, except for his wardrobe. He went at it all, especially the baseball part, with passionate commitment. With him, it was fun being a fan.

Sandberg Can't Be Sandbagged

I can understand Joe Morgan's ill-concealed jealousy of Ryne Sandberg. What eludes me is the way some put him down because he's not the most electrifying locker room orator since Knute Rockne. What's the problem?

What Sandberg did at second base was not second rate, even if he couldn't orate like Demosthenes, with or without a mouthful of marbles. He was marvelous at that position, the best keystone sacker I ever saw. That goes back to the last days of Charlie Gehringer at Detroit, through Flash Gordon, Bill Mazeroski—a Hall of Famer with credentials far inferior to Sandberg's—and Morgan himself, a cog in Cincinnati's Big Red Machine.

Morgan was great. Sandberg was greater. That's not a homer verdict on my part. Nor is it a minority opinion. A few years ago, I asked some baseball people to define the Cub superstar's place on the all-time list. The answers left little doubt that it was up there with Eddie Collins, Rogers Hornsby and Jackie Robinson. Among them were two of Sandberg's managers, Don Zimmer and Jim Lefebvre.

Zimmer—"In my 43 years in baseball, Sandberg is the best all-around second baseman I've seen. He's a quiet, tough guy. He will play hurt and no one knows except the manager, but that's the way he wants it."

Lefebvre—"Players like Jose Canseco excite the fans, but they don't have Sandberg's consistency. He takes pride in playing, and he has nine gold gloves to prove it."

Beside Ryno's contemporaries, the guys who had a total of over 150 years in the game provided some impressive testimony.

Ernie Harwell, baseball broadcaster since 1948—"He compares favorably with the best of them on offense and defense. I put him on a par with Jackie Robinson, the first truly great second baseman I saw in the National League. He has the same skills that made Charlie Gehringer the best in the American League for so many years."

Red Schoendienst, Hall of Fame second baseman and Cards coach—"He's such a great athlete, he could play polo. I don't try to compare players from different times because the game has changed too much, but Sandberg is as good as anybody I played against. Fans will always argue whether Willie Mays was better than Mickey Mantle."

No, I didn't get any verbal grand slams from Sandberg in 15 years of covering him since he got stolen from the Phillies in the

Ryne Sandberg transformed himself from a throw-in to Mr. Consistency of the Cubs with sheer effort. The acrobatic second baseman eludes Atlanta's sliding Dale Murphy to unload a double-play relay to first.

1982 trade that has to rank as one of the biggest steals since Bonnie and Clyde. The Cubs being the Cubs, they installed the greatest second baseman of his generation at third base, where he started off in a horrendous 1 for 32 slump.

So it was understandable that Wrigley Field fans figured this rookie was just another in the long line of losers who kept flunking the Ron Santo lookalike contest that had been going on ever since that outstanding hot corner guardian got dealt to the White Sox in 1974. Wrong. Once he moved from third to second, his natural position, "Kid Natural" naturally blossomed, coming back from his first retirement in 1994 to depart as the all-time leader in homers (277) at his position. Still, the "colorless" label lingered, so I addressed it this way:

Ryno's Bat, Glove Eloquent Enough
(Daily Herald, June 14, 1994)

Less than 24 hours before Ryne Sandberg dropped Monday's retirement bombshell, a writer complained about him.

"Yeah, I know how good Sandberg used to be," the guy said. "he's not the same. Besides, he's so bland and boring."

More proof that in this era of instant superstardom, a glib tongue is almost as essential as a bat or glove.

"That's stupid," I replied. "Look how consistent he's been. If Sandberg isn't a great player, nobody is. Why do we keep bum-rapping him for not providing the media with a post-game clubhouse sideshow?"

Well, now we won't have Sandberg to kick around anymore. I've seen some gradual slippage, to be sure, but that can't cloud his performance for these dozen-plus Chicago seasons. A great ballplayer, pure and simple. The rush-to-judgment media types who panned him for refusing to play the added role of a Mark Grace quote machine will have to find another target. Don't worry, they soon will.

Sandberg was a struggling rookie third baseman when I first met him in 1982. On an early-season trip to Montreal, he related how hard it had been to overcome that rocky start at the plate in his Cubs debut. Neither of us suspected he would become a premier second baseman, ticketed for the Hall of Fame. Over the last dozen years, I saw Sandberg routinely make far-from-routine plays.

Sandberg's favorite years were no surprise—1984 and 1989—when the Cubs won the division title prior to painful first-round playoff knockouts by the San Diego Padres and San Francisco Giants. The Cubs rode that crazy-quilt, roller-coaster cycle throughout his career. Through all those occasional ups and customary downs, Ryno was a model of consistency on a wildly inconsistent team. Sadly, Sandberg grounded out to quash a Cub rally in his last playoff at-bat, but he came through in the clutch more than enough.

He did it so well and so quietly, fans often overlooked him. Like almost all of the thousands of fielding chances that came his way, Sandberg handled that, too.

Quiet—Genius at Work
(Daily Herald, October 7, 1989)

SAN FRANCISCO—Ryne Sandberg has hit for the cycle already in this young National League championship series.

Heading into tonight's third game in the best-of-7 set, Sandberg's hitting .500, with a single, double, triple and homer in eight trips. He also has driven in 2 runs, scored 4 and flashed his usual Golden Glove at second base.

But his ex-Cub teammate, Giants right-hander Rick Reuschel, got more media attention after being pounded in the first inning of Game 2 than Sandberg did for the triple that ignited a 6-run outburst. That's the way it always seems to go for the 30-year-old Quiet Man.

"I'm used to it," Sandberg said, with no trace of unhappiness on his face. "Some letters from fans mention that I'm having an MVP year, but it looks like Kevin Mitchell (Giants outfielder) has it wrapped up."

If so, the taciturn Sandberg won't throw a tantrum. He's been playing the fringe of the spotlight for so long, nobody seems to know he's closing in on all-time totals for fielding, hitting and durability.

In Chicago, Basketball's Spelled M-E-Y-E-R

I hope Johnny Wooden's admirers don't take this personally. I share their regard for the man who went from All-American player at Purdue to all-conquering coach at UCLA.

But there's a man in Chicago who has done more for basketball in general and college hoops in particular than Wooden, Dean Smith, Adolph Rupp or even the real superstars since the dawn of TV—Dick Vitale and Michael Jordan. His name is a lot less secret than his fame should be.

Ray Meyer did much more than put DePaul University on the map. He kept college basketball alive in Chicago when tickets were not easy to give away. His Blue Demons lured people into Alumni Hall, a nifty little jewel close to the el tracks on Chicago's North Side. OK, it wasn't quite as cozy—or as charismatic—as Loyola's bandbox Alumni Gym, right under the el a little further North, and so tiny it almost fit into one of those CTA trains that rumbled overhead.

With its 1920s YMCA-style overhead running track and support columns strategically placed to block maximum views for the minimum crowd in that scenic shoebox, Loyola's gym seemed like a movie set, shipped directly from a Hollywood backlot. It also had some great coaches for first-rate Ramblers teams, cool dudes like George Ireland, Jerry Lyne and Gene Sullivan.

But the one and only Ray Meyer was No. 1 except for 1963, when Ireland's underdogs upset mighty Cincinnati to win Chicago's only NCAA basketball championship. Long before and long after that, Meyer was sowing the seeds for basketball's big-time breakthrough, recruiting kids the Big Ten wouldn't accept and fitting them into winning teams. His career record at DePaul—42 years, 1,078 games, a 724-354 record—sparkles, though that's far from the real story.

For my money, Ray Meyer was the best thing for the college game since James Naismith hung up his first peach basket. Contrary to rumor, I wasn't there to get quotes from basketball's inventor on the day he spawned a way to make winter blasts more bearable, at least when shivering fans came in out of the cold to red-hot action on the court.

Ray Meyer, De Paul's head coach for 42 years, patiently brought Chicago college basketball into the big time, along with another pioneer, George Ireland of Loyola.

But I was here for much of the Meyer era, before he handed over the DePaul dynasty to son Joey in 1985. Ray and I talked a lot in his cramped office on the second floor of Alumni Hall, and the tales flowed like wine at grape-stomping time. One thing we never had to do was worry about Coach Ray complaining about our stories or, even worse, cutting off quotable contact with us. He knew what we were writing and saying, but it was not his way to whine and complain—unlike many of his coaching colleagues.

A totally unpretentious man, Meyer did not need to have his ego stroked by puff pieces. He let his record speak for itself, another reason why I've always been a Meyer admirer. That's not to say he couldn't make his own case. All you had to do was ask, and to-the-point answers would fill your notes with quotes from Chairman Ray. My favorite: "Most of my 42 years as basketball coach at DePaul was like a paid vacation."

So Ray's pleasure at learning that the new fitness and recreation center, across the street from Alumni Hall would bear his name, was genuine, despite a tinge of bitterness. When Joey got fired in 1997 without warning by DePaul, it led his Dad to cut ties with the university, move out of the office where he'd held court for a half century and stop serving as color commentator for WGN radio's broadcasts of Blue Demon games.

"I owe everything to basketball," the senior Meyer said. "Naming this building for me is a great honor. I had wonderful years at DePaul, even though there's still a little heartbreak in those memories."

Not for Ray Meyer fans. Those were the Good Old Days.

Hey! Hey! We still Miss Brickhouse Today

Maybe I'm mistaken to include the plural "we" in that line, but I don't think so. Yes, I'm aware this is a bare-knuckle, rip-and-slash era of journalism, both print and electronics, with no rock unturned to probe what might crawl out from underneath. That's the way it is on the sports page, too. So we've all had to get more vicious, personal and unforgiving in our stories.

Hey! Hey! A superstar doubleheader, for sure, when Jack Brickhouse (left) and Ernie Banks got together in the Wrigley Field broadcast booth. Brickhouse counted his call of Mr. Cub's historic 500th homer as one of his personal top kicks. Both of them provided plenty of memories, but a World Series for the Cubs was not one of them.

But that's not the way it was when Jack Brickhouse ruled the broadcast booth in Chicago for almost six decades. Harry Caray said it, but Brickhouse personified the fun-at-the-old-ballpark approach more than anybody. He was not Mr. Sunny Side Up on the air and a totally different, snarling egomaniac once the mike got switched off.

I found that out when I asked Jack to write a foreword for my first book in 1975, entitled *The Bulls and Chicago: A Stormy Affair.* Not only did he read the proofs before writing, but he sent me a thoughtful, well-written analysis of the book and the people who played roles in the Bulls' hoop opera that was so exhaustive, I regretfully had to trim some of it.

That was the real Brickhouse. He was my friend, so I'm not pretending to be objective, but Chicago lost an irreplaceable asset when Jack died at 82 on August 6, 1998. I last saw him standing in the Cubs dugout a few days before that, so I walked up, said hello and hugged him. I don't claim to be a psychic, but I was alarmed by his lack of vigor, so the blow was softened for me because I got that chance to say farewell.

In the big ballpark in our minds, where the fun and games never end, I can hear his "Hey Hey" signoff for a Cubs homer. When the Brickhouse exhibit opened at Chicago's Museum of Broadcast Communications, I got the chance to stroll down memory lane:

A Brickhouse of Memories
(Daily Herald, April 13, 2001)

Jack Brickhouse did so much play-by-play, it's a wonder he ever found time to play.

But Brickhouse did, occasionally at least, during a Chicago broadcasting career that began in 1940 and just kept going. Stories about the intensely human Brickhouse tossing his golf club in disgust, tearing up a losing race track ticket or schmoozing with show-biz legend Jimmy Durante at the lone-gone Chez Paree night club are timeless.

So was he. Nobody knows that better than Vince Lloyd, his sidekick on and off the air for decades.

"Jack and I worked seven days a week, doing wrestling and boxing, after the Cubs' season ended," Lloyd recalled. "Once he showed me a calendar, marked off for 13 straight weeks on the air without a break.

"Jack had the greatest outlook on life of anyone I ever met. He didn't want to miss a minute of it."

Brickhouse's widow, Pat, along with the rest of the WGN clan, joined friends and fans at the broadcast museum in the Loop to open a permanent Jack Brickhouse exhibit. The brainchild of museum president Bruce DuMont, it offers hundreds of photos, trophies and memorabilia gathered by sports author and broadcaster George Castle. It's a slice of Chicago sports history well worth seeing and hearing, especially audio and TV clips of the unforgettable Brickhouse voice, giving Ernie Banks' historic 500th homer his hey-hey seal of approval, along with many other timeless moments.

An incredible career, starting in 1934 at Peoria radio station WMBD would be reason enough for this tribute. The real reason why this unique man won't be forgotten was summed up by his pals.

"Jack Brickhouse was the man you wanted as a friend, a brother, a father or a co-worker," said Jack Rosenberg, his producer through decades of losing Cubs telecasts that Brickhouse somehow transformed in winning memories.

"Jack had that divine devotion to whatever game he was calling," said *Sun-Times* columnist Irv Kupcinet, who teamed with Brickhouse to do Bears games on radio for 24 years.

After Brickhouse died, DuMont called Pat to set in motion the feast of sight and sound that will be open to the public.

"When I was a kid in Chicago, I wrote Jack, asking for advice on how to break into broadcasting," DuMont said. "He told me to stay in school, look for a job in a smaller market and work hard."

"I've been a Brickhouse fan ever since."

He's not alone.

Ditka Toughest on Himself

Stories of Mike Ditka's competitive ferocity make up a big part of his legendary status in Chicago. When someone qualifies for that exclusive spot in the hearts and minds of Windy City fans, he—or she—stays there. That sort of fame has to be earned, but it never dims. So Bears fans still get their fire lit by hearing over and over the way Ditka went ballistic on the sidelines, challenged players, coaches, fans, and the immediate world and never, ever quit.

That attitude made Da Coach as big a fixture as Chicago-style pizza, and just as nourishing to victory-starved Bears loyalists. It's what brought him back to Chicago as a coach, because he left town as a player embroiled in a salary squabble with Bears owner George Halas, notorious for nursing those nickels. But when Halas saw Ditka blowing his top as a Dallas Cowboys assistant, he made a mental note that (a) nice guy Neill Armstrong had to go and (b) if No More Mr. Nice Guy would be his policy, Ditka was his man.

That had more to do with Ditka replacing Armstrong in 1982 as boisterous Bears boss than the celebrated letter Iron Mike wrote to Papa Bear. If Halas hadn't already been leaning in Ditka's direction, the Gettysburg Address would not have changed this stubborn Bohemian's mind. When it came to stubbornness—and toughness—Halas and Ditka could have been father and son.

I had plenty of chances to see Ditka run with the Halas legacy. Or snort, stamp, fume and struggle with it. He would do anything to win, pushing himself even harder than his players, because he learned you had to go to war every day as a kid in steel mill suburbs around Pittsburgh.

The image I can't forget got burned into my brain on October 30, 1998, in Foxboro, Massachusetts. Doug Flutie, the undersized, overachieving quarterback who had been hounded off the Bears by sneering veterans two years earlier, got revenge that afternoon. Flutie threw a bomb on the first play from scrimmage and passed the Bears dizzy, leading the New England Patriots to a 30-7 romp.

It was over so early that I followed other writers to the tunnel leading to the Bears locker room while the meaningless final minutes ticked off. When it mercifully ended, the beaten Bears trudged off, followed by their coach. Ditka's face was an alarming shade of gray. A few days later, he had a heart attack.

Like every other obstacle he's encountered, before or since, Ditka worked his way through that crisis. Nobody was surprised, least of all the players who knew him as a young, ferocious tight end:

Like Da Coach, Tough is a 5-Letter Word
(Daily Herald, November 3, 1988)

"Within two weeks, Mike Ditka will be up and back to coaching, as though nothing happened," predicted Rudy Bukich. "He's a very tough guy."

Quarterback Bukich was one of the 1963 NFL champion Bears honored here Wednesday. Topic A among Ditka's reunited teammates was the heart attack that had stricken the Bears coach a few hours earlier. Ditka was the tight end on the team that went all the way, toppling the New York Giants 14-10 for the title in frigid Wrigley Field.

"Mike came to practice one day with a cast on his leg, just so he could catch the ball and be with the guys," Bukich recalled. "Another time, he had a dislocated shoulder that must have hurt like hell, but we couldn't keep him away from the field."

Ted Karras, who helped Ditka throw the blocks that cleared a path for running backs Ronnie Bull and Joe Marconi, had trouble believing the news.

"We all thought George Halas would live forever, and Mike is just as tough as the Old Man," Karras said. "No matter what kind of shape you're in, I guess that pressure gets to you. Mike was out there hollering at the Bears every day, driving them to work as hard as he did. He'll have to realize none of us can carry on all our lives the way we did when we were young."

Can Ditka bank the fire and ease his all-out tempo?

"Mike was the epitome of the intense football player, and his coaching style is exactly the same," replied center Mike Pyle,

Ditka's road roommate in their playing days.

Bull understands how time has taken its toll on the 49-year-old Ditka.

"When something this serious hits, you have to stop and think," he said.

Rolling Sloan Gathers No Loss

Jerry Sloan has grown from an all-out, Ditka-style battler on the basketball court to one of the NBA's coaching elder statesman with the Utah Jazz.

I'm not surprised. This product of the Southern Illinois farms and oil fields has the sort of inner strength that pulled him through four-plus decades of all-out effort as a player and a coach. No matter what, the man I dubbed the Evansville Hustler when he was the Bulls' defensive battering ram (1966-76) found a way to get it done, playing through pain until his battered knees no longer could stand the strain.

When Sloan took over as head coach in 1979, the Bulls gave up on him too soon. He was learning on the job, adjusting to a new generation of players that had to be motivated, instead of bringing it with them every night. That's the way Sloan and his backcourt partner, Stormin' Norman Van Lier, took basketball as a never-ending challenge. But Chicago fans never gave up on either of them. They bestowed superstar status on Sloan because he earned it. I summed up his career this way:

On D, No. 4 Was No. 1
(Basketball Times, 1977)

CHICAGO—How do you write a Jerry Sloan retirement column?

In my case, reluctantly. The last part of my youth and most of my remaining illusions vanished during the decade when Sloan was flinging his body in the path of NBA behemoths.

When fate decreed he was never going to play on a championship Bulls team, I realized John F. Kennedy was right when he said, "Nobody told me life has to be fair."

Sloan's title dream faded, because the Bulls never even got to the NBA finals in his 10 years here. Sloan is the last man who'd ask for sympathy. He hid his hurts, mental and physical, playing as hard and as long as he could. When his aching knees couldn't work, he walked away with his head up, as always, win or lose. The players he hounded relentlessly on defense are glad they don't have to face him again.

Sloan molded himself into the NBA's top defensive guard by working longer and harder than anyone. Watching No. 4 unleash that reckless D was so eye-popping that many, even in Chicago, failed to notice he was a complete basketball player, scoring 10,233 points and grabbing 5,385 rebounds for the Bulls. I saw Sloan play most of his 696 games in that uniform. I never saw him give less than maximum effort. And the Bulls' organization never came close to matching the class he displayed.

Soldier Field – Payton's Place

So much has been written about the way Walter Payton lived and died. Little of it did the man and the legend total justice.

There's not much I can add, except to note I share the frustration that his life got cut short at 45. When liver failure claimed Payton on November 1, 1999, it closed the door on a list of amazing accomplishments.

The saddest part was that the best was yet to come. When Payton became an NFL owner, as he surely would have, his fellow moguls would have been hit with a blizzard of fresh ideas, as well as an occasional whoopee cushion on their well-padded chairs. Walter's sense of humor and his fondness for practical jokes was just one facet of a complex man.

His Sweetness nickname belied an awesome total of 16,276 career rushing yards over 13 seasons with the Bears. Along the way, he became the playing symbol of the team, the way George Halas was the coaching symbol.

The crowd around Payton was so deep during my years as a backup Bear writer that I seldom got a chance to go one-on-one with him. Still, I saw enough of his blend of outward affability and inner sense of protecting his privacy. The way he blended those conflicting traits, never letting either interfere with the business of carrying the football better than anyone else, past or present, convinced me "Sweetness" was the right label for this package of talent. A brief nugget from a college football story proves my point:

Hoosier Favorite Bear?
(Chicago Tribune, September 3, 1987)

BLOOMINGTON, Ind. —Walter Payton, a believer in reaching for new heights, is helping Indiana to get over the hump this season.

Two Hoosiers, tailback Anthony Thompson and linebacker Kevin Kelly, ran up and down Payton's hill in the summer. The Bears superstar joined them on the steep landfill near his Barrington home, providing an example that could elevate Indiana in the Big Ten. Payton works out frequently with Kelly, a 200-pound special teams standout from Barrington High. Thompson also was invited to test the punishing hills, impressing Payton when he galloped up and down 15 times without stopping.

"I was in heaven," said Thompson, who stamped himself as an NFL draft possibility by topping 100 rushing yards in the Hoosiers' last five games. "Walter Payton encouraged me to prove what I did last season was no fluke."

A Fine Kittle of Frank's and Fisk

No, Ron Kittle was not a superstar, except in popularity polls among White Sox fans. Catcher Carlton Fisk, a Hall of Famer, and

Walter Payton made the long journey from Jackson State to Chicago look easy with his blend of talent, charm and unfailing good humor. The folks in Jackson, Mississippi, showed their feelings for the Bears running back by celebrating his return with a special day.

Frank Thomas, sure to join him eventually, definitely belong in that category.

It would be hard to find two images that contrasted more sharply, at least to the ticket-buying public. From the day he switched Sox, from Red to White, in 1981, when Pudge stroked the first of his 214 homers in Chicago flannels in his first game for them, he gained instant admittance to the South Side lodge. That's not easy, because White Sox fans jealously guard the prized tag of Our Guy they choose to bestow on a favored few players.

Right from the start, Fisk was one of them, and still is. His penchant for picking fights with the front office, especially Sox chairman Jerry Reinsdorf, further endeared him to that hard core of demanding, knowledgeable fans. And the way the catcher, field general, handler of pitchers and clutch hitter did his job on the field made him a solid favorite. This was one of many Pudge pinnacles:

Sox Star Hits 2,000 on Sock Market
(Daily Herald, July 18, 1989)

Carlton Fisk gave Comiskey Park fans a moment to remember Monday night.

The rest of the White Sox contented themselves with remembering how to win. They celebrated Fisk's 2,000th major-league hit by treating the crowd of 18,070 to their fifth straight victory, a 7-3 romp over the New York Yankees. Fisk added a single and double, giving him 905 hits for the Sox, 11th highest total in team history.

"Getting 2,000 hits means I must have made 5,000 outs," the 41-year-old catcher said. "Some day I'll look back on the big hits (a reference to his game-winning homer off Fenway Park's left-field foul pole in the 1975 World Series) but tonight was bigger, because my family was here to share it."

That was in sharp contrast to the way things have gone for Thomas. Despite hanging up batting totals that compare favorably with Babe Ruth, Lou Gehrig and other all-time sluggers, the Big Hurt often got slapped with the title of Big Pain by a noisy minority of Sox fans. They saw Thomas' preference for doing things his way as evidence that he was a selfish, moody performer, more interested in his own stats than where the Sox stood in the AL. It was a bum rap, in many regards, although once that cat's out of the bag, it's not easy to stem the torrent of catty remarks.

The David Wells controversy in 2001 added more venom to the stew of a Sox flop, especially after the way they stormed to the AL Central Division crown a season before. Wells was wrong, a fact he sullenly admitted, after hinting it wasn't a bigger hurt when the first baseman tore a right triceps muscle. He needed season-ending surgery, but his critics suggested snidely that a personality transplant also might be advisable.

Thomas weathered the storm, declining to get into a shouting match with Wells, a confrontation that couldn't have helped him. If Thomas can boost his average to .250 in the public relations league, superstar feats on the field might ease the animosity and smooth his path to Cooperstown.

When the Big Hurt rejoined the Sox in 2002, he brought a better attitude, plus his booming bat. Skeptical Sox fans still need to be convinced.

A Highly Motta-vated Coach

Bulls fans are too busy lamenting the post-Jordan depression they're stuck with to reflect on the past. If they did, some with long memories might demand that Dick Motta be summoned from retirement to lead the Bulls back to the playoffs.

In the unlikely event that Motta would consider coaching the Bulls for a second term, things would get a lot more interesting in the United Center. They sure were in Chicago Stadium, Motta's stomping ground during his eight-year term as the firebrand of the NBA.

Plain and simple, Motta saved the Bulls from the slaughterhouse. He could be as contentious off the court as he was on it, but that would add some badly needed fun to the dreary Bull situation. Fans would start packing the place again, and the Bulls would start playing defense again. Besides that, Motta's meaty quotes would get plenty of exposure. Try these snippets from my last Q and A with him:

"I don't give a bleep what people think of me. I know who I am. My problem is I don't go buy people drinks and kiss their asses. At one time, I thought my candor and availability were respected in this town. Nobody likes to be split open and displayed in public."

You get the idea. Motta often left himself open for jabs, and today's go-for-the-jugular school of sports writing would nail him to the wall daily.

Finally, a new crop of superstars keeps coming along in Chicago. I always enjoy seeing how up-and-comers like Bears linebacker Brian Urlacher handle the media hordes. After some praise for his hard hits, Urlacher responded, "You (media) guys always see the good things."

He'll learn.

Dick Motta's all smiles in this meeting with his assistant Phil Johnson (center) and General Manager Pat Williams (right). But when the power struggle ended, Motta was both coach and GM of the Bulls, leaving Williams out in the cold.

6

Knight Games

Writing a newspaper column is easy—or so most people think. Mostly, that's because they've never tried to write one, especially under deadline pressure.

What's supposed to be different about column writing is the alleged freedom the pundit gets to pass along his ponderous pronouncements on all topics, great and small. That supposed line of demarcation between a just-the-facts-ma'am news story and a let-'em-have-it opinion column is a myth. It's the kind of thing unaware editors keep telling themselves, in between mumbling their mantra and attending focus meetings.

Actually, the writers out there in the trenches, trying to tell readers what's really happening, know their daily stories are loaded with opinion. Fans who seek only to learn who won the game usually are satisfied with a wire service story. The vast majority, from rabid followers of a team to those seeking mild diversion on their lunch hour, wants punchy, inside stuff.

I use that description only because a *Sports Illustrated* editor once described the book I wrote about the Bulls as "punchy inside stuff". Or perhaps he really thought I was punchy for trying to get inside SI's lofty standards with an except from my book on the

1974-75 Bulls, who should have won the NBA championship, but didn't.

So this must be a column, because I'm opining that SI employed erroneous editorial judgment. More to the point, it's a deep background column, because unidentified informed sources can be trotted out at any moment to make my case. Of course, I'm kidding, because some columnists wouldn't hesitate to use psychic sources in a bid to induce their readers to keep on reading.

It's clear by now, I hope, that a column means whatever the author wants it to mean. Unlike a news story, it doesn't have to be about a game or an event, which requires an attention-grabbing lead paragraph, along with some more or less pertinent details such as the final score. All a column needs is readability, an elusive quality, indeed.

The following columns I've written over the years cover a wide spectrum of subjects, times, places, and degrees of intensity. Sometimes I wrote for the sheer enjoyment of putting one word next to another, or just to see whether the butler (Jeeves, not Kevin) really did it, or for some other inscrutable purpose. My good friend, Larry Donald, an outstanding editor and nationally respected publisher of *Basketball Times*, and *Baseball Bulletin* used to give me wide latitude for such double-drivel (in basketball columns, of course) as crummy puns. Other times, I could wax indignant with the best of them, especially if the supply of wax didn't wane. And at no time did I gloss over the facts. Well, maybe sometimes, especially when Bobby Knight was at it again:

Time to Call It a Knight
(Daily Herald, February 28, 1998)

BLOOMINGTON, IN. – It's time for Bobby Knight to give up coaching college basketball.

I'm not writing that to stir up controversy, although the mere mention of the Indiana coach assures it will. What I saw Tuesday night in the IU Assembly Hall convinced me that the final meeting of the "Good-bye Bob Club" can't be postponed much longer. True, Knight's outburst might have been provoked by referee Ted Valentine's bad judgment, but it was inexcusable, unacceptable and downright scary. Preventing the Big Ten's prestige and national image from plummeting to the level of the World Wrestling Federation calls for action. Now, not later.

The conference should suspend Knight from the Hoosiers' next game, Saturday at Iowa. And the Big Ten's Council of Presidents should send him a letter of reprimand. If that doesn't work, Indiana University should fire him.

Forget the usual channels—the athletic directors and Big Ten Commissioner Jim Delany. They're powerless to curb Knight's tantrums because IU president Myles Brand insists Bob's indispensable. His players graduate, his teams win, and he's not such a bad fellow as the media portray him. What I'm saying is that kids imitate what they see on television. My guess is a lot of them are replaying Knight stalking menacingly toward Valentine after getting thrown out of Tuesday's game with Illinois.

But kids now have guns and knives. Knight's display of rage could convince some of them it's OK to settle a dispute with violence. I'm not anti-Knight. He earned his berth in college basketball's Hall of Fame. The way college basketball should be presented, played and coached no longer is Knight's way. Regardless of the provocation, no college coach should storm around the court the way he did.

Referee Valentine pulled the ejection trigger on Knight too quickly. That can't justify Knight's display of childish fury, his arm-waving tirade and his crowd-inciting exit. Instead of going out the shortest way to the Hoosiers' dressing room, the ousted coach milked the last ounce of bad sportsmanship and ham acting from that theatrical departure.

Basketball, after all, is only a game. Colleges, especially the Big Ten, have a responsibility to set and enforce standards of conduct by teachers and coaches.

This one drew strong reactions from across the country—mad in Denver, glad in Boston:

It's Not Easy Being Anti-Green
(Basketball Times, 1977)

CHICAGO—Open letter to a National Basketball Association coach:

Mr. Larry Brown, c/o Denver Nuggets, McNichols Sports Arena

Dear Coach Brown:

Welcome to the lodge.

Your recent blast at the NBA in general and the referees' competence—or lack of it—in particular was evidence that you're learning. You and your team now belong to a league that has two conferences.

No, not the East and West Conferences. In reality, the NBA consists of the Boston Conference and the All the Others Conference, sometimes known as the Great Unwashed.

You were perceptive in discovering that the Celtics seem to get a higher percentage of crucial calls than any other team, especially in Boston Garden. The reason you attributed to that phenomenon after the Nuggets lost in the Gah-den (that's what Beantowners call it, but visitors prefer terms of endearment like "Snakepit" and "Chamber of Horrors") was faulty. As an observer of a team which has been losing faithfully in the Gah-den for 11 years, I'd like to point out a few laws of nature, NBA style.

You said, and I quote, "There are two sets of rules, one for NBA teams and the other for ABA teams. It's dishonest. It stinks."

Wrong, coach. There ARE two sets of rules in the NBA, all right, but one is for the Celtics and the other for all of you peasants, regardless of the color of the red, white and blue beachball some of you used to play with.

Many explanations have been offered over the years. Personally, I don't believe the problems stem from dishonesty on anyone's part. What it comes down to, pure and simple, is that the Celtics are the aristocracy of pro basketball. They have ruled this kingdom for two decades, surviving a few lean years when Crown Prince Tom took over for Emperor Arnold, and nobody ever accused them of being benevolent despots.

I mean, the Celtics beat you. They went out and won the championship, year after year, by wanting it more. If anybody doubts that, it's in the record book—13 NBA titles in the last 20 seasons, eight consecutively. You could look it up.

The point is, nobody builds a monument like that with press clippings or homerism or anything else except sheer effort. A lot of people outside Boston may not like it, and there's no question that such a stranglehold on the throne room was not the best thing that could have happened to the league, but the Celtics earned what they got.

So please don't hand us that stuff about "They're picking on us poor little ABA outsiders." Last time I looked at the standings, the Nuggets weren't faring too badly. No ABA team has disgraced itself in this season of transition, not even the Nets, where Kevin Loughery is too busy molding a bunch of castoffs into a competitive club to compliant about the officials, except maybe Manny Sokol.

I understand how you feel, Coach Brown. It's disheartening and frustrating to play as well as your guys did in the Gahden and still come up empty. That sort of thing has happened before, though, and will again, because the Celtics are the Celtics. They come to play and you've got to beat them, not the refs or the fans or the NBA Establishment or any other real or imagined adversary.

The only guys you have to worry about are the ones in those green shirts, coach. They represent excellence, something that should be preserved and respected in an era when too many people make too much money for doing little and caring less.

You've got a fine team there in Denver. I can't speak for the rest of the NBA, but it would be silly of me to look down on them after the way they've mangled the Bulls this season. Pardon the free advice, but the Nuggets will get the recognition you hunger for when they prove they deserve it on the floor and on the scoreboard —not at the debating rostrum.

See you in the playoffs, coach. Good Luck,

Bob Logan

Pete Rose pushes a lot of hot buttons. I know most of my media colleagues and a sizeable majority of fans want his plaque hung in baseball's Hall of Fame today, if not sooner. I don't. The argument about a lot of drunks and bad guys already being here, so why not Rose, does not work for me. Here's why:

A Rose by Any Other Name—Except Hall of Famer
(Daily Herald, April 4, 1992)

One thing about Pete Rose is perfectly clear.

As the all-time leader in hits, he belongs in the Hall of Fame. What he did on the field for so many years is what America is—or used to be—all about.

Effort. Guts. Willingness to work, take risks, and get more out of his ability than anybody suspected was there. That was Pete Rose, the player, a Rose that bloomed in the clutch, a scrapper who Rose to the occasion.

If that's the only factor, no problem. He would have been eligible—a unanimous first-ballot selection this year, including my vote.

Then Pete Rose the manager clouds the picture, and I start having problems. It has more sides than just Rose's alleged gambling addiction. The transformation of Charlie Hustle into Pick 'em Pete creates disturbing questions about whether any standards still exist in sports or anywhere else.

For aging squares like me, the dilemma has sharp, clear-cut edges. We recall Connie Mack, sitting in the dugout with his high-button collar and bowler hat, waving his scorecard to position outfielders for more than a half-century. While Mack was winning nine American league pennants and five World Series titles over that span, the Tall Tactician of the Philadelphia Athletics became a symbol of the game and how it was supposed to be played.

They called him Mr. Baseball, although his rules applied with equal ease to the game of life. You did not cheat or intentionally hurt an opponent. Neither did you sit in your clubhouse before games, phoning bookies with big bets and using your inside knowledge to beat the odds.

I'm aware that some fans reading these words have no idea who Connie Mack was. Others would laugh at the notion of an old man managing a major-league team in a suit and tie. Still

Two of baseball's best—Baltimore's Brooks Robinson (5) and Cincinnati's Pete Rose.

more might snicker over Mack's antiquated image, one that never varied from his managerial debut with the Pittsburgh Pirates in 1894, right up to the end of his unprecedented reign as owner-manager of the A's in 1950. Since then, a lot of the beliefs taken for granted by Connie Mack seem to have vanished along with him.

Born Cornelius McGillicuddy during the Civil War, the stringbean kid started out working 16-hour days in a New England shoe factory. He became a big-league catcher, then a baseball immortal, with the name shortened to Mack, so it would fit into a box score. In his day, individuals were considered responsible for their own actions, good or bad. Rule-breakers, like Shoeless Joe Jackson and the rest of the 1919 Black Sox, paid the price.

Nowadays, there's a built-in set of excuses for the Pete Roses of the world, from petty thieves to mass murderers. He or she was culturally or emotionally deprived—perhaps both—or maybe it was the victim's fault for being there in the first place.

And Rose the gambler? Well, gee whiz, he wasn't doing anything the rest of us haven't done by plunking down our hard-earned cash to bet on a sporting event, was he? So what if Rose wagered heavily, even on baseball? Why use that as an excuse to keep such an otherwise superbly qualified player out of the Hall of Fame, a shrine already overpopulated by off-the-field boozers, rowdies and skirt-chasers?

For many fans, the ethical line Rose allegedly crossed is so blurred that it hardly matters. To me, it matters a lot. If there is clear proof that Rose bet on baseball games while he was managing the Cincinnati Reds, I will not vote to put his plaque in the Hall. If it turns out that Rose bet on other sports, but not on baseball, I will vote for him sooner or later, probably later.

Those who play by today's anything-goes rules will disagree with me. I accept that.

I just don't believe Connie Mack would disagree with me.

The world has whirled many times, even doing flip-flops and assorted bizarre gyrations, since I wrote this column in 1970. It paints a picture of a way of life that's as extinct as the dinosaur, the dodo bird or the quaint notion that our own shores were safe from enemy attack. It's about the first NBA All-Star game I covered, but mostly about a code of dress and conduct incomprehensible in 21st Century America.

Willy-Nilly in Philly
(Chicago Tribune, January 21, 1970)

PHILADELPHIA—The ballroom is crowded and noisy. Over in one corner a dance band is sawing away, murdering a Cole Porter ballad.

The talk is about basketball and the big men in the room are players, the best in the business. This is a reception in a Philadelphia hotel on the eve of the NBA's 20th annual All-Star game. It is an affair of the type known to newspapermen as a freeload. The freeloaders are out in force.

On your right in a chair ranged against the wall is Lew Alcindor, awesome rookie center of the Milwaukee Bucks. On his right is Jimmy Walker, Detroit Pistons playmaker, and his stunning wife. On their right is Elvin "Big E" Hayes of the San Diego Rockets, who will start at center for the West team because Nate Thurmond of the Warriors is in a San Francisco hospital, recovering from knee surgery.

Alcindor slouches, shades glinting in the light, waiting for the media to come and pay its respects. The media is too busy rushing the bar, so the former UCLA superstar gives up and rushes the chow line.

Tom Van Arsdale (or is it Dick?) enters with his gorgeous wife. Dick (or is it Tom?) trails his twin brother. Similarly dressed, it's impossible to tell which is which. Dick will wear the red suit of the West squad and Tom the white East threads, marking the first time brothers have opposed each other in an All-Star game.

The babble grows louder. Oscar Robertson of the Cincinnati Royals enters, shakes hands and says yes, he still is president of the NBA Players Association. They'll soon meet to take a position on merger rumors, raging between the NBA and its pesky rival, the American Basketball Association. The position already is clear. The players have threatened to strike and probably will file a Curt Flood- type lawsuit to block the merger if it cuts off the flow of big bucks both leagues use as weapons in their bidding war for talent.

Voices of owners, general managers, and writers rise, trying to top each other's stories. The booming tones of Marty Blake, Atlanta Hawks general manager, cut through the din: "So this scout says to me, 'I need six tickets for tomorrow night.' So I say to him, 'But you're a lousy scout.' So he says, 'OK, give me four tickets".

Two new members of the NBA expansion committee come by to talk turkey. Elmer Rich of the Bulls and Ray Patterson of the Bucks want to make their hard-line merger stance clear, with Patterson adding, "By merging or expanding, we don't improve the quality of the NBA."

Jerry Colangelo, general manager and coach of the Phoenix Suns is saying, "Nothing would please me more than for Phoenix and Chicago both to make the playoffs. What do I care about Los Angeles and San Francisco?"

John Havlicek of the Boston Celtics leans against a wall, telling me how appearing in a TV commercial has made him an overnight celebrity. In the middle of the room, Alcindor towers over the other East center, Willis Reed of the Knicks.

The dance band switches to assault and battery on a Jerome Kern tune. It is time to leave. Another freeload beckons at a hotel across the street.

Some Big Ten people thought I was putting their conference down in this column. Not true. After 30-plus years of covering the Big Ten, I've built up a huge reservoir of respect and affection for the old Western Conference. What I was trying to say here was that Notre Dame's decision to keep going it alone was the only way to go. Notre Dame bashers let me know I was a sucker for the myths and faded glory of Rockne, Leahy and Parseghian. Maybe, but I still admire the ideal, even when reality falls short.

Notre Dame Stays Where it Belongs
(Daily Herald, February 6, 1999)

SOUTH BEND, Ind.—Notre Dame has a well-defined set of standards.

The Irish do not always live up to them, as detractors gleefully point out, but they're there.

The way things are now, it's pretty clear that being right is not essential. Regardless, I'm glad I was right in predicting Notre Dame's polite, "Thanks, but no thanks," to the Big Ten's welcome aboard overtures. Why? Because I believe in standards.

They're higher at Notre Dame. That doesn't mean it does everything right, or that Golden Domers are superior people, as some misguided Irish undergrads seem to think after swilling a few brews.

What it means is that Notre Dame has a smaller pool of high school athletes to tap. The recruits are aware there are no snap courses or professors winking at the empty classroom chairs of star players. ND's graduation rates for athletes are at the top, year after year. It also awards degree to a high percentage of black athletes, the backbone of big-time sports, both college and pro.

The difference between Notre Dame and the Big Ten is largely academic, pun intended. Illinois, an outstanding university with a proud athletic tradition, has had a lengthy list of classroom non-qualifiers on its teams in recent year. That's no shameful, isolated situation. It's typical. The Big Ten, Big East, Big 12 and the rest of the biggies battle ferociously to recruit marginal students who are exceptional athletes. Most of those high school hotshots don't consider Notre Dame. The defense of all this promise-him-anything recruiting by the win-at-any-cost football and basketball factories sounds like an excerpt from the politicians' handbook: "Everybody does it, so what's the big deal!"

The list of major football powers that make the dean's list Top 10, and occasionally go that high in the AP rankings is slim— Stanford and Notre Dame. Northwestern has been there a few times lately, unlike Rice and Duke. Harvard, Yale, Princeton, Penn—not since the Ivy League opted years ago to try winning college football games with actual students.

I've been on the soapbox in this space for a long time, dropping not-too-subtle hints that all college sports ought to operate on that premise. Except for big-time football and basketball, they generally do. But with so much money and pressure to win in those sports, we find ways to lower the standards and kid ourselves about the real reasons why. Well, Notre Dame has not lowered its standards. If it did, there soon wouldn't be many academic standards.

Loss of support from the athletic hierarchy was one reason why Lou Holtz abruptly quit after 11 years at Notre Dame. He kept pressuring the admissions office to bend the rules for substandard football recruits like Randy Moss. Academics won. Holtz lost. Exit Holtz.

So I applaud Notre Dame's decision to keep going it alone. I don't blame the Big Ten for trying to keep up with the Joneses in SEC football and ACC basketball. People who figure college games are life-and-death events—probably because they bet on them— slap labels like elitist, arrogant, pompous and hypocritical on Golden Domers.

And the fiasco of George O'Leary's 20-minute tenure as Irish football coach gave ND bashers lots more ammo.

When I read that stuff, I think about the stories of young black kids getting ridiculed and shunned by their peers if they "act white" by trying to excel in the classroom, I wish there were more places like Notre Dame for those kids to learn that life's winners—and losers—are not determined until long after the college games are over.

Now that Ty Willingham, a winner at Stanford, is the first black head coach under the Dome, it's time to win more than football games.

Sometimes a column can be, and maybe should be, just plain nonsense. Many newspaper columns, including some of mine, unintentionally turn out that way. When I wrote this more than 15 years ago, it read like overstated satire. Now, amid endless pitches prolonging games past four hours, it might be all too true:

The Snide Side of Sports Spieling
(Basketball Times, 1984)

CHICAGO—"Good evening, sporting fans. This is your friendly neighborhood sportscaster, Kerr Mudgeon, with you once more for the opening night of another sensational NBA season.

"We're right here at courtside in quaint old Chicago Stadium, which reeks of basketball atmosphere, including a pot—

pardon the expression—of other odors. My color man for this colorful curtain raiser is next to me at mikeside, so here he is, Mr. Mike Side."

"Duh, when do we eat, Mudge?"

"Thanks, Mike. Go color your color man's coloring book for a while. Fans, Mike Side's incisive analysis has been brought to you by Jerko, the junk food for everybody in the wide, wide world of sport and/or size 53 triple-X trousers. Remember, fat is where it's at, so slurp some Jerko right now. After all, wide not?

"A little humor there, folks. That was the Tons of Fun Pun of the Game, from the official NBA punshop, 'Hoke About That?' at the corner of Hook and Crook, on Da great Nort' Side of Chicawga, as the real Mayor Daley used to say.

"Well, the big moment is here. After a station break, sponsored by Gimme a Break, we'll be back for all of the fast-breaking action. Remember, fans, next time a juice man breaks your leg for stiffing him on your 2,000 percent interest loan, call GAB, so we can rush right over to set the bone and give you a free wallet transplant. Don't worry if you're broke. We'll give you a break—the other leg.

"This is what you've awaited, fans, ever since the Chicago Butts lured a throng of over 289 thrill-seekers to their heartbreaking 289-29 season-ending loss to the Baltimore Ballots, the team that votes early and often. We'll return with the starting lineup after this word from It Figures, the official accountant to discerningly dishonest agents. Besides those tricky tax tips, we also get you a free trip to the state pen. It Figures is not a corporation, because when they do both sets of your books, the Inc. is invisible.

"Before this titanic tussle gets underway, we'll pause to select the Booty Rest overpaid star of the game. Who's the lucky guy tonight, Mike?"

"Duh, uh…"

"Right, Mike. It's Guy Lucky, that crowd-pleasing guard who can really play the D, but never does, because coach Lefty Drywit won't put him in.

"Now, without further ado, who's on the disabled list, here's tonight's starting lineup for the Chicago Ands Ifs or Butts, brought to you by Shrinkem and Thinkem, official NBA headshrinkers. If you're a head case and you don't lie, or even tell the truth, on our couch, coach, you should have your head examined.

"OK, the Double Vision Optical Co. referees of the game can't see their way to starting yet. One just tripped over his seeing eye dog, jumped up and whistled a T on the puzzled pooch.

"At forward for the Butts is Slow Moe Schmo, sponsored by the South's top trailer rental company 'You Haul, You All.' The other forward is Ike Spike, who led the league in beer commercials last year, so he's always a threat at foam games. At center is 7-foot-7 tower of tedium Nick 'No-Neck' Knack, peerless pitchman for Pigout Pizza.

"Back at playbreaker is En Youface, who really can dish out those assists, but won't, preferring to unleash off-target 30-foot jumpers. En endorses our big-bounce brand, Double Drivel, the talking basketball that gives you a line of jive while you drive. Last but least, here's Shifty Slinker, just like a coach on the floor, especially one who just fell off his barstool.

"One more commercial, fans, and this pulse-pounding season will start to cure your insomnia. Tired of the burnt coffee your insignificant other recycles for breakfast, along with her special mother-in-law sandwich—cold shoulder and tongue? Hustle your buns to McMac's. Take a McMac Pack to work. It's diet foot that works, because nobody can get past the first bite.

"And, if anybody still cares, there's the opening tipoff, courtesy of Tripoff Travel Agency. Their motto is, 'If you want a vacation ripoff, call Tripoff.' Knack, the Knicks' last draft pick before they barely managed to unload him on the Butts, commits the season's first turnover. He wins tonight's Badhands Insurance award, a no-cut contract with Guillotine razors. How do you see this roundball rumble shaping up, Mike?"

"Duh, looks to me like a hard-fought contest between two evenly-matched squads. Back to you, Kerr Mudgeon."

For every let-'em-have-it column over the years, I've written four or five others dealing with the fun side of our fun and games. I look on sports as entertainment and competition rolled into one. Yes, it matters a lot which team wins or loses. If it didn't, as a smart man once pointed out, why bother keeping score? Still, now and then, something outrageous, like the strike/lockout that probably killed a long-overdue World Series in Chicago, needs to get what it deserved:

Fans Treed by Baseball's Greed
(Daily Herald, March 11, 1996)

It's good to know baseball players have been ordered by their mean, nasty bosses to be nice to the fans this season.

That should repay White Sox rooters for the never-happened 1994 World Series their team might have played in. We'll always wonder about that, because players and owners were too busy making obscene gestures at each other to stage the playoffs.

Now the marketing mopes and the pollsters and the shills for what once was America's pastime swear on a stack of 1994 postseason scorecards that we've forgiven them for striking out our game. I've got news for them. We haven't. At least not those of us who love baseball, the game, as opposed to the greedy, grubby business it's become. We're the ones who got the business.

And we know that neither the entrepreneur ballplayers nor their onerous owners appear to have learned a thing from the huge hole they tore in the fabric of baseball. A lot of tradition and loyalty oozed from that wound, and the bleeding hasn't stopped yet. The blank spot in the record book is an X-ray of the numb skulls of twin numbskulls Donald Fehr and Bud Selig. It's a vanished page of baseball history that can't be rewritten.

Fans who face facts know that the only thing they have to fear is Fehr himself. The players' czar admittedly doesn't care what fans want, a lesson he learned from his tutor, Marvin Miller. But neither do the owners, despite their pious bleating. For them, baseball is a money machine, fueled by TV cameras and fat corporate cats in skyboxes, making bleacher creatures as obsolete as the 5-cent cigar and as irrelevant as Bill Veeck's midget.

So a pox on Fox and its beefed-up TV graphics. All that will do is enable Bud Light commercials to put a heavier tap on our wallets. In the end, that's where baseball fans get it. We pay the price for the players' greed and the owners' stupidity.

Yes, I know all this was said in anger last year, when we got baseball back only because some NLRB paper shuffler, who had no business sticking his nose in it, decreed one side was right. We know both sides were wrong. It's being said now more in sorrow than anger. We'll get a full 1996 season, unless the players walk out again or their bosses opt to lock them out again. If there's a buck to be made by shutting out the fans, count on those grabby groups to go that route.

There's also a group of fans ready to forgive, forget and fork over dough for inflated ticket prices, setting themselves up for another emotional mugging. They're egged on by some self-serving media, demanding that we get over it and embrace arrogant players and owners "for the good of the game."

The game itself is good. The way it's being run, on and off the field, is bound to run off even the hard-core base of baseball backers. Don't expect real baseball fans to forgive or forget that.

Nothing cheers me up more, especially after another attack on the Chief Illiniwek tradition by lame-brained University of Illinois professors and their legion of if-you're-for-something, we're-against-it followers, than good news about this school. I've spent countless hours and days in Champaign over the last four decades, most of them enjoyable. Along the way, I've learned to respect the Illini tradition, its teams and above all the people who keep it heading in the right direction. Ron Guenther, the hard-driving U of I athletic director, is one of them. He's made big strides, both physically and emotionally, in the Illini sports picture, rebuilding optimism for the future:

Chiefly, Guenther's Heap Big Plans Coming True *(Daily Herald, December 18, 1999)*

At Illinois, the Christmas stocking is stuffed.

New buildings, new plans, new ideas cram the Champaign campus. It figures to be a jolly holiday season at the U of I, especially for sports, the tinsel on the tree of life. For all those presents, one presence deserves an Ill-lion's share of credit. He bleeds Orange and Blue, as my eardrums attest from his bellow of "D" whenever the Illini need a stop in Memorial Stadium or the Assembly Hall.

So here's a hearty Ho, Ho, Ho to Ron Guenther, the Go-Go architect of much of this overnight success. It was fortunate that Coach Ron Turner's football team reinvented itself in midseason, preventing a steep dive in the athletic budget that might have delayed Athletic Director Guenther's plans.

Likewise, Coach Lon Kruger's basketball team exorcised the demons (no, not Blue Demons) of a bad season with three straight stunning upsets last March in the Big Ten Tournament. Still, it took a lot of prioritizing in Guenther's office, along with barrels of midnight oil, to convert these plans from fantasy to reality. Evidence of Guenther's groundwork is in the Bielfeldt athletic administration building and the Ubben practice gym, combining separate but spectacularly equal practice facilities for the men's and women's basketball teams. It's as spiffy a collegiate workout setup as you can find, with an indoor football practice field in the works.

Impressive stuff, all of it, with more to come. A century ago, Daniel Burnham made Chicago into a world-class city with the magic of four soul-stirring words. He said "Make no little plans," and then brought that vision to life with an array of big plans.

Guenther is doing the same things at Illinois. It's working. High energy is in the air, spilling over from this clearing in the central Illinois cornfields to U of I alumni and supporters in the Chicago area and elsewhere around the country.

"Let's be honest," said Guenther, who's signed a contract extension. "Our package of sports facilities was not competitive. As proud a state as this is and as proud as this institution is, you can't get there unless you have all the things other people have. So we drew up a plan and it's framed in my office.

"Plans like that tend to disappear. When I look at what Illinois has accomplished, I'm very pleased."

He should be. I admire this man's respect for tradition. In fact, a Park of Tradition is part of Guenther's master plan, saluting the history of Illini athletics and the men and women who brought it to life.

Wouldn't it be something if that made a few people pause to ponder the legacy of this magnificent university, especially the ideas that flow from it to enrich the lives of those who wouldn't know an Oskie from a Wow-Wow? But let's not get carried away here.

I'm not expecting miracles, like the MTV generation suddenly realizing the world existed before Ricky Martin. It's just reassuring to know Illinois is trying to do the right things, athletically and academically, for the right reasons.

So I hope the university can withstand a constant assault on one of its best traditions by the small band of compulsive whiners who make the most noise. For the vast majority of those who really care about what the University of Illinois is and where it came from, Chief Illiniwek is a respected and revered symbol, not a mascot. Their feelings and wishes should count for more than the few complainers, but they obviously do not.

Despite that, if the Chief eventually falls victim to political correctness, the tradition will survive. Likewise, I hope the regeneration set in motion by Guenther keeps rolling after he steps down. it's more than bricks and mortar. Michael Jordan proved again and again that sheer force of will is the most powerful Bulldozer—pun intended—on earth.

As always, it began with an idea turned into reality by the vision of one person. Thanks to Ron Guenther, it'll keep happening at Illinois well into the new millennium.

Yes, I enjoy the NCAA Tournament's electricity, even after years of covering it in arenas from coast to coast. Now it's the biggest thing in college basketball by far, outstripping such moss-covered traditions as the Kentucky Derby and the World Series. The whole season preceding NCAA selection Sunday has shrunk to three months of jockeying for tourney berths by bubble teams and tourney seeds for those who know they're in. Here's why I regret that:

NCAA Tourney-The Monster That Ate College Basketball?
(Daily Herald, March 26, 1989)

It's too big. It's too long.

Too bad.

The NCAA Tournament is a great TV show. Longer than "Gone with the Wind", more entertaining than "Hollywood Squares," richer than "Wheel of Fortune," it keeps on growing.

From the Sunday they reveal the 64-team field to the Monday night when a national champion is crowned, college hoops hold center stage in the sporting spectrum for 23 days. In a country where new fads arrive every 23 seconds, that's astounding. So is the complete, cotton-pickin' cornucopia of this annual NCAA orgy. Maybe what appeals most to us is bottom-seeded Princeton coming within a heartbeat of stunning top-seeded Georgetown.

Whatever the secret of this coast-to-coast hoop-o-ree, fans can't seem to get enough. They peel off big bucks to cram into the Ditkadome or some other inflated gasbag. From way up in the rafters, the players look like rumors, but the money for those precious ducats looks plenty green. The postseason money machine has a green light to keep gobbling up the greenbacks, mostly from a staggering CBS pact. The bottom line—profit—is the ultimate arbiter, telling us what's hot and what's not.

If something in this scenario bothers you a trifle, you're not alone. It bothers me a lot. There's still time to save the best of this spectacle by toning down its gaudy excesses. The price college basketball pays in the yearly scramble to land an NCAA bid is too high. Normally sane athletic directors will do almost anything to join the party. Ego plays as big a role in their frantic quest, or maybe more.

Sure, they all want fistfuls of NCAA loot, $250,000 for a first-round game, way up to millions for Final Four fame. But they yearn just as feverishly to get a few seconds on TV, batting back softball questions from a network shill. Some ADs and coaches, plus lots of alumni, are not choosy about how they win enough games to punch their ticket to the Big Dance. If pictures of presidents on U.S. Treasury notes accidentally slip into

Megamope U's letter to a hot prep prospect's parents, well, that's how the recruiting game is played, right?

And if the team doesn't win in spite of such goodwill gestures, the coach gets canned. If they can't make the NCAA invite list, even coaches who run clean programs, try to keep their kids off drugs and make sure they occasionally go to class find themselves drawing unemployment compensation. How else to explain unloading such principled men as Bob Donewald of Illinois State and Dayton's Don Donoher? Then there's Northern Illinois, where coach Jim Rosborough got booted out.

If you believe the NCAA Tournament has nothing to do with this sort of throat-cutting, you're wrong. The thing has become so all-consuming that the tail end of the basketball season now wags the schedule dog. When TV moguls beckon, most athletic directors genuflect. In their ardor to get the tube time, they expose their own character, or lack thereof.

Regardless, turnstiles keep spinning. TV ratings keep escalating. Powder kegs piled around the NCAA Golden Goose keep heating up. The spark to detonate all of this could be lit by a crooked gambler, an unprincipled coach, or a point-shaving player. If that happens, you'll be able to buy all the tickets you want for the Final Two at Northwestern.

This column appeared before Joe Paterno replaced Bear Bryant as college football's all-time winner. It could have been written in any year of his tenure at Penn State. Paterno is my definition of the exception to Bill Veeck's lament that there are no more American heroes:

To Head in the Right Direction, Tell 'Em Joe Sent You
(Daily Herald, September 18, 1999)

In a world where integrity gets swept away faster than Carolina beachfronts, it's reassuring to hear Joe Paterno's gravel voice, unmuffled by a half-century amid the mountains of Pennsylvania.

Paterno stands taller than any of them, even the fabled Mt. Nittany, where his Penn State Lions have been feeding visiting teams to the sharks for so long. I hope he doesn't say "So long" until after I stop writing about fun and games. Very few coaches have such command of their programs and the determination to keep it totally aboveboard.

To survive in the snakepit of big-time sports, you have to cheat a little or a lot, mostly because the NCAA's incomprehensible book of recruiting no-no's is both thick and thick-headed. For most coaches, it all depends on how much they can get away with. They know winning beats rectitude by a mammoth margin in the job-security department.

So I'm glad to see Paterno is sharp as ever at 70-something, still cranking out Big Ten contenders in Happy Valley. It's hard for rip-and-rap media types to make Paterno look bad, because he's not concerned about making himself look good. We won't see his like again.

There's such pressure to win now on every level of competition, from T-ball to the Super Bowl, that everything in its path gets flattened, even ethics. Lose a game and you're a loser, personally and professionally. Somehow, Paterno stays above all that. When Penn State's team stumbles and the Joe-must-go whispers become audible in Not-so-Happy Valley, Paterno survives with a blend of common sense and mental toughness that will keep him coaching well into the new century.

There are plenty of good coaches and good guys around, but none of them is a Paterno. There's only one of him.

Every once in a while, I get up on the soapbox, a common failing for columnists. The response I got from this set of admittedly antiquated notions convinced me I had struck a nerve:

As a Society, Have We Gone Too Far?
(Daily Herald, March 6, 1999)

Just a simple question this time. No speeches, finger-pointing or tsk-tsking.

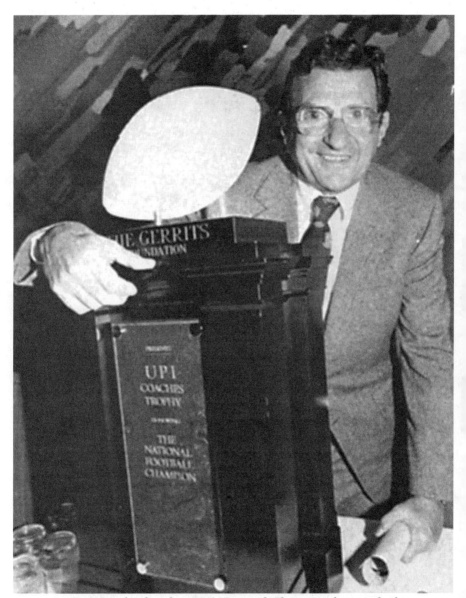

Joe Paterno clutches the 1986 National Championship trophy his Penn State football team earned for its memorable 14-10 Fiesta Bowl triumph over Miami. The Nittany Lions' coach has another of these in his Happy Valley trophy case from 1982.

The setting: Big Ten Tournament during Thursday's opening round in the United Center. Strolling around between games, I heard a few spectators, presumably college students, chanting obscenities directed at Bob Knight.

Indiana's controversial basketball coach is not this column's concern. He can match such pleasantries and often does in postgame media sessions. I'm asking only this: Do you, the students, alumni, fans and casual followers of Big Ten athletics care if this storied conference becomes a clone of the WWF?"

Like it or not, that's where we might be heading. It should take a while for staged midcourt shouting matches between rival coaches and scripted, simulated head-bashing, accompanied by torrents of profanity, to creep in. But trash-talking between players, widespread referee-baiting and increasingly rough play already are here.

I'm aware my outlook is hopelessly outdated. The time is long gone since Mom could cure her kids' experimental outbursts of shock language with an oral dose of Ivory soap. Nowadays, some enlightened thinker would get her jailed on child abuse charges.

Gone, too, is the era when kids would meet in the schoolyard, test the limits of four-letter free speech with their pals and kick around all that nasty stuff they knew better than to bring up at home. Lately, they seem compelled to let it hang out in public. From the T-shirts I've been reading at Big Ten games, the line between rabid rooting and vulgar abuse is disappearing faster than farmland in the path of suburban sprawl.

I'm only asking. People who try to define what's right and wrong, or even that there is such a thing, are not in high demand (Writer's note: One encouraging aftermath of the September 11, 2001, attacks on America, was the realization that we need to rediscover our real values).

I've been hearing those hyphenated words for decades in locker rooms, coaches' offices, dugouts and in press boxes, too. Censorship is not my bag.

Still, as someone who has been dealing with words and ideas all my life, I find it hard to believe there's no connection between thoughts and actions. When it's acceptable to act like a street brawler in the stands, how do we stop it from spreading to the playing field, and from there to everywhere else? Whether or not you think I'm overreacting, I'd like to know what my readers think about this.

I must admit I was troubled when I heard those young people, wearing shirts with the name of their university, expressing their version of free speech in the United Center. It seemed to me they were saying more about themselves than about Knight. But you can walk past a schoolyard anywhere today and hear grade school kids using the same epithets. Is this merely the way it is, not something to worry about?

Just asking.

Columns about books are not what I normally write. It takes a special book and/or a special person to break that rule. Both Jack Brickhouse and his book qualified.

Hey, It's a Winner
(Baseball Bulletin, 1984)

CHICAGO—It's not the custom in this space to plug books, beer, booze, blades or what have you.

However, I'm sure you've heard the one-liner Groucho Marx used to squelch vaudeville hecklers "I never forget a face, but in your case, I'll make an exception." In this case, the exception is Jack Brickhouse's "Thanks for Listening."

This is not collection of Cosell-style venom. Brickhouse, at 70, is the same sunny-side-up guy he always was during years of radio and TV broadcasting on Chicago station WGN. His inexhaustible store of one-liners, anecdotes and stories kept a TV audience tuned in on those already 11-2 Cub losses in Wrigley Field.

Lord knows there were enough of such disasters. Cub fans survived, and Brickhouse was the pied piper who helped them keep the faith. There never was the slightest taint of hypocrisy in his cheerful banter. Like the rest of his Cub-crazy flock, Brick believed each new season would be that long-overdue "next year" all North

Siders have been fantasizing about since 1945. If the temptation to rip off his headphones and roar, "This is the crummiest bunch of Cubs I've ever seen!" crossed his mind, Jack kept it to himself. Despite being off daily telecasts since 1981, Brickhouse still is one of Chicago's most recognized faces and voices. His style and "Hey! Hey!" punchline for a Cub homer made him a family member, with that familiar voice booming from every TV set on the block for endless summers. "Thanks for Listening" takes you back at the same relaxed, leisurely pace, without bum-rapping even such deserving targets as Leo Durocher.

For my money, the chapter on Bob Elson is worth the price by itself. Titled "The Commander" (Elson's nickname, from a Navy stretch in World War II), it's a grab-bag of funny, affectionate remembrances of the long-time White Sox broadcaster. I used to play poker with easy-going Elson and other writers on Sox road trips, once going broke in Baltimore, but winning my money back before we got to Cleveland. My favorite Elson tale, direct from the book:

> The late Vince Garrity, for years a loyal city employee, once told me of the night he was invited to accompany Elson on a speaking junket 50 miles outside Chicago.
> "Why not go along and keep me company?" offered Bob. "All you have to do is introduce me at the banquet. I don't know what they're paying, but we'll split it 50-50."
> I emphasize that Garrity and Elson each respected the other's cunning. Garrity made the intro and while Elson was speaking, the dinner chairman told Garrity, "Please give this envelope with his fee to Mr. Elson." Garrity went to the men's room, opening the envelope containing $150, and stuck $50 in his pocket. When Elson finished, Garrity handed him the envelope.
> Now Elson went to the men's room, found $100 in the envelope and put $50 in his pocket. He came back to Garrity, opened the envelope again and banded him $25.
> "Here's your half," Elson said. "Let's get the hell out of here. These bums only gave us $50."
> Hey! Hey! Those were the days.

Jack Brickhouse (left), a man for all seasons, welcomes two more Chicago icons to his WGN show, long before sports talk gab and chatter filled our airwaves. This trio of Windy City luminaries includes Bill Veeck (center) and George Ireland, coach of Loyola's 1963 NCAA basketball champions.

I guarantee this will stand as my first—and last—millennium column:

Hopey New Year, Century and Millennium
(Daily Herald, January 1, 2000)

MIAMI – This is the first time I've started a millennium column with a dateline.

If it works, I might try it again, just in case I'm lucky enough to be working for a newspaper in 3000. Chances are the term "hot news" will have a meaning all its own by then, but I figure to be surrounded by a lot of my fellow hoop, grid and diamond scribes, all of us hoping the place will really freeze over.

Anyway, the dateline here happens to be Miami. The 20th Century is gone, but I hope the need for professional gypsies like me to tell people like you what happened, and why it happened, won't vanish with it. So instead of ringing out the old by wringing my hands over a list of leftover problems, I prefer to ring in the new with a one-word solution: Hope.

Hope is what got us this far. I intend to ride that trusty steed to the finish line, win or lose. Hope keeps Cub fans coming back to Wrigley Field year after year, and now century and after century, confident that this is their year, or maybe their millennium.

Hope fills the seats at renovated Allstate Area to watch DePaul try to recreate the magic formula that took Ray Meyer's Blue Demons to the 1979 Final Four. Hope makes me suspect Bears fans believe Dick Jauron is the reincarnation of George Halas. Hope keeps women athletes reveling in the revelation that they can compete as hard and as successfully as their brothers.

Hope helps South Siders visualize their White Sox winning again, finally exorcising the memory of the 1919 Black Sox. Hope convinces Subway Alumni diehards, still faithful to the legend of Rock and the Gipper, that Notre Dame will silence the jeers of Irish bashers with a strong of 10-2 seasons and New Year's Day bowl bids.

Finally, I hope we all find the inner strength and sense of purpose to turn every day into an adventure instead of an ordeal. Happy New Year.

7

A Santo Claus for Good Kids

Lou Boudreau and Vince Lloyd, two of Chicago's all-time Good Guys, called each other "Good Kid" on the air for so long, it became a Chicago catch phrase. That's fitting, because Vince and Lou were among the best of that colorful bunch.

Actually, Good Guys come in all shapes and sizes. I was lucky enough to deal with them almost every day of my 40-plus years on the Chicago sports scene. There were, and still are, far too many to mention, but I can see their faces even now, while I'm sifting through the mountain of memories that piled up for so many sizzling summers and frigid winters in the Windy City.

I still love this toddlin' town, an affair that began on the day I drove in, looking for a newspaper job. That was in 1961, and the only complaint for me since then was the way it all went by too fast. Now when I stop to wonder what happened, I realize it was the Good Guys and Good Gals who turned Chicago into an even better version of Hemingway's Parisian moveable feast, because I could drink Scotch without having to speak French.

Anyway, the Good Guys had one thing in common, despite their many differences. Being around sports somehow brings out the kid in them, in me and most likely in all of us, except the Scrooge clones who refuse to sample the sheer joy of rooting, playing, winning, and yes, even losing. The kid comes out in Jerry Manuel, after a tough loss for the White Sox, when he talks about coming back the next day to turn things around.

Good Guys believe it will happen, if not tomorrow, then the next day. I'm the same sort of optimist by nature, so sports keeps me young. Regardless of age, though, the Good Guys help you get through good days and bad. Without Johnny "Red" Kerr to coach the Bulls and the writers in that wild, wonderful 1966-67 expansion team's NBA debut, it wouldn't have been nearly as much fun.

My list of Good Guys needs no long-winded intro. Most Chicago sports fans feel like they're old friends, just like I do. Sportscaster Chet Coppock's wry sense of humor came up with the right line for all of them with this tongue-in-cheek fanfare for a football game:

"No buildup needed when these old rivals get together."

You said it, Chetster. This All-Star lineup of Good Guys can speak for themselves. Speaking for myself, I'm grateful for being allowed to hang around with them.

Santo: Third Base, and First-Rate

Cub fans don't boo Ron Santo anymore, but they used to. He was a visible target in his 14-year tenure as the best third baseman ever to wear a Chicago uniform.

Santo was so durable, consistent and productive over that lengthy span that Wrigley Field regulars knew they could count on him. When he went into a slump, they were less forgiving than they always were with Ernie Banks, the beloved Mr. Cub, or with Sweet Swinger Billy Williams.

Maybe that's because Santo wore his heart on his sleeve, letting his emotion—and his frustration—show. He worried about his performance more than the spectators did, though not because he was one of the players who figured going 2 for 4 was a good day, regardless of the final score. Santo brought an intense will to win with him to Chicago, and never lost that outlook. You can still hear it in his voice from the WGN radio booth—up when the Cubs win, down when they lose.

That's why Cub fans have come to appreciate their best-ever Hot Corner guardian even more now than they did then. They like the way he's concerned with people and worthy causes, notable the Juvenile Diabetes Foundation, and worthwhile events in his adopted city. Chicago has adopted him, too, as one of its favorite sons.

The disappointment of not getting voted into the Hall of Fame is still there, of course. Santo got my vote when he was on the baseball writers' ballot, because he had the numbers to deserve a plaque in Cooperstown, along with the other great third basemen. He's the one I'd want out there every day, even though in Robin Ventura's prime with the White Sox, he had the softest, surest hands of any third baseman I've ever seen.

But Santo had the intangibles, mainly the mental and physical toughness and the courage to be in the lineup every day. He never gave in to diabetes. He coped with that lifelong affliction as a player, and he's still doing so, despite the leg amputation that further crimped his less-than-Olympic speed, but not his mercurial spirit. Enough has been said and written about that to make it clear that people now know the price he's paid. The one thing that never changed was Santo's ability to make the best of a tough situation and enjoy every day.

I found that out a long time ago. In 1970, my first year on the baseball beat, Santo was battling a slump when we had our first conversation. I was impressed by him then, and I still am.

Santo Wants Hits to Chase His Boobirds
(Chicago Tribune, June 23, 1970)

Ron Santo sat in his underwear, feet propped on his locker, in the fast-emptying Cubs clubhouse after yesterday's 9-5 Wrigley Field loss to the Mets.

Ron Santo (right) and Pat Hughes, a matched set of Good Guys, are WGN's radio rascals, keeping Cubs fans into the game with their blend of snappy patter and insight to the inside strategy of baseball. Even when things go wrong for the Cubbies, Santo always figures a winning rally is right around the corner.

It was more than just a third straight defeat, and Santo knew it. The expression on the co-captain's face told the story of a 3-0 Cubs lead dissipated and another hitless day for him.

When Santo stepped to the plate in the first inning, boos from the crowd of 24,864 rivaled the cheers for the Chicago third baseman. The darling of Wrigley Field fandom last season, Santo suddenly has been targeted by a growing number of hecklers. How does it affect him?

"I hear them, all right," Santo admitted. "They're booing me because I'm not doing my job. I'm not hitting. They expect me to be me."

Santo's trying everything he knows to get back in the power groove. Fortunately for the Cubs, the plate paucity has not affected his fielding skill. In Sunday's doubleheader against the Cards, for instance, he roamed his territory to make brilliant defensive plays. Even so, each time he came to bat then and again yesterday, the boos boomed out over the applause.

The fans know what I should be doing," Santo said with no trace of bitterness. "Every time I come to the park, I feel today is going to be the day."

Norm's Storms Subside

Norm Van Lier has been one of my favorite people since the day the Bulls made him their fifth-round draft choice in 1969. I called him up at St. Francis that afternoon, the small Pennsylvania college that had sent Maurice Stokes to the NBA in 1955, only to see that budding superstar's career and life cut short by a rare disease.

Fifth-rounders don't rate training camp headlines or even phone calls. I forget which scout told me this Van Lier kid had quickness and the spunk to make the big jump to the pros. He was half right. The firebrand I soon dubbed Stormin' Norman never dazzled anyone with his speed, but he won respect for his physical and mental toughness. That blend of temperament made Van Lier a Chicago fan favorite when he returned in 1971 from a stint with the Cincinnati Royals. It was a break for the youngster, enabling

Norm Van Lier and author Bob Logan talk it over in Chicago Stadium. As a Chicago Tribune sportswriter, Logan covered Stormin' Norman and the rest of the Bulls on their tempestuous journey through the NBA under Dick Motta's Us-Against-The-World coaching style.

him to serve his pro apprenticeship under Royals player-coach Bob Cousy, the greatest playmaker in NBA history. Yes, Cousy was better at that tricky art than Magic Johnson, Isaiah Thomas, and the other playmaking wizards. The Cooz led the charge of the Celtics to a dynasty that made Boston a basketball bastion in the 1960s.

Nobody, not even Michael Jordan, ever has earned eight straight championship rings and 11 in the remarkable 13-year run that lasted from 1956 through 1969. Cousy was the Boston Garden's parquet floor leader for the first half-dozen of those NBA titles, and his killer instinct left a legacy of push-it-up, attacking, fast-break basketball. Those lessons were not lost on Van Lier, an apt pupil of that aggressive style. So when Moving Van moved back to the Bulls early in the 1971-72 season, it was the start of something big in Chicago's pro basketball saga, giving the Bulls the horses firebrand coach Dick Motta needed to make a run at the NBA crown.

Van Lier and Jerry Sloan teamed to become the best linebacking duo outside of the NFL, a backcourt to be reckoned with—and wrecked by. With a front line of scoring standouts Chet Walker and Bob Love, bolstered by underrated Tom Boerwinkle in the middle, these guys should have gone all the way at least once.

Unhappily, they didn't, adding a frustration factor to the fireworks generated by Motta's burning desire to win. That set the stage for a smoldering Motta-Van Lier feud. Their sideshow spats added to the enjoyment while the Bulls scrapped, struggled and swashbuckled a path through the NBA. Along the way, they were feared and even hated elsewhere, but came close to cult status in Chicago Stadium. Fans packed the joint nightly, scrambling for seats that had gone begging a few years earlier, when the Blackhawks were in and the Bulls on their way to some other uninterested city.

Stormin' Norman almost always was in the middle of the wars that kept erupting, inside and outside the Bulls. He feared nobody and took on everybody who challenged him. The combative side of Van Lier made for much better writing and reading, so that image overshadowed other aspects of this complex man. Back home in Midland, Pa., a hard-scrabble steel town, the local gendarmes didn't have to fear the wrath of Jesse Jackson, and a full-court media press, when they cracked down on alleged "black militants."

It wasn't hard to pin that label on a fiercely independent young man. Van Lier reacted to their reaction, refusing to swallow his pride, as a lot of black athletes were forced to then, in order not to jeopardize promising careers. Years later, many of them told tales of the humiliation inflicted on even such superstars as Oscar Robertson, one of the all-time greats in both college and pro basketball. It was a bitter pill to swallow for him, Henry Aaron and many others with less talent, who got scarred just as deeply by such bigotry.

Along with lots of unaware white sports fans, I didn't know much about the mental and physical barriers built by such hateful, hurtful racism. Van Lier and I like each other, so we talked a lot after our first conversation on draft day, 1969. He told me about invading the Midland police statement to protest unfair treatment, probably not the best way to get it done. But Norm the Storm sometimes let emotion override better judgment, so he got used to serving time in the NBA penalty box, as well.

Van Lier helped me understand the repressed rage that sometimes boiled over for black people, athletes or just plain working folks. We're still friends, and I enjoy listening to Norm telling young players to avoid the mistakes that dotted his own career. The struggle his generation went through made things better for today's players of all colors, races and religions.

And Chicago fans still share my respect for Stormin' Norman. They fondly recall the battles waged by him and the rest of the Motta-era Bulls. As for Van Lier, the feeling is mutual.

"The fans kept me going, and I won't forget that," he told me after the Bulls put him on waivers in 1978. "Fans are fickle, up when you're winning and down when you lose, but in Chicago they appreciate players who lay it on the line every night."

That includes him.

Good Kid, Great Player

I went to Cooperstown, N.Y., to cover the story when Lou Boudreau joined baseball's Hall of Fame in 1970. Time stands still in that sleepy, upstate New York village, where Abner Doubleday allegedly did, but almost certainly didn't, invent baseball in 1939.

That fiction has served us well since the Hall of Fame was dedicated a century later. Cooperstown a spot that seems frozen in the 19th Century, is the perfect place to preserve our illusions and our youthful fantasies about baseball. That's why the game had such a hold on people who grew up in my generation, including me. We were unencumbered by the big-business baggage that most likely will spell the death of the major-league system, now beginning to totter on its greenback foundation.

Trite as it sounds, baseball was still a game when Lou Boudreau was elected to the Hall of Fame. It was that way, too, in 1955, when I first saw the imposing brick building, in the legendary setting where James Fenimore Cooper lived and wrote about the last of the Mohicans. Ted Lyons, an all-time White Sox mound mainstay, was in the group to be enshrined that year, along with Joe DiMaggio and others.

I hear the word "Cooperstown" and recall the image every year, when I fill out my Hall of Fame ballot. A picture of Otsego Lake flashes into my mind. I'm standing on a hotel balcony overlooking the lake on July 27, 1970, the big day for Boudreau, a former All-American basketball player at the University of Illinois. On the lawn below, commissioner Bowie Kuhn is munching breakfast and scribbling welcome notes for Lou, the only man to get the required 75 percent of that year's vote.

The comish invites us down to his table for coffee and some background about his running feud with cantankerous Oakland A's owner Charles O. Finley. For Kuhn, Charlie O.'s initial translates to "O Boy, here comes trouble." Regardless, internecine warfare will not cast a cloud on Boudreau's reward. I can't remember much of the windy speeches, but the booming voice of Casey Stengel comes through clear as a bell.

The Ol' Perfesser, who enriched baseball by deciding not to become a dentist in Kankakee, Il., works the crowd, shaking hands, telling stories in his matchlessly indecipherable brand of Stengelese.

"That fella could play some shortstop," Stengel says of Boudreau. "He had a pretty good idea of the right fella to get a clutch hit, for which he was a pretty smart manager."

Casey's syntax was scrambled, as always, but his meaning was unmistakable. With a game or a pennant on the line, Boudreau wanted one man at bat—himself. Cleveland's player-manager led off the 1948 one-game AL pennant showdown against the Red Sox with a homer in Fenway Park, adding another to send Bill Veeck's Indians to a World Series triumph over the Boston Braves. No wonder one of the congratulatory telegrams Boudreau got said simply, "It's about time they put the best shortstop in baseball in the Hall of Fame."

No surprise who sent it, either. It was from Ron Santo, a rookie third baseman on the Cubs in 1960 when Boudreau managed the team. A typical touch of class by Santo, although he's still wondering more than 30 years later when he'll start getting those welcome-to-the-Hall salutations.

Boudreau's credentials were impeccable. The "Boy Wonder" manager of the Indians at the tender age of 24 when he took over in 1942, Lou grew on the job, becoming a canny tactician. He invented the shift that frustrated Ted Williams, moving three infielders to the right of second base. Lou guessed correctly that the left-handed Splendid Splinter would try to beat the shift rather than bunt for singles or slap the ball to the unprotected side. And despite chronically weak ankles, Boudreau made sensational defensive plays when the Indians needed them most.

I admired Boudreau on the field, but even more in the broadcast booth, where he had a long and productive second career, telling fans what the Cubs really were up to. Often, that was hard to figure out. The best of Boudreau came during rain delays, when WGN sidekick Vince Lloyd would let the old shortstop spin yarns, about his treasury of American League lore. Like Boudreau at bat, it was a clutch hit.

Red's Hot and Still Rolling

He was a smash in Syracuse, a blast in Baltimore and a phenom in Philly.

But when Johnny (Red) Kerr came home to Chicago, he became a hometown hero. Well, maybe more like the neighborhood kid who made good, returning to familiar sights and sounds—and above all, people.

I've met few guys in sports who can match Kerr's knack for making everybody around him feel at ease. He's a pip of a people person. The Old Redhead could have been ambassador to anywhere, a Good Will man without the used furniture and a Good Humor man without the ice cream. He's as comfortable as a well-worn davenport and as refreshing as two scoops of strawberry on a hot afternoon.

For sophisticates in the crowd, suspicious that Kerr might turn out to be a goody-goody type, too relaxed to enjoy, fear not. Just listen to him paint real color on a Bulls' telecast and you'll get the idea. I first used this line about Kerr in my book about the Bulls' struggle to survive in Chicago, written more than a quarter-century ago:

"I've been traveling around the NBA for years, searching in vain for somebody who doesn't like Johnny Kerr. So far, no luck."

All these years later, that's still true. Hiring Kerr as the first coach of the expansion Bulls in 1966, a shaky NBA franchise in a skeptical city, was a stroke of genius. His quotability quotient, an inexhaustible supply of one-liners and exhaustive knowledge of the league and the players made him a natural.

I recall walking with Kerr and the Bulls' ace publicist, Ben Bentley, along with a few other writers to lunch at the old Sherman House Hotel. He could have held his own with a lot of the standup comedians who played that famed nightspot in its heyday. The Bulls' new coach had a smile and a quip for the La Salle Street crowd that paused to wish him well. Most of his self-deprecating humor took note of a prediction that the Bulls would not win 10 games in their NBA debut.

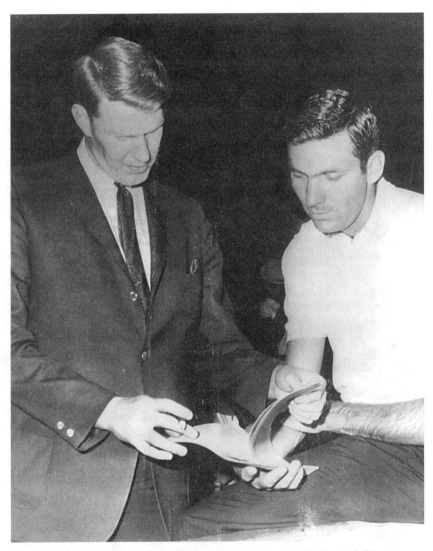

A pair of former Big Ten standouts, Johnny (Red) Kerr of Illinois and Jerry Lucas of the Cincinnati Royals, share some info. Kerr's playing career was ending for his role as coach of the brand-new Chicago Bulls.

The gloomy forecast came from Richie Guerin, coach of the St. Louis Hawks, and the last of the two-handed set shooters in his playing days. Kerr and Guerin had collided on the court often enough to have a healthy respect for each other and their rivalry was about to enter a new phase.

"Richie's a smart guy, but he's wrong this time," Kerr told lunchtime passers-by. "I'm not going to play center for the Bulls, so I know we'll win more than 10 games."

Coach Kerr was mostly right. The Bulls won 33 games in 1966-67, an unprecedented success level for expansion teams in any sport. If the 6-foot-9 Kerr had been in his prime, enabling him to fill the same dual role Guerin did for the Hawks, the Baby Bulls would have grown up faster. But Kerr always had some kid in him, no doubt accounting for the way he was able to enjoy life every day, instead of falling into our familiar trap of postponing the good times until next month or next year or until it's too late. He met his wife, Betsy, when they were both students at Illinois. From that day till she died in 2000, John and Betsy had a lifelong love affair. I saw the grief in Kerr's eyes months later, when he told me how hard it was to get used to sleeping alone.

Betsy was his best friend and chief cheerleader. From his Illini stardom to an NBA title in Kerr's rookie year with the Syracuse Nats and throughout a long, though not always fun-filled pro career, they were a winning team. Tragedy dogged the Kerrs, especially the death of their first son, three-year-old John Jr., in 1960. An adopted niece, Laurie, was the victim of any unsolved 1975 murder, casting another shadow on the family.

So the Old Redhead sometimes had to smile in public to conceal the tears he and Betsy shed together. Their love got them through everything, right up to the end of this storybook romance. Not even Kerr's nationwide legion of friends, acquired through decades of travel across America, could shield him from the pain of that loss.

Pals still get together, of course, and Kerr still leaves them laughing. He smiles with an aching heart while recalling Betsy's outrage when Bullets coach, Paul Seymour, ended Kerr's then-record streak of 917 consecutive NBA games by benching him on November 5, 1965, in Baltimore's Civic Center.

"It's better all around, " said Seymour, shrugging off their long-time friendship, after shattering the string for no discernible reason.

"Besides me, the only other guy that record will mean something to is the player who breaks it," Kerr responded, characteristically refusing to point a finger of blame at Seymour. "I have to admit the first 900 were the hardest."

When the Old Redhead gets around to writing his autobiography, *15 Years in the Pivot Without the Ball*, it will be crammed with wry remarks suitable for easy listening and lots of laughing while sipping rye on the rocks. When you go to the bookstore for a signed copy, Kerr will hold up the line while he tells you he always was a center in his years with the Syracuse Nats and Philadelphia 76ers "Until 1 a.m. on January 13, 1965." That's the exact time Wilt Chamberlain was traded to the 76ers, where the Big Dipper promptly would become the center of attention, as well as the center of the team. "At that moment, I became a forward."

Whatever position Johnny Red played on the basketball court, he also was—still is, for that matter—the man in the middle of the all-time Good Guys squad. I went to his house in the Chicago suburb of Riverwoods when he was named NBA Coach of the Year for getting the 1966-67 Bulls into the playoffs, capping a sensational pro debut for the team and its freshman coach. His family and neighbors celebrated while we talked:

Nice Guy Finishes First

"I've never been associated with a team that finished last," John (Red) Kerr said when the newly minted coach was asked how his Chicago Bulls would fare in their first NBA season. "I don't intend to start my coaching career that way."

He didn't.

Skeptics are finding something else to laugh at besides the Bulls, because Kerr was right. His vow, made before the Bulls took the floor against NBA opponents, looks pretty good in print right now. So do the Bulls. Instead of the anticipated pushovers, Kerr molded a young, hungry, running team, gaining grudging NBA respect in just one season.

Success is far from an unheard of word to Kerr. A winner as a player at Illinois and in the NBA, he brought that attitude to his hometown team. So at 34, he's riding a crest of success reached by few first-year coaches. Say, Red, do you do for an encore after the first act is a hit?

Kerr knows that next step is the hardest.

"In high school, my team (Tilden Tech) won the Public League title," he said. "In college, my team (Illinois) won the Big Ten title. In my first years as a pro, my team (Syracuse) won the NBA title. I want to coach an NBA champion."

Bears Boast Good Guys to Spare

Pro football players are crazier than almost all of their brethren in other sports. This is not a knock. They almost have to be, just to survive a few NFL seasons. Reckless, almost foolhardy disregard for physical pain is a prerequisite for playing the game at that level.

When a writer called it "a contact sport," Vince Lombardi scoffed. "Dancing is a contact sport," barked the former watch-charm guard (at 165 pounds) for Fordham's front line—the impregnable Seven Blocks of Granite. "Football is a collision sport."

As usual, St. Vincent, still the patron saint of Packerland, all these years later, was right. I recall standing on the sidelines at Platteville, Wis., in 1984, the first year the Bears shifted their training camp to the land of beer, bratwurst and cheeseheads. Collisions between behemoths, from that close-up vantage point, made us wonder what the human body is not capable of withstanding. And those guys were between 260-280 pounds then, many without the finely chiseled muscle mass you see now, from virtually living in the weight room plus the metabolism-altering effects of steroids, in many cases. The rookies come in at 300 pounds and up of solid steel, soon discovering that's not enough to survive, except for the fortunate few who have the rare blend of strength and speed.

Brian Urlacher is an obvious exception to the rule. He covers the field, sideline to sideline, faster than any linebacker I've ever seen. That includes a lot of great ones, from the incredibly tough Chuck Bednarik to the Bears' championship trio of Larry Morris, Bill George, and Joe Fortunato, on to Lawrence Taylor—the modern standard—and, of course, the incomparable Dick Butkus.

They might be making 'em bigger and faster than Butkus now, but he surpassed the saturation point in ferocity even as a two-way player at Chicago's Vocational High, a Rose Bowl victor at Illinois, and a bulwark for the Bears, where he won nothing save acclaim for the passion that set him apart.

"Uncle Dick still bleeds Orange and Blue, so I know he's proud of us," nephew Luke Butkus said after he and the rest of the Illini shocked the college football world in 2001 by storming to their first outright Big Ten Crown since 1983.

But Butkus and Bears owner George Halas, a couple of hardheaded guys, locked horns often, mostly over salary. Playing through constant injuries took its toll on Butkus. With a winning team, he could have slid much sooner into the good guy role he's played often in a lengthy career as an actor and TV pitchman. On the field, Butkus shared the frustration of the Soldier Field fan who yelled after a 26-0 whitewash by the Los Angeles Rams: "The three players the Bears need are the Father, Son and Holy Ghost."

Noting the 1973 ticket price, Butkus lashed back, calling those unhappy customers, "$7 animals." It's true, though, that time heals such wounds. Butkus left limping, with his Good Guy ranking intact. When they call Urlacher the next Butkus, it's the supreme compliment, even though they're different players from very different NFL eras, each with his own unique style.

Lots of Good Guys took up space on the Bears roster in the years I wrote about their trials, tribulations and occasional successes. Few were on the same talent level as Butkus. All-time running back Walter "Sweetness" Payton, occasionally Jim McMahon and perhaps in time, Urlacher belong.

Dick Butkus already was polishing his pounce-on-'em ferocity at Chicago's Vocational High School. The All-American, All-Pro, All-World linebacker went in a straight line from there to Illinois to the Bears to the Hall of Fame.

One obvious exception was Dan Hampton, who could play in any era, proving it with relentless effort on battered knees. Like George Connor, a ferocious lineman from an earlier Bears era, Hampton took on all comers and won most of his battles, at least on the field. Danimal's insistence on telling it exactly like it was stirred up some storms, notably when he rapped quarterback Jim McMahon's practice habits during the 1986 season. The Bears tried in vain to reprise their Super Bowl shuffle of the previous year, only to get unceremoniously shoveled out of the playoffs in the first round by the Washington Redskins.

But Danimal's candor paid off in the end. It landed him a second career as a colorful color analyst on WGN radio in Chicago and elsewhere. His style is a refreshing change from the tendency of some ex-jocks to preach sermons about football as some sort of a Holy War. In the process, they wring out every semblance of entertainment value, making it sound more or less what it was to them on the field, an exercise as joyless as a tax audit. Not so with Hampton, happily joining Pro Football's Hall of Fame in 2002.

Sweet Swinger a Solid Citizen

If I had faced Billy Williams during my mercifully brief minor league pitching career, I wouldn't feel like ranking him among Chicago's most deserving of the Good Guy label. Chances are lefty swinger Williams would have decapitated me with one of his patented line drives off my southpaw slants. I saw him slam enough of those off shell-shocked pitchers in Wrigley Field to shudder silently at the thought of what he might have done to what was laughingly known as my fast ball.

I'll miss seeing that familiar No. 26 on the field and in the coaching box at the Friendly Confines. Now that Williams has moved up to a new role in the Cubs' front office, it'll limit the pregame talks we had about anything and everything. I enjoyed his stories of big hits—and misses, too—against such Hall of Famers as Sandy Koufax, Bob Gibson, and lots more. For a baseball fan like me, it was storybook stuff, and the Sweet Swinger wrote one of the most productive chapters while quietly slugging his way from Whistler, Ala., to baseball's Hall of Fame.

"When I was on one of those line-drive sprees, the ball looked as big as a grapefruit coming up to the plate," Billy told me. "And I never had much trouble hitting left-handed pitchers."

When he was in that groove, Williams punished them all — right, left or ambidextrous. He delivered in the clutch through the 1960s as often as Sammy Sosa does now. Because the media swarmed around quotable Ernie Banks, volatile Ron Santo, knowledgeable Don Kessinger, loquacious Randy Hundley, and other members of that media-friendly Cub club—with the obvious exception of irascible manager Leo Durocher—Billy more often than not got overlooked. That made him no less a fan favorite in Wrigleyville, as witness his No. 26 flag, a permanent memorial atop the right-field pole as an equal partner to Banks' No. 14 in left. His reserved, gentlemanly manner did not keep Williams out of the Hall of Fame, along with teammates Banks and Fergie Jenkins. I was lucky to record some of the memorable moments that got Williams there.

One I didn't enjoy was writing the story on the afternoon in Wrigley Field when the Sweet Swinger closed the book on his National League record of 1,117 consecutive games. It was well short of Iron Horse Lou Gehrig's supposedly unbreakable skein of 2,130 games for the Yankees and even further behind the mark of 2,632 in a row racked up by the Orioles' Cal Ripken, whose constitution obviously included a trace of titanium. Regardless, under the rigors of only-day, everyday baseball in Wrigley Field, where the Cubs often had to start a homestead in broiling summer sun after flying in hours earlier after a night game on the road, it was a fantastic feat.

Not a surprise, though. In my book—and this is it—Billy Williams is that rare blend of classy character and consummate clouter. He accepted the end of this record consecutive-game streak with the same approach that brought him through slights and snubs from minor-league ignoramuses on the way to stardom with the Cubs:

Billy Williams' No. 26 is flapping in the Wrigley Field breeze and the Cubs fixture is ready to recall the Good Old Days with Bob Logan.

Billy's Streak Strikes Out
(*Chicago Tribune, September 4, 1970*)

Billy Williams will start another consecutive-game streak this afternoon in Wrigley Field, when the Mets arrive for a showdown with the Cubs.

It won't be as long as the one that ended yesterday under gloomy, dripping skies. The long-playing left fielder sat it out while the Cubs were whipping the Phillies 7-2 behind the four-hit pitching of Ferguson Jenkins.

The crowd of 10,675 chanted "We Want Billy!" in vain with the ninth inning coming and going, calling a halt to one of baseball's noteworthy individual feats. Williams had been a part of the last 1,117 Cub games, so the box score accompanying this story is the first one since September 22, 1963 without his name somewhere in the Chicago lineup. He couldn't hear the fans' exhortations.

"I came into the clubhouse in the seventh inning and listened to the rest of it on radio," the steady veteran said. "If I had stayed on the bench, I would have started thinking."

Manager Leo Durocher said he elected to bench Williams "when I made out the lineup this morning. I just decided not to play him. If we had been behind today…"

Twice earlier this season, Williams had been held out of the starting lineup, only to appear as a pinch hitter each time. Had the situation demanded it yesterday, his NL record would be rolling on.

"I wanted to make it clear this was my choice," Williams said, as always, keeping his eye on the pennant race instead of his own ego. "Herman Franks (Cubs coach) made it plain Leo would let me play if I wanted."

The Sweet Swinger also shrugged off his 0-for-12 mini-slump as a factor.

"Nothing wrong with my swing or timing," he said. "The strain was there, physical and mental. It could be both. If I start a new streak tomorrow, I want it to include some World Series games."

Williams is the only National Leaguer ever to perform in 1,000-plus contests. Ernie Banks was one of the few Cubs still around to see the streak end and begin, with a rare 0 for 5 against the Milwaukee Braves almost seven years ago.

"We know Billy thinks first of the club winning," Mr. Cub said.

Alas, Williams never got to that World Series in Chicago, but finally saw playoff action for the 1975 Oakland A's at the tail end of his brilliant career. That was a thrill never shared by Cubs teammates Banks, Jenkins, Santo, Hundley, Beckert and others. At least Fergie's run of six straight 20-win seasons (1967-72) for the Cubs, plus 3,192 career strikeouts and 284 victories was enough to get him into the Hall of Fame. The voters overlooked a 1980 conviction for cocaine possession in his native Canada, preferring to reward Jenkins' impeccable pitching credentials.

"The Cubs felt I was through at 30 after one bad season," Jenkins said of the 14-16 record in 1973 that led them to trade the lanky right-hander to the Texas Rangers. As happened so often, they were wrong. "Washed-up" Jenkins gave American League batters a 25-12 bath that season. His popularity with North Side fans landed him a front-row perch in their Good Guys gallery.

Ditto for Dandy Don Kessinger, the smooth shortstop who anchored an outstanding Cub infield that seldom was out standing around while grounders zipped past. The good gloves of Banks at first, Glenn Beckert at second, Kessinger at short and Santo at third bailed pitchers out of many jams in their near-miss string of seasons, starting in 1969. Kessinger, a soft-spoken southerner who played basketball at Mississippi State, brought that fluid grace to the diamond. He made some near-impossible plays from deep in the shortstop hole by whirling like a ballet dancer in midair to unleash a strong throw to first. I've never seen anyone else pull off that maneuver with Kessinger's style.

But, along with some other Cubs, Kessinger felt the no-lights reality of Wrigley Field, the last big-league holdout (until 1988) for day baseball, cost them at least one NL pennant. In the first 14 years since arc lights landed on Wrigley's roof—still a sore point with Cub traditionalists—the North Side nine said "Nein!" to postseason play a dozen times and got swept out in the first round both seasons (1989 and '98) they did get in. That doesn't add much credence to Kessinger's lament.

"I always lost weight in September," the stringbean shortstop recalled. "I'm convinced the heat took so much out of us that we couldn't hang in there (in 1969) and maybe a couple other years when we should have won the pennant."

Like Kessinger, Bruce Sutter was first-rate at his job, only to taste nothing but frustration in five seasons as the Cubs' premier reliever. One of the first pitchers to keep throwing dirt in hitters' eyes with his split-finger fast ball plummeting from the strike zone into the dust, Sutter saved 113 games and won 32 more for the Cubs. Incredibly, they thought $900,000, relative peanuts even in those days before $100-million-and-up contracts, was too much to pay baseball's best bullpen bulwark.

So they dealt Sutter to St. Louis, where he helped the Cards to trump Milwaukee in the 1982 World Series. The right-hander later raked in the jackpot, a $25 million Atlanta Braves pact, until his career got shortened by a shoulder ailment. That trade set up another heartbreak for Cub fans, bringing in first baseman Leon Durham to make one of the most memorable errors ever, while the San Diego Padres roared from an 0-2 deficit to win a best-of-five NL playoff series in 1984, casting a pall of playoff gloom over Chicago.

Lots of Good Guys wore Cub flannels in the 31 seasons that have come and gone with startling rapidity since I first lugged a portable typewriter into the old Wrigley Field press box on the third-base mezzanine level. Catcher Randy Hundley belongs on that list, with second baseman Glenn Beckert and a versatile utility infielder, Paul Popovich.

But the group would be incomplete without Jim Hickman, a resounding success story when the Cubs picked him up for peanuts off the NL reject pile. Hickman, a soft-spoken gentleman farmer from Tennessee, was ready to forget baseball and go hitch up the plow on the family homestead's back 40 when manager Leo Durocher interceded to get the outfielder a few more thousand on his 1969 contract. Hickman repaid Cub fans with nonstop hustle, also propelling 92 of his 159 big-league homers for them—along with a textbook lesson on how to respect the game and the fans.

The D. Klein and Fall of the Bulls

If effort made the difference, Dick Klein's Bulls should have won those half-dozen NBA championships in his first six years as their creator—mostly with smoke and mirrors—dreamer of illusionary dreams, true believer and eternal optimist. His sojourn read like the script of a B movie, with Gene Lockhart as the likeable, bumbling owner who hires grown-up Boy Scout Fred McMurray to lead a team of inept amateurs to triumph at the final fadeout.

As we're all sadly aware, nursing our own bitter bumps and bruises from clashes with reality, life isn't like that. Klein, the man with supreme confidence in his ability to tilt at NBA windmills, ended up unhorsed—or in this case, unBulled—his jousting pole severely bent. About the only thing that survived Klein's head-on collision with pro basketball's power elite was his unbreakable, unshakable spirit.

And one other thing. Against long odds, the Bulls franchise survived to plant deep roots in Chicago and eventually become the dynasty of the '90s. It was a long, hard fight for an unpopular operation seemingly doomed to get buried in Chicago. It was known as the graveyard of pro basketball, planting earlier entries under the competing weight of the Blackhawks, Bears, Cubs and White Sox, along with tons of college teams.

Klein was long gone before the Bulls won their live-or-die lottery. They've played home games in the International Amphitheater at the old Union Stockyards, the Coliseum, Chicago Stadium—all three structures since demolished—and now in the plush, posh, pricey United Center, where the life-size statue of Michael Jordan draws more spectators in a week than Klein's Bulls did in their first few seasons. And even though the Bulls have been worse —much worse—since Jordan moved on to the Washington Wizards, nobody's talking about the franchise moving to Keokuk or Podunk or anywhere else.

Maybe that's the most impressive monument to Klein, who never got the credit he deserved for selling some rich guys on this version of a Ponzi scheme, chipping away until some caved in, ponying up enough greenbacks in 1966 to meet the NBA's asking price of $1.5 million for admission to the lodge. Now, that's not enough to pay the yearly salary of an undersized, overpaid shooting guard. Then, it was ridiculously too much to toss into Lake Michigan on a venture that had no chance.

That's what most fans figured, along with the sports establishment. Klein proved them wrong by making the right decision for the wrong reason. He infuriated easy-going coach Johnny Kerr— not an easy task—enough to drive the Old Redhead to Phoenix for a reunion with another Chicagoan, Jerry Colangelo, so he needed a new bench boss. Klein found one he thought he could control in Dick Motta, toiling in virtual obscurity at Weber State College in Ogden (where's that?), Utah.

Motta, nobody's fool and especially nobody's puppet, saved the Bulls by ignoring Klein and doing things his way. Motta's way turned out to be an ordeal for his players, but a delight for newfound Bull fans, suddenly flocking to the Stadium to watch the combative coach's team beat up on NBA visitors with slam-bang basketball. It was both vindication and the kiss of death for Klein, because Motta wanted to get rid of him, and did, as soon as he got enough backing from other Bulls' owners.

That wasn't what Klein envisioned in the giddy days after NBA commissioner, J. Walter Kennedy, emerged from a stormy league meeting to shake his hand and say, "Welcome, partner," This is what he had in mind:

Bulls Can Win: Klein
(Chicago Tribune, February 6, 1966)

Dick O. Klein, a certified optimist who's general manager, part owner and total booster of the Bulls, wants to sell pro basketball to Chicago, a project that has frustrated the hopes and depleted the bankrolls of others through the years.

This is an undertaking of considerable magnitude. The NBA, a league conceived in confusion and dedicated to survival of the richest, frequently has been its own worst enemy. When the Bulls got their horns 10 days ago, they also got the shaft. They won't have a chance to draft Michigan All-American Cazzie Russell, a Chicago native and outstanding prospect in this year's senior crop.

Instead, NBA solons graciously will allow the Klein syndicate to buy two players from the bottom five on the 12-man rosters of the other nine teams. The Bulls also will complete their expansion lineup by drafting last in each round next May, when college players come aboard, except for the second round, when they get the No. 3 and No. 4 picks.

With that sort of second-hand, second-rate talent, many already have concluded the Bulls shortly will slink into the slaughterhouse, to be remembered as just another bum steer. Klein has reached no such conclusion. "It doesn't scare me," he said. "A smart, aggressive team can beat one with better physical attributes."

After two years of empty seats, Good guy Klein hired Tough Guy Motta. Good-by, Good Guy. Life is tough, in and out of the NBA.

Sox Keep Roland Along

Roland Hemond is living proof that nice guys don't always finish last. He's first in the esteem of just about everybody who knows him, in or out of baseball. That kind of reputation can only be earned, never bought or inherited. Hemond's earned it with over a half-century of high-class service.

So even those hard-bitten South Siders were pleased when Hemond returned to the White Sox for another tour of duty as assistant, consigliori and invaluable experience conduit for the rookie general manager, Kenny Williams. Roland's seen it all and been through it all in this game, and he's still game for more.

Vintage proof is on view outside Comiskey Park's Bards Room, where the writers gather to eat, swap tips and gossip and gear up for another typical three-hour-plus Sox home game. It's the champagne-soaked suit Roland wore in the clubhouse celebration after the Sox clinched the 1983 AL West title, punching their first postseason ticket since the 1959 World Series. No word on whether the bubbly was domestic or imported. Either way the joy on Hemond's face while he got soaked with the stuff was ample evidence of how much he savored the team's success.

Hemond, like me, was another name on the long list of Veeckophiles who studied at the feet—actual at the fertile brain—of Bill Veeck. These two very different men shared the same fierce love of competition and a mutual respect that anchored their partnership. When things were going good, Roland's quiet competence kept everybody around him from feeling overconfident and/or arrogant. When they're going bad, as in the Sox injury onslaught of 2001, he offers this sort of reminder that baseball goes in cycles:

Sox Injury Parade Worst Hemond Can Recall
(Daily Herald, May 13, 2001)

Roland Hemond has seen just about everything in baseball from a front-row seat in various front offices for 50 years.

But he can't recall watching another team go through this season's painful parade. One calamity after another keeps dragging the White Sox down from their lofty perch as 2000 AL Central champs to an also-ran array of walking wounded. Now making a comeback with the Sox as an executive advisor, the 71-year-old Hemond shakes his head in dismay at the gory Comiskey Park spectacle unfolding almost nightly. Patience is one of many lessons he's learned en route to elder statesman status.

"I was talking to (former Phillies GM) Lee Thomas about all the injuries his team suffered through one year and still came back to make the World Series," Hemond said. "But our total of arm injuries, one after another, is new to me."

The Sox pitching staff has been decimated, with starters Cal Eldred, James Baldwin, and Jim Parque in addition to relievers Antonio Osuna and Bill Simas going down. Worst arm ailment of all was the torn right triceps sustained by slugger Frank Thomas on April 27.

"Strange things happen, and the White Sox have had their share of catastrophic injuries before this," Hemond said. "When Mike Epstein ran over Dick Allen and broke his leg in 1977, it cost them a shot at the playoffs."

Thomas is expected to be out for the season after upcoming surgery. Parque faces arthroscopic surgery in hopes that damage to the southpaw's rotator cuff or labrum proves repairable. Cubs flame-thrower Kerry Wood seems to be recovering from 1999 elbow surgery, blowing away NL batters with a fast ball clocked at up to 97 mph. Similar comebacks cheer up sore-armed pitchers, even though the history of such arm, shoulder or elbow miseries tilts the odds against them.

"For every recovery by a Kerry Wood, 10 other pitchers never make it back," Hemond said. "You don't hear about those guys, because they just fade away. In the old days, the ones with sore arms just tried to pitch through the pain. The term then was 'He threw his arm out.' Nobody knew how to treat it, so they were out of the game. The Tommy John surgery saved a lot of careers."

John was first among them. When the ex-Sox lefty's elbow ligament snapped almost 30 years ago, it was replaced by Dr. Frank Jobe, a Los Angeles orthopedic surgeon, who promptly became the patron saint of pitchers.

"That technique added 16 years to Tommy's career," Hemond said. "People forget that Roger Clemens had the same injury early in his career, and he's still striking out batters. But what happened to Frank Thomas was just a freak accident."

First baseman Thomas damaged his right triceps muscle when he dove to snare a line drive and hit the ground hard. MRI exams showed a career-threatening injury that silenced critics (especially blowhard Sox pitcher, David Wells, later a victim of his own chronic back problem) who accused the Big Hurt of refusing to play hurt.

"It's a blow, but you have to stay positive," Hemond said. "Sometime losing a superstar like Thomas gives other players a chance. I was with the Milwaukee Braves in 1957 when (center fielder) Billy Bruton got hurt. We wanted to bring up Ray Scherer to replace him, but our veteran minor-league manager, Ben Gerahty, talked us into taking another kid. Ben said, 'This guy's a streak hitter, and he's hot right now.'

"It was Hurricane Hazle. In our last 41 games, Bob was a real hurricane, batting .403 with seven homers and 27 RBI's. Without him, the Braves wouldn't have beaten the Yankees in a terrific seven-game World Series. And the Seattle Mariners didn't fold their tent when they lost Junior Griffey, Randy Johnson and Alex Rodriguez, three of the top players in baseball."

Regardless how high players' paychecks soar, Hemond's perspective is priceless.

The Sox usually were short of victories and playoff-bound teams when I covered them. Still, there seldom was a dearth of Good Guys in the clubhouse or the manager's office, including the present incumbent, Jerry Manuel. Of them all, a pair of classy pitchers, Wilbur Wood and Terry Forster, were my personal favorites. Another would have to be Ron Kittle, an unheralded outfielder who added punch to the lineup with rooftop homers in old Comiskey Park and pungent humor to the clubhouse via an irreverent, on-target sense of humor.

Pitcher Cal Eldred added stability while Sox kids proved they could play by knocking Cleveland off the AL Central throne in 2000. The veteran right-hander could have defused the unrest stirred up by malcontent David Wells a year later, but Eldred's arm was beyond repair, so he went back home to Cedar Rapids, Ia., after he and his wife gave the University of Iowa money to install lights at the baseball field. His departure created a maturity gap on the Sox roster.

Third baseman Herbert Perry will be missed, too, for his cheerful updates on farming conditions back home in Florida and yarns about SEC football days. At least one more football fan can be found in the Sox radio booth, where former pitcher Ed Farmer teams with John Rooney to provide game accounts as enjoyable as the ones Pat Hughes and Ron Santo spin for the Cubs.

Farmer was startled when I told him I covered his big-league pitching debut. A lifelong Notre Dame booster, Farmer was a standout athlete at Chicago's St. Rita High School before working his way to the majors. That career included successful stints with the Sox, but here's how it started:

Sox Scalped Again
(Chicago Tribune, June 10, 1971)

CLEVELAND—If there's anything more troublesome for the White Sox right now, other than missed scoring opportunities, it has to be guys named Foster.

For the second straight night, a Foster did them in. This time it was Alan Foster, pitching Cleveland to a 3-1 victory, on the heels of Roy Foster's three-run homer in the series opener that gave the Indians a 5-3 verdict over the Sox.

And just to rub it in, a former Chicago prep star, Ed Farmer, entered to fan Sox catcher Tom Egan for tonight's final out with the tying runs on base. It was the first major-league appearance for the husky right-hander.

In the ninth, Jay Johnston's two-out single broke Foster's shutout, so he departed with two runners aboard. Manager Alvin Dark summoned hard-throwing Farmer from the Indians' bullpen, where he's been waiting for the chance since being re-called 10 days ago from Wichita. The 21-year-old rookie's first pitch was a fast ball, despite the slider signaled by catcher Ray Fosse. It sailed past the startled receiver for a wild pitch, moving the runners up, but Farmer redeemed himself inducing Egan to strike out on a slider that ended matters.

"I wouldn't say I was nervous," Farmer smiled while duck-ing barbs from veterans for crossing up the catcher. "I was just plain scared, but I knew the Indians brought me up for a reason.

"Actually, I wanted to play for the Sox when I was growing up in Chicago," Farmer said. "I always went to their games, but I attended the White Sox boy's camp in 1963 and they told me I'd never be a pitcher."

Another Good Guy Gone

Gene Sullivan is a Chicago guy. Not just because he lived in the same Northwest Side house until his death in 2002.

Sullivan, a fighting Irishman if ever there was one, was a walk-ing, talking—he talked a lot—map of Chicago. He had big dreams, but always knew how to scuffle, deal with reality, handle people and, above all, survive. A lot of like-minded people and the way they turned adversity into opportunity is the main reason why Chicago became a world-class city.

Besides that, Sullivan was fun to be around. He saw the big picture, and described it with an Irish gift of gab. I enjoyed cover-ing Loyola games when Sullivan coached the Ramblers, not just because of their nifty, phone-booth sized Alumni Gym, but be-cause he held court afterward, hanging around as long as at least one notebook was still being scribbled in. What Sullivan had to say and what he did for all those years places him high on my Good Guy gang:

Sullivan Seeks Chicago-Style Talent
(Chicago Tribune, February 11, 1985)

Take your pick:

1—Gene Sullivan is a breath of fresh air, blazing new trails in college athletics.

2—Gene Sullivan is a bag of hot air, interested mainly in rocking the boat and promoting himself.

Because Loyola's fiery 53-year-old basketball coach has stepped on a lot of NCAA toes, Proposition 2 would get some votes. Just don't try to sell any "Good-bye Gene" buttons around Loyola's Alumni Gym. Sullivan's unique blend of guts and grace inspires near-fanatic loyalty from the players and assistants he has welded into winners during five hectic seasons as head coach of the Ramblers. His unranked, unsung, unpaid team, all 11 from the city or suburbs, has a shot at its second straight 20-victory campaign.

The Ramblers even got some rare national publicity with back-to-back December upsets over Illinois and Louisville. Sullivan's explanation uncovers the zest for battle underneath his smile.

"DePaul scouts every game played by a high school kid in Florida," Sullivan said of Tom Hammonds, a coveted 6-8 forward. "One trip there is more than my whole recruiting budget. Ours is gas money. Anyway, we try to find kids the world hasn't heard of."

Take Alfredrick Hughes. Sullivan did in 1981, when few others wanted the 6-5 forward from Chicago. Hughes will end his Loyola career as one of the all-time top college scorers. When he blossomed, other opponents in playground games boasted of money, cars, girls and other inducements they got for choosing big-time basketball factories.

"Rick (Hughes) told me 'Coach, the young players asked why they couldn't get stuff like guys at other school.' Nobody gets a dime to play here."

Sullivan admits his unsuccessful crusades have attracted more attention than his team's successful record. That's a challenge on the same level with proving Notre Dame wrong when they spurned his 1971 bid to fulfill a dream—becoming the Irish basketball coach. Digger Phelps got the job, and Sullivan still smarts.

"I was in there with the athletic board, pleading my case, and their news service was sending out a release that Phelps was the new coach," recalled Sullivan. "They wouldn't even give me a fair hearing."

Sullivan won't wallow in self-pity. Shaking off bad breaks has been routine since the age of 10, when a friend rammed a hockey stick into his right eye, leading to its eventual loss. While he works to get Loyola more exposure, his restless nature keeps finding new causes, like limiting home games, so colleges can't assure NCAA tourney bids by loading their schedule with pushovers.

"The big ones all want to win 20 games, so they can claim six teams from their conference deserve NCAA spots," he said.

Sullivan keeps on fighting, even when his projects fail. Why?

"You have to reach out beyond your own concerns," he said. "I guess Senator George Norris put it best: 'To sin by silence makes cowards of us all.'"

That's one thing Gene Sullivan will never be accused of.

8

Feature Creatures

Feature stories can be hard-hitting exposés or ponderous preachments.

They also can be whipped cream pie, giving sports page readers their just desserts. Then there's the two-part, three-part or even longer series, examining an issue in depth. This gives the writer the chance, along with the obligation, to tell the story from every available perspective.

I've done those, along with just about every reporter who's spent any time at all on a newspaper staff, whether sports or news. One of the most enjoyable assignments I ever handled was a celebration of Comiskey Park's 75th birthday. Built in 1910, the place was falling apart by the time it reached that venerable age, with White Sox chairman Jerry Reinsdorf digging into his deep pockets to keep the roof from caving in.

Actually, there was little danger of that happening. The era of state-of-the-art stadiums was dawning across the country, which meant that Comiskey Park, already the senior citizen among existing big-league structures, would have to be toppled soon. One by one, those venerable ballyards went down—Ebbets Field and the

Right up there with the Wrigley Building and the Water Tower, Wrigley Field's mammoth, hand-operated scoreboard is a symbol of Chicago.

Polo Grounds in New York, Shibe Park in Philadelphia, Braves Field in Boston, Crosley Field in Cincinnati, Sportsman's Park in St. Louis —to be replaced by new-age, electronic arenas like Toronto's Skydome.

So I got to go on a 1985 tour of America's four remaining old-time baseball nostalgia storehouses, starting with Fenway Park in Boston. I went on to Detroit's Tiger Stadium before returning to Chicago for a sentimental look at Wrigley Field and finally, Comiskey, timed to run on the 75th anniversary of Opening Day at that landmark on 35th Street and Shields Avenue. I doubt the readers had as much fun reading each installment of this series as I had writing them, but I got letters from around the country telling me those old ballpark tales had touched a nerve and brought back good memories.

Another feature, coming up later in this chapter, tells of my sentimental journey to the park where I grew up in Philadelphia. But features take on all shapes and sizes, covering an endless variety of topics—just about everything under and beyond the sun. I once wrote a long feature story about Alaska that did not get into the *Chicago Tribune*. But one of mine that made it into the Sunday magazine was an in-depth study of the Jobs for Youth Program on the near West Side that turned some youngsters away from gangs and toward productive careers.

For the most part, though, my features were about sports and the sometimes weird world of people inhabiting that quixotic universe. Here are some of them:

Irish Ayes

I've always had a soft spot for Notre Dame. I realize that could put me on the outs with half of the people reading this, because there seems to be no middle ground when it comes to that place. College football fans either love it or hate it.

Personally, I enjoy legends like the Gipper and the Four Horsemen. A lot of people now specialize in debunking such folklore. I'd rather preserve them. Anyway, I wrote this about Frank Leahy's grandson, a few days before the Irish beat. Florida State 31-24 in a 1993 Notre Dame Stadium classic that could have been the biggest collegiate clash of the '90s:

Leahy Link to Notre Dame Glory
(Daily Herald, November 12, 1993)

SOUTH BEND, Ind.—A common thread runs through the legend of Notre Dame football.

Or, to be more precise, a common man thread. It's not about knights in shining armor.

From Knute Rockne and Gus Dorais in 1913 to Kevin McDougal and Lou Holtz in 1993, this is the tale of ordinary people from a little school who somehow became larger than life.

There's a lot of hoke and hype woven into the fabric of Irish gridiron glory, too. Those who scoff at the legend proclaim the whole thing is little more than a hypocritical hustle.

Those who believe don't need explanations or justifications. That's why offensive guard Ryan Leahy will limp into action Saturday against Florida State with torn cartilage in his right knee. The 6-foot, 290-pound junior didn't want to hear medical options, only that he was cleared to start for the Irish.

"Seems like I've been waiting all my life for this game," Leahy said.

No wonder. He's the grandson of Frank Leahy, a vital link in the coaching chain between Rockne and Holtz. In 11 years at the Irish helm, interrupted by World War II Navy service, Leahy's teams won four national championships (1943, '46, '47, '49) and just missed another (1953). The Irish went unbeaten in six Leahy-era seasons and rolled up an incredible 37-0-2 streak, stretching from a 26-6 season-opening victory over Illinois in 1946 to a 28-14 loss to Purdue in the second game of 1950. With that kind of pedigree, it's understandable how Ryan Leahy feels about losing.

"Can't stand it," he said. "Losing makes me go out and do stupid things."

For him, losing to No. 1 Florida State would be extremely stupid. The feeling must be hereditary because Grandpa Frank was so determined to make old Notre Dame win over all that life-threatening illness forced him to retire in 1954.

Leahy's "lads," as he called them, were driven by this relentless coach even harder than Holtz rides herd on today's Irish. Chicago Fenwick product Johnny Lattner won the Heisman Trophy in 1953, when Leahy's career ended on a 9-0-1 note.

A memory Lattner recalls vividly, more than 40 years later, is Leahy's hunger for perfection, even on the practice field. He played no favorites, frequently flaying star halfback Lattner as an example to young players.

"John Lattner! John Lattner!" Leahy would bellow. "Don't you want Our Lady's school to win?"

That sounds familiar to Ryan, who gets the same kind of heat from Joe Moore, crusty coach of the machine-like Irish offensive line. But Leahy didn't come to Notre Dame, all the way from his Yakima, Wash., hometown, to rest on his grandfather's laurels. He's earning respect as a starter on what has become one of Moore's most formidable offensive lines.

"Ryan Leahy might be the most unemotional player I ever coached," Holtz said. "He sure didn't talk the way Frank Leahy used to, so one day I told him, 'You must have been adopted.' But when we moved him to guard this season, we found out he's quite a player."

Leahy happily accepts that compliment. "I want to win a national championship for my dad (Jim, a reserve lineman for Ara Parseghian's 1968 Irish) and my grandfather," he said. "I was only a year old when he died, but my grandmother made sure Pat (Leahy's brother, a pitcher on Notre Dame's baseball team) and I heard all about him."

Chances are most of the freshmen who just got their first glimpse of the Golden Dome never heard of Frank Leahy. They're getting a crash course in Irish history from his grandson, who might imagine hearing another voice when he goofs up in practice:

"Ryan Leahy! Ryan Leahy! Don't you want Our Lady's school to win?"

Like I said a few pages earlier, feature stories can be fun. Whether they should be is a subject I'll let editors worry about in those endless meetings they love to stage, but this one was pure fun for me. Running into situations you didn't expect produces this sort of zany stuff:

Bulls a Dog Team?
(Chicago Tribune, February 14, 1974)

NEW YORK—The Chicago Bulls went to the dogs today.

Literally.

They really stepped in something when they arrived at the hotel across the street from Madison Square Garden, where they were scheduled to meet the Knicks tonight. The lobby of the Statler Hilton was swarming with canines, in town for the 98th Westminster Kennel Club Show.

All breeds, shapes and sizes. The place was a veritable barking lot. Dogs had taken over, keeping their owners on short leashes and making sure they were well-heeled enough to pay the room tabs. The Bulls knew they had mutt their match.

Center Tom Boerwinkle returned to the registration desk shortly after getting his room key, a peculiar look on his face.

"There's a dog in my room," Long Tom said.

There was indeed—a big one. The 6-foot, 11-inch, 275 pounder had no intention of judging whether the beast's bark was worse than its bite.

"From the noise it made, I'll bet that dog weighed 150 pounds, Boerwinkle said. "I wasn't about to open the door."

This was not exactly what Coach Dick Motta had in mind when he said on the flight here that he expected a dogfight with the Knicks. What with watching while they're walking while this giant kennel slowly emptied of show-weary pooches, the Bulls tried to paws and reflect. This week's NBA schedule is so ruff, they can't afford to dog it.

While a doggoned weary reporter was waiting for man's best friends and their two-legged escorts to vacate the room as-

Tom Boerwinkle (18), hounded by Kareem Abdul-Jabbar, was top dog in rebounding for the Bulls. Despite that, the 6-11 center "mutt" his match at the Westminster Kennel Club show.

signed to him, he looked out the window at the fabled sidewalks of Fun City.

It wasn't even raining, but there were poodles all over the street.

The Ills at Illinois

Most features require a lot more work than the fluff piece above. I put a lot of research into this one and the results (I hope) speak for themselves:

CHAMPAIGN—Neale Stoner's reign over athletics at the University of Illinois is stone cold dead, but his legacy of controversy, confusion and turmoil lives on.

It's been two months since Stoner quit under fire as Illini athletic director. The problems he created while reviving moribund U of I sports fortunes still hang around, with no quick fix in sight.

"It was different from what I expected," admitted John Mackovic, the coach hired by Stoner to grapple with the crisis-plagued Illini football program. "I'm not in the decision-making process, but I'd like to have the wheels in motion for a smooth transition when the new athletic director steps in."

Instead of expediting their quest for a blue-ribbon AD to prop up the sagging image of Illini athletics, school officials are juggling this hot potato. Instant decisions by the all-powerful Stoner, czar of the virtually autonomous Athletic Association, got things done for eight years.

Suddenly he's gone, leaving things in limbo while various boards and watchdog groups nervously shuffle papers and simultaneously their feet. The committee in charge of finding Stoner's successor is still discussing procedures, not interviewing candidates. The group looking at athletic reform won't report until the end of the fall term.

For fiscal 1989, an unbalanced budget was forced by a $1.45 million shortfall. And the deficit could soar higher than the projected $189,676 if football ticket sales keep lagging. What happened? How did the early success of the Stoner regime come crashing down around the university's ears?

"When the people in charge realized Stoner would have to go, they tried to sweep things under the rug," said Loren Tate, sports editor of the *Champaign News-Gazette*.

From his first day on the job in 1979, Stoner started turning losing Illini teams into winners. Dazed with gratitude, alumni rallied around to donate big bucks, skyrocketing grants-in-aid from $600,000 in 1980 to $3 million now. Grandiose plans were laid to pluck the feathers of this golden goose.

"Illinois officials took the easy route—capitulation," educator Philip A. Nathan said in a *News-Gazette* commentary. "Since 1979, the university has pursued a relentless win-at-any-cost policy."

Stoner came to Illinois from Cal State-Fullerton and soon began turning Champaign County into eastern California by bringing in Mike White to coach the Illini into the 1984 Rose Bowl. It seemed like the Orange and Blue victory blight was gone for good. On the contrary, Stoner's troubles were just beginning. Some of White's recruits proved more adept at barroom brawling in Champaign than they were at sacking quarterbacks in Columbus or Ann Arbor.

Sports frenzy peaked in 1984 with a long-awaited Big Ten football championship and a share of the conference basketball title. Pied piper Stoner could do no wrong. And if White's staff occasionally played fast and loose with NCAA rules, so what? It was fun while it lasted, but Illinois is paying for that corner-cutting spree with an emotional and financial hangover.

Football success got overshadowed by disciplinary and classroom problems. The NCAA stepped in, alerted by Big Ten coaches who wanted to blow the whistle on White. Slowly, then with alarming speed, the Stoner "miracle" unraveled. More charges leveled at White forced the coach out after a 3-7-1 record in 1987. Stoner summoned squeaky-clean Mackovic to sweep away the aura of suspicion.

But Stoner's days were numbered, as well. An accumulation of such escapades as a free-spending Hawaii junket to golf with cronies at $75 per round greased the skids for him. One thing is clear amid all this soul-searching: the head of whatever Illini athletic setup that emerged from the ashes will never again wield Stoner-style clout.

Sometimes a straightforward feature can provide a reaction of disbelief not long after, because life is so unpredictable. After September 11, 2001, Americans were forced to admit that life also is fragile and precious. It's happened to all of us on the sports beat and the news side as well. We write a story about an athlete, an entertainer, a politician and the next thing we know, he or she is dead.

Payne Stewart was at the pinnacle of pro golf and the prime of life when he played in the 1998 Western Open at Cog Hill in Chicago's western suburbs. There was no premonition in this upbeat feature story about the tragic fate that awaited him when his private jet landed.

Stewart, Like Pro Golf, Has Game in Good Shape
(Daily Herald, June 25, 1998)

The way things are now in pro sports, those Bad Boys from the Detroit Pistons who terrorized the NBA in the late '80s might seem no more offensive than the Spice Girls.

But Payne Stewart insists pro golf is an exception to the Rodmanization of play-for-pay games.

"We put the other sports to shame," Steward said Wednesday. "Look at us (the PGA Tour) as a whole and compare it to what's going on (elsewhere in sports). We're heads and shoulders above any of them in showing how to have some class, how to be gentlemen, how to be adults.

"We realize there's a right way and wrong way to act on the golf course. Yes, there are times I get mad out there, and so does everybody else."

Not too long ago, though, Stewart's speech wouldn't have been credible. Now he looks, sounds and feels different. The 41-year-old veteran of 17 tour seasons is here, cool, stylish and sincere in his trademark knickers for today's Western Open.

That's because Stewart's reaction after last week's U.S. Open in San Francisco was far more impressive than his performance in a disastrous final round. The sportsmanship he displayed was a refreshing change from the tantrums thrown by other millionaire athletes when adversity strikes.

Leo Durocher didn't say "Nice guys finish second."

But Stewart found out at the U.S. Open that a nicer guy can finish second. After blowing the tournament to Lee Janzen, many onlookers expected the surly side of Stewart to emerge. He's been known for such things, especially after letting the Honda Classic get away last year.

"I couldn't sleep that night," Stewart admitted. "Letting a tournament get to me that much made me take a step back and say 'Wait a minute. This is ridiculous.' I didn't want that to affect the way I act around my kids or my wife and friends. So it opened my eyes to the fact that I have a beautiful family.

"I'm looking more at that and playing less golf. My son (Aaron, 9) asked me to pick 15 tournaments this year and play well in them.

"I had a premonition I'd get paired with Mr. Janzen this week, Lee and Frank (Nobilo) are great guys to play with and I have no problem with the pairing."

So no more fits of pique, no matter what happens in the Western or the upcoming British Open?

"People are coming up and congratulating me on the way I conducted myself," Stewart said. "It means more than the way the tournament ended. I've matured a lot. Some of you (media) have been around me in those past situations, but I'm older and wiser now."

Howard Cosell? No, Hardsell

Howard Cosell stormed into the Soldier Field press box, waving a feature story I had written a few hours earlier and foaming at the mouth. I didn't get there until later, but early-arriving writers described the scene. Apparently, Cosell picked up an early edition of the *Chicago Tribune* on his way to do this 1972 Bears-Vikings Monday night football telecast.

It was clear that his Everest-sized ego had been bruised by my account of his virtuoso performance at the afternoon's pregame luncheon. In his book *Like It Is*, Cosell devoted a couple of pages to pointing out deficiencies in the story and holes in my head. All of that without mentioning my name. Cosell also depicted this discussion of the story with my boss, *Tribune* sports editor Cooper Rollow, as a polite, calm rebuttal. Those who heard what he really said told me—gleefully, of course—that it was a full-blown Cosell rant and rave, worthy of the Pulitzer Prize for Friction, replete with undeleted expletives. They probably were overstating the case.

Howard had to save his best barbs for the nationwide TV audience swilling a few pre-game brewskis to either prepare to enjoy or anesthetize themselves from his tongue-lashing. As a backdrop and occasional reference point for Cosell's tireless tonsils, the Bears and Vikings huffed and puffed to a 13-10 victory for the home team, a rare breakthrough in Abe Gibron's dismal 4-9-1 coaching debut.

But even the sizeable minority of fans turned off by Cosell turned him on. Whether it was on Monday football, his burlesque interviews with Muhammad Ali or Olympic drama, he was one of America's most listened-to voices. That's the ultimate tribute to him. Here's a slice of Cosell at his best—and worst:

Caution—Exploding Ego
(Chicago Tribune, October 24, 1972)

The Howard Cosell Show played to a standing-room-only audience at the Chicago Today Quarterback Club luncheon yesterday. It had to rank as one of the most entertaining monologues since the Gettysburg Address.

Maybe it won't finish 1-2 with Mr. Lincoln's message when final ratings flash from that big TV network in the sky, but Howard gave 'em what they came to hear. The man who makes the sports establishment tremble cut loose at many victims—and he didn't spare the decibels.

The Cosell style transforms him from windbag to prophet with dizzying frequency. He delivered it in two ear-splitting sermons, diluting the impact of his thought-provoking filibuster. Cosell's star quality almost—but not quite—outshone the abrasiveness.

"I remember baseball, Chuck," Cosell told White Sox manager Tanner, who served as a preliminary verbal sparring partner before the heavyweight champion of pedantry took full charge. "Baseball was No. 1 in the '30s and it will be again when our civilization is destroyed by nuclear bombs and we're back to the era of 'Clang, Clang, Clang Went the Trolley.'

"Football is what people want now because it's the game of our times—violence and motion. Monday Night football is No. 1 in the ratings," Howard thundered. "Those sporting scribes from another generation with the dugout mentality won't affect us. If the Bears upset the Vikings, a dying team, it won't solve the Viet Nam War.

"Don't tell us sports is Camelot!"

The final ovation was reserved for a question hinting Cosell might deal more in hot air than hot news. The crowd loved his fiery comeback.

"Shill! Shill! Shill! he barked. "That's all we broadcast journalists hear. Where's the qualifications of the people who say that?"

Humble Howard got one more roar of approval with this prediction about his Monday Night Football future: "If I want it, it's mine in perpetuity."

Comiskey Fans' Diet Strictly, "Hi, Cal"

Cal Ripken has been baseball's version of Jack Armstrong, the All-American boy, for two decades. Now that his remarkable career, capped by the incredible streak of 2,632 consecutive games, has ended, baseball badly needs a new Ironman. A durable jerk won't do. Ripken left behind a legacy packed with much more than record-shattering consistency. He was wall-to-wall class from start to finish of 21 years as Mr. Everyday for the Baltimore Orioles.

Ripken was so good, he made streaking respectable. He handled the hoopla over breaking Lou Gehrig's long-standing mark of 2,130 straight games with a rare blend of dignity and humility. No upset, therefore, when the long-term shortstop, switched to third base for his final seasons, coped with the adulation he got everywhere around the AL in 2001.

It was no different when Ripken played his final Chicago games. The red-carpet treatment came from the media, the fans and especially from the heart:

These Ironmen Doff Caps to Ripken

In Syracuse, N.Y., Johnny "Red" Kerr's wife, Betsy, would reach out the front door on bitter winter days for snow to rub on throbbing ankles, helping to keep his NBA consecutive game streak alive.

In Cincinnati, Billy Williams hobbled into the Crosley Field clubhouse after fouling a pitch off his foot, determined to keep his NL consecutive game streak alive.

And in Chicago, Bears running back Walter Payton would run up and down a steep hill to the point of exhaustion, honing the superb conditioning that made his NFL consecutive game streak possible.

All of these Chicago ironmen talked with Baltimore's ironman, Cal Ripken, over the years. Understandably, a major topic was playing in pain, playing through the pain, but almost never playing completely without pain. The Sox will pay tribute Sunday to the Orioles' perpetual motion machine, but Williams and Kerr didn't wait that long.

"When I talk to Cal at old timers' games, we'll be on the same page," said Williams, who set the NL record of 1,117 straight games from 1963-70, since broken by Steve Garvey. "I know what he went through to stay in the lineup, day after day."

Kerr concurred. He's in the hang-in-there lodge, too, with the previous NBA record of 917 games in a row.

"I had a tough time keeping it alive, even playing a couple of games with a broken foot," the Old Redhead recalled.

Over Payton's protests, an injured toe kept the spectacular rookie out against the Pittsburgh Steelers on October 19, 1975, the fifth game of his inaugural NFL season. For the next 12

Walter Payton, the Iron Horse of the Bears, was rolling up records for dependable durability in the NFL while Cal Ripken's quest to set baseball's all-time endurance record of 2,632 consecutive games grew. Ripken did it for the Baltimore Orioles, topping legendary Lou Gehrig's 2,130.

years and 185 consecutive games (175 as a starter), pro football bruisers rocked, pounded and pummeled Sweetness, piling painfully on him, to pull, twist, tug and do everything except yank him from the lineup.

"Walter was in a different category," said Bears teammate Dan Hampton, recalling the era that ended when Payton gained the last of his 16,726 career rushing yards in 1987. "I put Ripken on that same level, even though baseball is a totally different situation. In football, you get 80 violent collisions every game, the same as a car going 40 miles an hour.

"Baseball is more of a wear-and-tear thing. Ripken belongs with Walter, one of those super athletes."

Williams faced the same struggle to stay healthy daily. The former Cubs left fielder learned early that such consistency also carried a heavy load of responsibility.

"I'm sure Cal would agree with me on this," the Sweet Swinger said. "If I wasn't in the lineup every day, I felt the Cubs would lose. People get to depend on you to keep producing, so you don't want to let them down. It becomes an obligation to ignore a sore back and all the other aches and pains."

Fans wouldn't wait for Ripken's last hurrah, either. As soon as his head emerged from the visitors' dugout before Friday night's Sox-Orioles series opener, cheers erupted. They didn't stop until the best thing from Baltimore since crabcakes got a hit in his final Chicago at-bat, two days later. Before that, Ripken greeted the media with some well-chosen words.

"There are a lot of secret moments in baseball," he said. "One of them is the bond between players and fans. The way a kid's face lights up when you sign the paper he's been waving is one of the rewards I'll take with me. "The (retirement decision) was gradual, but in the last few years, it became crystal clear.

"I have fond memories of (old) Comiskey Park, especially that 1983 playoff with the White Sox," Ripken said. "If Tito Landrum hadn't hit that homer (to end the best-of-five series in four games) we would have had to face La Marr Hoyt. Who knows what would have happened?"

All Sox fans knew was more heartbreak. They forgave Ripken 18 years later, mainly because he won't be around to beat them anymore.

Weeb's Web of Unbearable Truth

One of my most enjoyable assignments was covering the 40th anniversary celebration of the Mid-American Conference. The gathering of former players, coaches and officials in the summer of 1986 brought an impressive group of people together in Toledo, Ohio, close to the MAC's roots.

MAC member Miami of Ohio earned fame as the cradle of coaches, and the evidence was on display at the reunion—Woody Hayes, the Ohio State legend, Bo Schembechler, the Michigan legend and Ara Paraseghian, the Notre Dame-Northwestern legend. Lots of others from all sports and all parts of this Midwestern group of grass-roots colleges were there.

For a sportswriter, it was like being a kid at a Marx Brothers double feature. Everywhere you turned, there was another former MAC player or coach, anxious to open a trunkful of memories. The stories flowed of tough games and good friends, piling up faster than I could write them down. Luckily, I had a tape recorder, and it's filled with MAC gems, including Paraseghian's reasons for going for that 10-10 tie when he coached the Irish in that unforgettable 1966 clash at Michigan State.

There's enough for another book, and maybe I'll get it done. Right now, here's what another former Miami coach had to say. Just like Woody, Bo, Ara and a lot of other first-rate MAC people, he was right:

Bears Won't Repeat, Ewbank Says
(Chicago Tribune, August 26, 1986)

Mike Ditka, don't take this personally.

It's just that Weeb Ewbank does not believe the Bears will repeat as NFL champs despite the prod provided by your emotional brand of coaching. Ewbank, the first coach to win titles in both the NFL and the AFL, found out the hard way that repeating is much tougher than getting there the first time.

"I don't expect the Bears to play with the same intensity for the next two or three years," Ewbank said. "Things will happen that Ditka or anybody else won't be able to handle. It's human nature."

What makes it difficult, if not impossible, to rack up back-to-back championships?

"The doggoned players are overpaid," Ewbank replied. "They forget the close games they maybe shouldn't have won. Only an instant was the difference. Maybe this season it doesn't happen that way. The breaks the Bears got in 1985, they don't get in 1986."

"The players are thinking, 'We can make it happen again whenever we want.'" They'll find out it's not that easy. You can't turn it on and off like a faucet."

Even though he's been away from coaching for 13 years, Ewbank, 79, remains one of the sport's most respected elder statesmen. His warning to the Bears carries weight because Ewbank twice grappled with the same challenge Ditka faces for the first time.

Ewbank's Baltimore Colts had Johnny Unitas, the NFL's best quarterback, when they beat the New York giants in sudden death —the 1958 title game credited with triggering the pro football boom. The Colts repeated in 1959, but their budding dynasty ended there. The bubble burst a lot faster for the New York Jets after Ewbank steered those AFL upstarts to a stunning triumph over the Colts in Super Bowl III. That 1969 upset shook the program to its foundations, giving the AFL instant credibility.

With flamboyant Joe Namath at quarterback, the Jets became America's team, especially on the Playboy circuit. Instead, they proved to be one-shot wonders.

"I had a long talk with (Michigan coach) Bo Schembechler, and we agreed I coached at a better time," Ewbanks said. "Bo told me he's glad he's not starting out as a young coach today. He's not having the same problems with players at Michigan other coaches deal with, because Bo won't let them get away with anything."

What's happening to erode the Vince Lombardi mold of a coach as the dictator?

"It's worse since I retired, but I could see the changes in my last few years with the Jets," Ewbank said. "Now even the agents get into the act. Some of the dances players did in the end zone happened because their agents told them, 'Let the people know you're out there.' When a guy does that, he's not a team player."

The disgust in Ewbank's voice went all the way back to the 1920s, when he was a Miami player, then a teacher and coach. All roles were clearly defined then. Players really were student-athletes, drilling unquestioningly on fundamentals.

"We used Bob Zuppke's book on physical education in 1925, when they patterned a course after the one Zup taught at Illinois," Ewbank recalled. "Still have the dog-eared thing somewhere."

If Ewbank coached against Ditka, he'd use the NFL champs' strength to his advantage.

"The Bears are a blitzing team," he noted. "I'd get a quarterback with as quick a release as Namath and never get caught with only one back pass-blocking. I'd go into the game hoping the Bears would blitz."

Ewbank must have been a little more tolerant than he let on, especially with Broadway Joe Namath, who completed even more passes off the football field. Angered by the New York writers' insistence on keeping score for his after-dark escapades, Namath called them "$100 a week creeps." He got his comeuppance when a grid scribe shot back, "You're right about that, Joe, except you got the salary too high."

A Gummed-up Escapade

Somebody should have turned the Philip K. Wrigley-Leo Durocher romance into a TV sitcom. Maybe they weren't a serious threat to Laurel and Hardy, Abbott and Costello, Martin and Lewis or even Madonna and Sean Penn, but there was something extraordinary about the affinity between these two totally different men.

Phil Wrigley, the millionaire gum tycoon, was plain as an old shoe. He had only one wife, loved to tinker with cars in his garage and answered his own phone. I know, because I called him at his Lake Geneva, Wis., mansion, and he answered the phone. Wrigley's only seeming peculiarity was this baseball team he inherited. An intensely loyal man, P.K. tried everything under the sun—but not under the lights—to turn the Cubs into winners. When he hired Durocher to manage them in 1966, he thought that would do it.

So did Durocher. Probably the most self-centered man I ever met, he had supreme confidence in himself and not enough in his players, especially young pitchers. Leo the Lion loved stick-it-in-his-ear guys like Sal "The Barber" Maglie and disliked kids who wouldn't knock hitters down when they dug in.

When the Cubs fizzled in 1969, not even Wrigley's total support could keep Leo—and the Cubs—from unraveling. The Boss even took out a full-page newspaper ad, telling the "Dump-Durocher" crowd to chill out. Too late. Leo was a toothless Lion by then, so the Cubs' frustration kept growing, even after he left early in 1972.

But in his final days, the cloak-and-dagger intrigue grew thicker than Lake Michigan fog. Rumors swirled of secret meetings between Wrigley and Durocher, with the fate of the Cubs and/or the outcome of the Cold War hanging in the balance. This mild goose chase is one example of the way we—well, almost—always solved the mystery:

Bond Banned From This Spy Saga

Ever fantasize of being a James Bond-style spy?

You know how it's done… slither through dark afternoon fog, casting furtive glances, trench-coat collar turned up. Somewhere out there, your man is lurking. Your mission, fan, should you decide to accept it, is to track down Leo Durocher and Phil Wrigley at their summit meeting. Just ferret out the secret Chicago yearns to know and flash the news to Cub fans, as thousands cheer.

Sounds glamorous? Forget it. There was more intrigue in "Rebecca of Sunnybrook Farm" than you'll find in this assign-

Philip K. Wrigley, the easy-going Cub owner, and his son Bill swap pennant predictions with Ernie Banks. P.K. kept Leo Durocher on as his manager until both Leo the Lion and the Cubs were toothless —and winless.

ment. Sure, it sounded promising. When you're summoned off the copy desk in the midst of writing headlines for the first editors, with deadline time nearing, you know the chase is on.

"Go with Ace Photog Ed Feeney to the Wrigley Building and see what you can find out on the Durocher situation," says Dave Moylan, the hard-bitten assistant sports editor, speaking gruffly to conceal his heart of gold.

This is it—the break you've awaited. Come up with a scoop on this yarn and even the Pulitzer Prize people might take notice. Concealing your excitement, because newshawks are supposed to be unflappable, you trek across Boul Mich with Feeney, take the Wrigley Building elevator to the 16th floor and approach the lair of P.K. himself, the Cub owner who answers his own phone and writes his own newspaper ads.

Alert, ready for anything, you lose a wrestling match with the glass door of Mr. Big's office, just like Peter Sellers in "The Pink Panther" and case the receptionist. From then on, it's all downhill. No gorgeous blonde sitting there, so you could curl your lip into Bogey's sneer and snap:

"OK, sister, I'm here for the lowdown on the Durocher caper. Spill it."

Instead, a pleasant lady, not even slightly blonde, greets you with a smile and directs you to a seat. There you languish with two other reporters and some photographers drifting in and out until the pleasant lady gets up just before 5 o'clock to go home, suggesting you do the same.

The only inside info gleaned from the vigil is that Feeney scored the second hole-in-one of his golfing career Wednesday on the 134-yard third hole at Medinah's No. 2 course, with a 7-iron.

"The hole played longer—like about 150 yards" Feeney discloses in an exclusive interview with fellow lensmen.

The one thing you know definitely is that Wrigley and Durocher are not on the premises or anywhere nearby. Before you scram, a big decision remains to be made. The pleasant lady offers you gum from a plentiful supply on her desk. It isn't Dentyne, but that's not the problem.

Will you go for Spearmint, Doublemint or Juicy Fruit?

Holtz, That Tiger

I sat in Lou Holtz's office at Notre Dame, just before 1988 spring practice began, talking with the coach about prospects for the upcoming season. I remember remarking, "On paper, this isn't a national championship team." To which Holtz replied:

"National championships aren't won on paper."

I was working for one newspaper when I wrote that spring practice story. By the time the season opened, I was working for another newspaper, kicking off a 13-year stretch of covering Notre Dame football. It was that kind of season, both for me and for the Irish. They rolled over everybody to a 12-0 record and their 11th national championship.

Holtz got them there by putting relentless pressure on his players and assistants, but mostly on himself. He did not add that coveted 12th crown to the Golden Dome, despite losing just one game in each of three subsequent seasons—12-1 in 1989, 10-1-1 in 1992 and 11-1 in 1993. Holtz quit in 1996 with a 100-30-2 record for the Irish, five victories short of Knute Rockne's 13-year (1918-30, 105-12-5) total. So, despite a career matched by few coaches, an agonizing 41-39 loss to Boston College in 1993 prevented this prophecy I wrote in 1998 from being fully realized:

A New Notre Dame Legend?
(Daily Herald, November 28, 1988)

LOS ANGELES—It's too early to start comparing Lou Holtz with Knute Rockne and Frank Leahy, the first two coaching immortals in 99 years of Notre Dame football.

Or is it?

In three seasons as Irish head coach, Holtz has a 24-10 record. But all of the losses came in 1986 (5-6) and 1987 (8-4), while Holtz was reshaping the program after coming in from two years at Minnesota. If the 51-year-old fireball sticks around for another decade, more unbeaten seasons—the only acceptable standard for fanatic Notre Dame fans—seem possible, if not likely, in this era of college football parity.

In less than three years, Holtz has assembled a powerhouse that compares well with what Rockne or Leahy accomplished in any single season. After Saturday's convincing 27-10 win at USC, the Irish are 11-0, in firm command of the No. 1 spot in the polls and on target for the 1988 national title. One more victory over West Virginia in the Fiesta Bowl on Jan. 2 will wrap it up.

Giving Holtz that much time to prepare guarantees the Mountaineers will face an array of mental, physical and psychological secret weapons in this winner-take-all showdown. Underdog Notre Dame's romp over USC was a coaching clinic by Holtz. He didn't miss a trick, on or off the field, to build a Trojan horse for the Trojans and Rodney Peete, their Heisman Trophy candidate.

When it ended, the dazed losers talked the same way Miami did after an emotional 31-30 early-season setback in Notre Dame Stadium. "We played against ourselves today," said USC tailback Aaron Emanuel, unaware that he had fallen into Holtz' trap. That's the way he likes it. It suits the crafty coach's purpose not to be compared right now with the best big-game coach ever—Rockne.

Exhaustive preparation paid off with an 11th straight Irish victory in the LA Coliseum. The major game-plan gamble was the decision to blitz Peete repeatedly, something the Irish defense did not do to Steve Walsh, Miami's pass-happy quarterback. Scouting reports convinced Lou it was the way to negate Peete's explosive blend of rollout speed and a strong, accurate arm. It worked to perfection. Peete, sacked three times and intercepted twice, got taken out of the game by a relentless pass rush that beat him up physically and mentally.

The master pregame stroke, another identifiable Holtz fingerprint, was recycled from a gambit Holtz used at Arkansas a decade ago. When Irish tailback Tony Brooks and flanker Ricky Watters strolled into last week's team meeting fashionably late, laid-back California style, they never figured Holtz would crack down on the team's leading rusher and receiver. That's exactly what he did, shipping both suspended stars back to South Bend.

Along with lifting the rest of the players to a feverish pitch, it showed them who was boss.

"The coach draws a line," said Irish guard Tim Grunhard. "If you cross it, you're in trouble."

Despite all he poured into it—every attribute of mind and body—Holtz couldn't recreate the magic of 1988. Repeated close calls only hastened his burnout, so he departed. With five mostly frustrating Bob Davis seasons magnified by the here-today-gone-tomorrow George O'Leary coaching fiasco, Irish athletic director Kevin White turned, almost in desperation, to Stanford's Tyrone Willingham, the first black man to become head coach of any Notre Dame team.

Except for an insignificant minority, Notre Dame's diehard rooters worried only about Willingham's ability to produce winning football teams, not his color. For them, and the vast majority of fair-minded people across the country, the only black-and-white issue was on the scoreboard.

Chicago, an All-Star Town

Chicago's been the scene for other baseball All-Star games since it began there in 1934, as a promotional gimmick for its Century of Progress Exposition. Played on both sides of town, this gathering of the diamond elite was a big-time event.

An extra spotlight shone on the game when it came back to Wrigley Field in 1990. The first two Friendly Confines star shows were daylight affairs. This was different:

Wrigley Stars to Light Up the Sky
(Daily Herald, July 8, 1990)

From George Herman "Babe" Ruth to Ryne Dee "Baby Ruth" Sandberg, hundreds of baseball's best have entertained millions of fans with All-Star heroics on two of the game's top stages, Wrigley Field and Comiskey Park.

The still-new Wrigley lights and the eyes of the nation will shine Tuesday night on the Friendly Confines for the 61st AL-NL All-Star Game. It's the third Dream Game to be hosted by the Cubs, spanning an eventful era from the 2-1 AL victory in 1947 to the AL's repeat 9-4 verdict 15 years later to this return match, another historic first under the arcs.

Next time the stars shine on Comiskey Park, it won't be the same, mainly because the setting won't either. Comiskey II, now being built just across 35th Street, will replace the original "Base Ball Palace of the World," built in 1910.

"Hard to believe Comiskey Park will be gone," said Billy Pierce, the stylish left-hander who won 186 games for the South Siders. "So many memories in this place. I understand the new park will fit the needs of the Sox, but I'm convinced it was a lot more fun in the old days for the players and the fans.

Fun.

That's been this season's missing ingredient on the North Side. Aside from astonishment over Sandberg's power surge at the plate, along with the All-Star second baseman's routinely sensational glovework, midsummer frustration is alive and well and living in the outfield ivy. So the timing is right for Tuesday's TV spectacular, enabling fans with tickets and those across the country to replay memories during the telecast.

"I wasn't good enough as a player to have any All-Star highlights," said Cubs manager Don Zimmer, who grounded out in his only Dream Game trip to the plate in 1961, a year before the scene last shifted to Wrigley Field. "But when Roger Craig (manager of the Giants and this year's NL stars) asked me if I wanted to be his third-base coach for the game in our park, I jumped at it.

"To me, there's no bigger honor, after 40 years in baseball, than being on the same field with these players."

With all the hoopla, nonstop parties all over the area and a frantic scramble to get into jam-packed Wrigley Field, it's still a competitive game.

"The truth is, nobody loses an All-Star game," said Pierce, who pitched six scoreless innings as an AL's starter in 1953 and 1955. "It's a show for the fans, and they never forget it."

Comiskey Park's name and legacy lives on in Comiskey Park II, home of the White Sox since 1991. Right across 35th Street from the old edifice, this modern facility still searches for the lore and legend of Comiskey I.

A Horse on Me

A day at the races would be more fun if the bars on the pari-mutuel windows went all the way down to the counter, so the horse players, unable to slide wagers underneath, could be content to double their money by folding it and sticking it back in their pockets. Personally, I seem to bet on nags with short noses, who proceed to lose by a nose.

It's always enjoyable on a balmy spring day to see the horses saddled in the paddock and prancing toward the starting gate. I didn't escape the daily grind of hoop, grid and diamond scribing often enough to do that, or write much about the ponies. This is one of the exceptions:

Derby Winner Parks at Arlington

Trainer Carl Nafzger knew winning his first Kentucky Derby would have an impact rivaled by few events in America's overcrowded sporting life.

Nafzger admitted he's been staggered by the coast-to-coast outpouring of media coverage, overnight fame and just plain sentiment following Unbridled's upset triumph last Saturday at Churchill Downs. Trainer Nafzger and the colt's 92-year-old owner, Mrs. Frances Genter, became instant celebrities in the wake of Unbridled's flying hooves.

"It hasn't quit and we can hardly get control of the situation," Nafzger said Wednesday. "We're in a whirlwind."

TV shots of Nafzger and Mrs. Genter sharing the moment of victory triggered almost as much media coverage as the race itself. Unlike most one-shot Derby winners, they'll see a sizeable chunk of racing buffs and just plain fans rooting for Unbridled to sweep the Triple Crown.

"Mrs. Genter is such a great lady, I can see why people feel good about her horse winning," Nafzger said. "If I'm only supposed to win one Kentucky Derby in my life, I'm glad this was the one."

Nafzger was at Arlington International Racecourse to saddle Joel for the $75,000 added Dr. Fager Handicap, opening feature for the 134-day meet. Joel finished out of the money, but that won't deter him from returning. First, the trainer and his Derby sensation have a May 19 date in the Preakness at Pimlico followed by the Belmont Stakes in June.

"If Unbridled's sound, we'll give him a chance," Nafzger said. "He hasn't left an oat in his feedbag yet."

Nafzger realizes his bread and butter comes from sending out daily winners in claiming and stakes races, not transitory Kentucky Derby fame. At 48, the former cowboy and rodeo rider from Plainview, Texas, has a blend of humility and horse sense.

"Unbridled will end up at Arlington," Nafzger said. "Chicago is a great town. People are friendly and I like the pace of the Midwest. When Arlington Park was destroyed by fire (in 1985), Midwest racing turned tail. Now it's back and Arlington is the nucleus."

Home is Where the Ballpark Is

I tried hard not to warrant getting labeled as a homer in all these years of daily newspapering. But Philadelphia was my boyhood home and Shibe Park (please, not Connie Mack Stadium, the name it wore in its final years) was my home ballpark. Connie Mack's Philadelphia Athletics were my team. They vanished to Kansas City and then Oakland, but my loyalty has not, almost a half-century later.

I understand how Cubs and White Sox fans feel about their teams. This is how I felt about mine:

Happy Days With the A's
(Chicago Tribune, October 23, 1970)

PHILADELPHIA—On the cornerstone at 21st Street and Lehigh Avenue, these sharply etched words: "American Base Ball Club of Philadelphia. MCMVIII."

Time has not blurred that message. It's as legible now as on the day in 1908 when Shibe Park was dedicated as the home of the Philadelphia A's and hailed as one of the engineering marvels of the age.

Sadly, time has taken its toll on the rest of the place. Decaying along with the surrounding neighborhood, this ballpark which hosted some of baseball's greatest teams, is cold and dead, awaiting demolition. The American League A's left town after the 1954 season. The National League Phillies are moving to a new South Philadelphia stadium.

The final baseball game was played here October 1, although it was marred by a stupid orgy of destruction when 31,000 fans ran wild. They almost tore the park down while police watched helplessly.

Incredibly, Phillies' management provided the rioters with seat slats, intended as souvenirs. Clutching the weapons so thoughtfully placed in their hands, the customers gleefully put them to use. It was a sad way to close a rich chapter in major league baseball.

A visitor stopped by today to pay final respects to the spot where he spent many good days growing up in Philadelphia. The Phils' brass had fled for the day, which was fine, because the ex-fan talked his way in to walk through the field one last time, not to exchange small talk.

Besides, he was a rabid A's partisan and the Phillies were beneath him. Now that he lives in Chicago, the former fan smiles when he hears Cub and White Sox rooters exchanging insults. The visitor walks through a dark tunnel, up some rickety steps and into the home dugout, where manager Mack's scorecard waved for decades. The field is in good shape, but evidence of that last night's destruction is everywhere.

Whole rows of seats were ripped from their moorings. The big scoreboard in center field, the one Ted Williams cleared with the homer that put him ahead of Joe DiMaggio's lifetime total, is mutilated. So is the wooden left-field wall. One high-spirited scavenger was seen carting a urinal down Lehigh Avenue after the game.

No matter. The fan is standing on the mound where he saw Bob Feller strike out eight of the first nine A's he faced one night. He walks to the infield. A beer bottle is playing shortstop, with broken glass littering the second-base area where Pete Suder pivoted for double plays. The visitor remembers a double header in 1948, the year when the A's should have won a 10th AL pennant for Mack, but didn't.

The stands were packed. Player-manager Lou Boudreau of the Indians made an incredible stop to kill an A's rally in the first game and then summoned Satchel Paige from the bullpen to save the nightcap.

The park was renamed Connie Mack Stadium, but it will always be Shibe Park in one man's memory. Out in center field, a veteran groundskeeper is taking the batting cage apart. His name is John Godfrey, a 32-year member of the crew.

"We don't know whether the Phillies will keep us in the new stadium," he says. "I saw them all play here. Ruth, Mantle, Mays."

Carrying a broken piece of the left field wall the visitor makes a final stop in section 13, upper deck, first base side. From that wonderful vantage point, a youth saw DiMag, Lindell, Keller (all Yankees, the mortal enemy) smash homers over the left field roof.

The world was simpler then. A gentle rain falls and it's time to go. Thank you, Shibe Park, for the happy days.

9

These Games Not Bad, Dudes

The way the world is now, with everything standing on its head, no wonder words mean the opposite of what they used to mean.

I don't want to get trapped in semantics. Most, if not all, sports fans have been staring in amazement for years at their TV screens watching a routine play. In their ears, a spinmeister who's obviously watching a different game on some other planet, is screaming about "the greatest play since Willie Mays robbed Vic Wertz in the 1954 World Series."

Let's not get carried away here. The entire blame for turning the English language into a do-it-yourself project doesn't belong to TV, although the tube certainly hasn't helped. Too many kids spend too much time staring at TV to save any for reading. They're missing an entire world of magical, mystical ideas, where the written word paints pictures never seen on any screen.

My point is that some of this chapter's title might not mean what it says. Under the anything-goes method (I started to say "rules", but we all know such things as the rules of grammar are extinct), "Great Games" could mean mediocre games. As for the "Bad Dudes," everybody's aware that "Bad" now means "Good" in New Age patois, so some of the people in this mixed-up segment might turn out to be Good Guys. Or maybe not.

Anyway, it's best to take a look at a few great games (and people) along with others that might grate on you just a bit.

No Hits for Sox, Plenty for Fans

This won't go down as the no-nonsense no-hitter of all time. Maybe it has a fighting chance to end up on the bottom 10 list. For sheer, freaky entertainment, though, whatever it was that happened in the farewell season for old Comiskey Park on this scatterbrained Sunday afternoon was right up there with Madonna's underwear-turned-outerwear:

Wonder How the Hitless Wonders Won?
(Daily Herald, July 2, 1990)

The Hitless Wonders are back.

Not only that, but back in first place in the AL West, without benefit of a hit. Not even the original White Sox Hitless Wonders, who had the mighty Cubs scared hitless in wresting the 1906 World Series from them, could top that.

Very little short of sheer fantasy could have been more unbelievable than what actually happened Sunday in Comiskey Park. The dowager of big-league baseball arenas threw itself a smash-hit 80th birthday party, hosting a no-hitter thrown by Andy Hawkins of the New York Yankees and a 4-0 defeat tossed on the selfsame Hawkins' hapless head.

Even erudite Sox Manager Jeff Torborg couldn't hit on an explanation.

"Was this actually Comiskey's 80th anniversary?" Torborg pondered, as mystified as the rest of his hitless eyewitnesses, at the outcome of this sure-fire Top 10 strangest game in all of those eight decades. "I was trying so hard to get somebody on base that I couldn't get caught up in the excitement."

If so, Torborg's fingernails must have been the only ungnawed set on the South Side while Hawkins was gaining his no-hitter and losing his game. The way the Sox finally broke a scoreless tie in the bottom of the eighth inning—four runs, three errors, two walks, no hits—might confirm the suspicion that they are this year's team of destiny.

The Yankees left town Sunday night muttering to themselves. The series finale started as a duel between Hawkins and Sox starter Greg Hibbard. It built in intensity during the bizarre eighth. With the crowd of 30,642 hanging on every pitch, Hawkins got Ron Karkovice and Scott Fletcher on popups to come within four outs of his first no-hitter.

What happened between then and the winning Sox "rally" defies description, although Yankee third baseman Mike Blowers tried his best. Blowers was the man to ask, because his two-out error on Sammy Sosa's grounder opened the floodgates.

"What do you tell a pitcher after something like this?" Blowers shrugged. "Hawk pitched the game of his life and we couldn't get him any runs."

Neither could the Sox, until Hawkins walked the bases full after Blowers' boot. Then Robin Ventura stroked an opposite-field fly to left, where Jim Leyritz waited to put it away.

Oops!

"I hit the ball, started running to first and the next thing I knew, three runs were scoring," Ventura said.

That three-run, two-base error by Leyritz was the ball game. For the Yankees' next act, right fielder Jesse Barfield lost Ivan Calderon's hoist in the sun for a second straight two-base muff, admitting Ventura with the fourth unearned run off the unhittable Hawkins.

"When I came back to the bench, Andy told me, 'Hey, kid, these things happen,'" Leyritz said. "It looked like the ball was hit to my right, so I moved in that direction. Then the wind got it. I lunged, but the ball hit more of my bare hand than the glove."

At the end, Hawkins played better defense for the Yankees than they had for him.

"Why should Leyritz apologize to me?" he asked. "He wasn't out there dogging it."

Leyritz wasn't out there catching it, either. That's how the Yankees left Comiskey Park after all those years of leaving the Sox and their fans dazed and defeated. Imagine the legendary, fence-busting Bronx Bombers saying bye-bye by committing three eighth-inning errors to waste Whitey Ford's no-hitter and blow the game.

"Never saw anything like that in my life," said Yankees manager Stump Merrill. "We gave the White Sox six outs in that inning."

Thanks, Yanks.

The House of Krause

Nobody's suggested hanging that label on the United Center. Since Michael Jordan, the House His Airness Built quickly turned into a chamber of horrors.

So that enigmatic Buddha, Jerry Krause, has been getting more heat than usual while the post-Jordan Bulls keep getting posted up, pounded and pushed deeper into the NBA dungeon. In Boston, New York or Philadelphia, fans aroused by attack-dog media would be howling for Krause's head on a platter. In Chicago, the rotund boss of the Bulls mostly gets a pass.

In his days as a scout for the Bulls, self-styled "Gym Rat" Jerry Krause (left) ponders a draft pick with General Manager Pat Williams (center) and coach Dick Motta.

Some of that stems from the bunker mentality Krause adopted a long time ago. He distrusts most writers, including me, so they've given up on the frank exchanges of information that happen often around the NBA. Scribes and general managers need each other, so an amiable working relationship, or even friendship can develop. When things go wrong, the tendency to blame it on the media is always an option for coaches, managers, front-office types and occasionally, owners.

For Krause, such deep suspicion lingers permanently. He's been in a shell most of the time since 1972 when then Bulls coach Dick Motta delivered this blast at then-Bulls scout Krause: "Jerry Krause—the man who talked me out of drafting Nate Archibald."

That blunder didn't prevent Krause from getting hired and fired in short order as general manager of the Bulls by Arthur Wirtz, the real power behind the throne in pro basketball and hockey circles. Krause bounced back when new Bulls owner Jerry Reinsdorf hired him to run the show in 1985, with Michael Jordan preparing to dominate the NBA like no player before or since.

It took Krause six years to add enough supporting talent for Jordan to win the first of the Bulls' six NBA crowns. Without Jordan, how long will it take for Krause and new coach Bill Cartwright to get them back into the NBA playoffs?

Illini Give Badgers the Bounce

This could be my favorite Big Ten game of all. Since 1966, when I went to Bloomington, Indiana, to cover new Miami of Ohio head coach Bo Schembechler's debut against the Hoosiers, the total of afternoons (and mornings and evenings, since the TV moguls got control of the starting times) I've spent in press boxes around the conference has soared into the hundreds. It's a very enjoyable way to make a living.

Not all beer and skittles, though. There was the time Nick Vista, Michigan State's genial sports information director, had to be summoned from home to drive me around the Spartan Stadium parking lot in pitch blackness at 10 p.m. (it takes that long to write and file a football game story and notes) until I found my car. And the night when I got locked in Purdue's Mackey Arena. And lots more.

But once they went at it on the field, it was a lot more fun watching those collisions than being in on them. Sure, the Big Ten lacks a lot of the speed and some of the razzle-dazzle that you see in the SEC and other conferences. For me, there's no atmosphere like a Big Ten campus—except for Notre Dame—on a football Saturday. And when that war in the trenches becomes hand-to-hand combat, like it did in this Illinois-Wisconsin battle, you see why these stadiums are filled, year after year.

The incredible goings on at the end made this trip to Madison something special:

Turf Loss for Wisconsin
(Chicago Tribune, October 24, 1982)

MADISON, Wis.—The trick play that almost won for Wisconsin was worthy of an Oscar.

Illinois topped it Saturday with a Tony, breaking the Big Ten record for miracle finishes in a game. Each team came up with one.

Illini quarterback Tony Eason broke the Badgers' backs by completing 37 of 51 passes for 479 yards, enabling Mike Bass to break their hearts. Eason beat the clock and the Wisconsin secondary, so Bass could boot a 46-yard field goal in the final second for an incredible 29-28 Illini victory.

"I knew it was going through as soon as I kicked the ball," said Bass of his fifth field goal, tying a Big Ten single-game record first set by Walter Eckersall in 1905.

Just before that, the Badgers triggered hysteria in the overflow Camp Randall stadium crowd of 78,406 by recycling a dipsy-doodle maneuver from the Pop Warner playbook. Trailing 26-22 with less than a minute to go, quarterback Randy Wright tossed an apparent incompletion to receiver Al Toon on the sideline. Toon fielded the legal backward pass on one hop and unleashed a 40-yard touchdown strike to tight end Jeff Nault, alone behind Illinois safety David Wright.

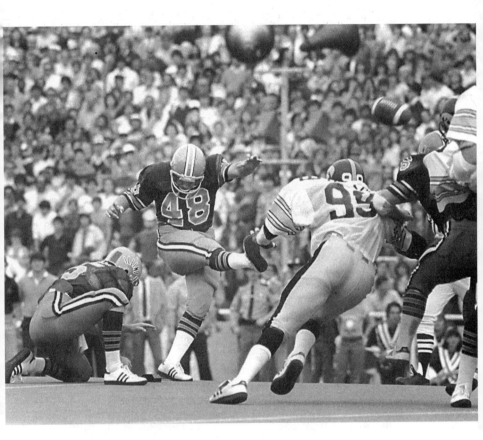

Mike Bass, a clutch kicker for Illinois, gives Iowa the boot from 3-point range.

Coach Dave McClain's team had been rehearsing this turf play all season, unveiling it here to mystify a regional TV audience, resurrect the Badgers' Rose Bowl hopes and roar from behind. Everything depended on a true bounce to Toon off the artificial turf, and they got one.

"We all thought the play was over," confessed Illini safety Craig Swoope, who tackled Nault just after he tumbled into the end zone. "We didn't recognize what had happened when the ball bounced."

McClain tipped off referee Otho Kurtz before the opening kickoff that the Badgers had something up their sleeves. The bounce pass ploy is legal if the receiver is behind the passer, making it a lateral that anyone on either side can recover. It worked when the defenders, lulled by Toon's nonchalant acting job, relaxed for the second it took Nault to get open.

"Al looked disgusted, like it was just a bad pass, so the guy rushing at him (cornerback Charles Amstedt) slowed up," Wright said. "Coach Dudley (Bill, UW's offensive coordinator) saw us throw new balls into the turf to soften them and he got the idea when they took good hops.

But after this bitter loss bounced the Badgers' faint chance to go to the Rose Bowl, depression replaced elation.

"That Eason," Wisconsin linebacker Jim Melka said. "Give that guy time to throw and he'll hurt you. We were in a prevent defense, but he just zipped the ball in there."

Green Light for Cubs

Dallas Green's hiring was hailed as a red-letter day for the Cubs when they hired him in 1981 to end their long-standing NL playoff boycott. The feisty Philadelphia import could have sold scrapple to hungry Cub fans then, even though that delicacy, made from unidentified hog innards, is considered edible only by City of Brotherly Love natives and Pennsylvania Dutchmen.

In the end, unfortunately, Green's regime proved strikingly similar to the 1966-72 tenure of manager Leo Durocher, with one major difference. Both were Wise Men from the East, allegedly capable of leading the Cubs out of the NL quagmire and into the promised land. At least Green steered the Cubs into the 1984 NL playoffs for the first time, although the aftermath of that hysteria-inducing drive to first place in the East Division was almost as bitter as the Durocher-led September foldup of 1969.

Green's "Building a New Tradition" theme was greeted with distrust until the Cubs suddenly turned things around in 1984. His Philly phalanx—superstar Ryne Sandberg, shortstop Larry Bowa, outfielders Bob "Deer" Dernier, Gary Matthews and Keith Moreland, pitchers Warren Brusstar and Dick Ruthven, plus coach John Vukovich—played major roles in the division-clinching season, with many a "Holy Cow!" from Harry Caray, grand marshal of the victory parade.

Another Philadelphia import, manager Lee Elia, was gone by then, unable to survive his second straight losing season in Chicago. The volatile Elia doomed himself by unleashing a profane blast at Cub fans on April 29, 1983. He lost it after the Cubs lost on a wild pitch by ace reliever Lee Smith, falling to 5-14 and out of the race before they stumbled through 20 games.

But Green's vindication began the following spring, one of those rare "next years" Cubs fans peek at as peaks to fend off their pique over decades of valleys. This time, the Cubs didn't fold until two games after the regular season. They swept the Padres twice in Wrigley Field and headed for San Diego, leading 2-0 in the best-of-5 playoff, with three shots at ending their 39-year World Series blackout.

Strike One! (7-1). Strike Two! (7-5). Strike Three! (6-3). Well, at least the Cubs crept a little closer in those last two games. Green's post-playoff lament that the Cubs had the Padres by the throat in the series led a frustrated Cub fan to wonder why his heroes seemingly played the last three games with one hand on their own throats.

Anyway, Green was convinced those scars would heal once his master plan got implemented.

"When we start getting a steady flow of young players developing in our farm system, the Cubs will be on the road to long-term improvement," the would-be franchise doctor prescribed.

A few years later, Green was back on his own farm outside Philadelphia and the Cubs were back to doing what they've done since the end of World War II—rebuilding.

Sundown for Suns

The drunks got a big head start in Boston Garden on Friday night, June 4, 1976. It probably came in handy to deal with the big, throbbing, hung-over heads tottering groggily out of the place early Saturday morning.

In their infinite wisdom, the TV barons decreed a 9 p.m. start for Game 5 of the NBA playoff finals between the Celtics and the Phoenix Suns. For years, Friday had been a combined basketball and fight night for Celtic fans, with the ball on the famed parquet floor and the brawls mostly in the stands. All of this action was punctuated by great gulps of foaming lager, bock, Pilsener or whatever else was on tap.

Fortunately, they poured the brew into paper cups before selling to the thirsty customers. Especially that night, brown bottles in the hands of the mob would have made the Boston Tea Party look like—well, a tea party. It didn't help that the late starting time enabled Celtics faithful to get an early start. They tanked up at various watering holes in the grimy blocks around the Garden, a building that looked as battle-scarred as the Celtics and Bruins backers who'd been unleashing their hostility there for decades.

Clearly, it would be aimed at the upstart Suns on this extraordinary evening. I walked out of the shoebox that passed for a Boston Garden pressroom with Bob Ryan, veteran *Boston Globe* writer, about a half-hour before tipoff time. Ryan glanced at the glassy stares we encountered on the way to our courtside seats, looked at me and shook his head ominously.

I was crammed into a postage-stamp workspace next to Joe Gilmartin, an old pro from the *Phoenix Gazette*. Along with the teams we covered, the Bulls and Suns, we had been losing skirmishes around the NBA for years, but this was shaping up as a full-scale war. The fans seated right behind us were in an ugly mood before the first foul got whistled by referees Richie Powers and Don Murphy.

Without exaggeration, we could smell alcohol fumes in the haze of smoke hanging over the court. The stage was set for something really ugly to happen. Instead, what took place was perhaps the most beautiful basketball game I've ever seen anywhere, played under the toughest conditions imaginable. Ex-Bull Garfield Heard, now with the Suns, emerged as the hero, even though his team lost. I'm not sure how, but this is what I told the world about it, before stumbling out of the Garden (except I was sober) in search of a flight to Phoenix:

Heard's Shot Heard Around the World
(Chicago Tribune, June 6, 1976)

BOSTON—Perhaps the supreme irony in what might have been the greatest pro basketball game ever was the pair of technical fouls called Friday night on Phoenix coach John MacLeod.

His Suns lost to the Celtic 128-126 in a triple-overtime classic that oozed championship action from every pore, along with sweat, a little blood and a few tears in the Valley of the Sun. Boston now leads 3-2 in an NBA playoff which has grown in stature each step of the best-of-7 struggle. It took a gigantic leap forward in Boston Garden, where a sellout crowd of 15,320, plus millions of TV viewers saw one of the all-time epics.

The Celtics were in their dressing room, celebrating a supposed 111-110 triumph after two extra periods, although a few seconds were left on the ancient Garden clock. Abruptly, they had to return and watch Garfield Heard's last-second, 25-foot miracle shot extend both sets of exhausted athletes to five more minutes of nerve-shattering drama.

(Writer's note: Four years later, Heard's miracle two-pointer would have been the game-winner for Phoenix. The NBA legalized the 3-point basket, for shots from beyond a line 23 feet, 9 inches away from the hoop, beginning in the 1979-80 season. It had been an ABA staple since that league opened in 1968.)

And yet, the Suns would have won 95-94 in regulation time if referee Don Murphy hadn't called a technical foul on MacLeod with 7:22 to go in the third period. They also would have prevailed 112-111 if MacLeod hadn't been forced to call a strategic timeout, paying for it with a technical foul and one free throw. That put Boston up by two points, so the Heard bomb, stunning the rabid crowed into silence, could only knot the score at 112-112.

Confused? Elated or outraged, depending on which team you're rooting for? You should have been here.

"Both MacLeod and Bianchi (Suns' assistant Al, an aide to Johnny Kerr in 1966-67, the Bulls' first NBA season) were yelling at me, but the coach used a four-letter word, so I had to call the T," Murphy insisted. Added his partner, Richie Powers, "It was the greatest game I ever worked."

Showing championship class, MacLeod and Bianchi went to the officials' dressing room to tell them they'd been superb. It was all the more laudable, because the Suns would be heading home with a chance to win their first NBA crown before a partisan mob, except for those two technical foul shots, converted by Jo Jo White of the Celtics.

So many incredible things happened before Boston's Jim Ard sank two clinching free throws with 31 seconds left in the third five-minute extra session. How much more effort these physically and emotionally drained teams could have scraped up is questionable. John Havlick seemingly had done it for the home team with a running 15-footer while the last second of the second overtime ticked away. It put Boston in command 111-110, sending a swarm of fans into the floor to salute their heroes' 3-2 series lead.

Not yet. The clock was reset to one second. MacLeod elected to take an automatic technical foul by calling time, so the Suns could bring the ball in from midcourt. A hopeless gamble, certainly, except to prove nothing is hopeless if people refuse to quit. The Suns gave TV onlookers, preparing to switch to the late movie, an extra, unforgettable second, while Boston Garden's uproar faded into a moan of disbelief.

MacLeod diagrammed a play which sends Heard streaking in for a back-door layup—except that the door was closed. So Heard wheeled to the top of the foul circle, took the inbounds pass from Curtis Perry, pivoted and unleashed an arching 25-foot bomb in the same motion.

Nothing but net.

If this historic arena had been a Hollywood movie set, the game—and the series—would have ended right there. It's real, so after Heard's miracle, the Suns' victory plea went unHeard.

Coach Tom Heisohn of the Celtics is one of the all-time class guys, a gruff teddy bear and fierce competitor who turns back into a painter and a delightful conversationalist as soon as the final horn sounds. If I had the luxury of rooting—something I don't believe a reporter should do—I would have felt good about Tommy Gun's team winning this game and going on to wrap up the championship in Game 6.

But John MacLeod is a special man. Since the day he came from the college ranks at Oklahoma to take over the Suns in 1970, I've liked him. It was not fun for me to watch MacLeod try vainly to resurrect Notre Dame's basketball fortunes around before getting fired in 1999.

Hull Lot of Hawk Hysteria

Walter Payton, Bears. Ernie Banks, Cubs. Michael Jordan, Bulls. Harold Baines, White Sox. Bobby Hull, Blackhawks.

Nothing more need be said about those five players and five teams. When you think of that team, you think of THAT player. At least over the last four generations, Payton, Banks, Jordan, Baines and Hull are the Fab Five of Chicago sports.

The Fab Five before them probably were all white guys. The ones to come will be all races, all colors, all origins, but (I hope), all Americans, and maybe even All-Americans, if they played college football. Sounds like progress to me. One of the best things I noticed about sports departments in all the years I've worked in them is the way we don't have to preach. All we do is report what hap-

The Golden Jet was the Hull show for the Blackhawks until they made the dumb—and costly—decision not to pay him what he was worth. At the peak of his career, Bobby Hull (9) skates in to slam the puck past Ed Giacomin, freezing the Rangers goalie on Chicago Stadium ice.

pens when everybody gets an equal chance to excel and the results speak for themselves.

My friend Wayne Embry pointed that out to me. Whatever Embry did as a college or NBA player, general manager, club president, businessman or co-champion patron (with Red Auerbach) of Chinese restaurants from coast to coast, was done with style. Until Wayne pointed out the obvious fact that in the NBA, the best players play, regardless of racial or other consideration, I never thought much about that.

But it's true. The NBA is living proof, even though it took baseball to give Jackie Robinson and a lot of great players, their long-overdue chance. What has all this got to do with Bobby Hull?

A lot, actually. Hull became the dominant player in his sport, ice hockey, on his talent and charisma. That's the way it should be. Since I was in Chicago Stadium to cover the Bulls, I seldom saw Hull play, except on TV. The exception was the night when he scored the goal that put him ahead of Rocket Richard on the all-time list. Naturally, the Stadium went berserk.

When I remember the roar, as the Madison Street Madhouse's farewell PR campaign implored us to, I still recall that bellow. It was right up there with the pandemonium when Tom Boerwinkle's last-minute layup gave the Bulls an undeserved 1975 playoff victory over Golden State. My *Tribune* co-worker, Bob Verdi, had a Hull rink full of Golden Jet stories, but not the one that tickled me the most.

When Hull was jetting toward his historic 50-goal season in 1962, Chicago got gripped by hockey hysteria, much like the Super Bowl schizophrenia over the 1985 Bears. Blackhawk fans planned to bombard their hero with all sorts of exotic gifts at the 50-goal celebration, to be presided over by Ted Damata, the *Tribune*'s veteran hockey writer.

Teddy, one of the best of the Good Guys, was taking this Hull thing seriously, so I tried to play it straight while reading the list of goodies to be showered on the Jet when his 51st goal shattered the NHL single-season mark shared by Richard and Boom Boom Geoffrion. I had to laugh out loud when I read about the lady who was baking 50 chocolate-covered pucks. Anybody trying to top that had to be out of puck.

The Hull-Chicago love affair was a two-way street at Madison and Wood Streets. Years after he left, only because the Hawks were too cheap—and dumb—to match the million-dollar contract from the World Hockey Association, Bobby longed to land back here. That era ended in 1972, but his halo still hasn't slipped for fans, despite lots of off-the-ice controversy.

The memory of Hull, a blond Adonis at 5-feet-10 and 195 pounds of muscular motion, won't fade. Neither will the word picture, painted by WGN announcer Lloyd Petit, of the Golden Jet barreling down center ice at 30 miles per hour to blast his fearsome 118 MPH slap shot past helpless goalies.

"I should have asked the WHA for $5 million," Hull lamented of his 15-year superskate in Chicago. "Leaving was a big mistake."

Much bigger for the Hawks.

Hooten and Hollerin'

The Cubs lost on Opening Day, 1972, with the season's start pushed back to April 15 by another of the labor disputes that keep turning off baseball fans and turning ballparks dark. With their patience taxed to the limit and their wallets tapped by the IRS, only 9,583 shivering fans turned up two days later on a raw, dank, dark Wrigley Field afternoon.

Suddenly, just like in that song about foggy London Town, the sun was shining everywhere. The turnabout came from Texas, not taxes, in the chubby person of Burt Hooton. The rookie right-hander made the Phillies knuckle under with something called a knuckle curve, helping fans feel warm all over. It would be another dozen years before the Cubs finally erased the gloom of their 1969 foldup, but on this bad-weather, good-news day, their never-say-die faithful got some psychic income to live by:

No Game? No, No-Hitter
(Chicago Tribune, April 17, 1972)

"To think we almost called it off," sighed Cub vice-president John Holland, "The forecast called for rain until 2 p.m., but we had a $25,000 advance sale, so I told the umpires 'Go ahead and use your best judgement.' "

"He just walked to the mound in the first inning and took charge," marveled manager Frank Lucchesi of the Phillies.

"I went out to talk to him in the seventh inning after he walked two straight batters and he looked at me as if to say, 'What are you doing here?'" chuckled acting manager Pete Reiser of the Cubs.

"Congratulate Burt for me and tell him to stop by the office in the morning to sign a new contract with a $2,500 raise— and give Randy Hundley $500 for catching him," ordered Cub owner Phil Wrigley in a phone call to Holland.

"You have to compare Hooton's knuckle curve with a Sandy Koufax curve ball," Hundley pointed out. "It starts at your head and winds up on the ground."

"Here's Fergie Jenkins, winning 20 games five years in a row and never had one of these things," philosophized Phil Regan, the Cubs' bullpen veteran. "Then along comes this kid and does it in his fourth major league start."

"I was kind of burned up about walking seven batters," Burt Hooton said calmly. "It's true that I dreamed about pitching a no-hitter (Saturday) night. In my dream, I didn't walk anybody. First, I dreamed I hit a home run."

In case you spent the weekend spelunking or something, those comments concerned a chunky, steel-nerved 22-year-old pitcher named Burt Carlton Hooton. Bursting onto the Chicago sports scene with the impact of a Bobby Hull or a Gale Sayers, Hooton became an instant superstar yesterday in Wrigley Field.

All the kid from the University of Texas did was hurl a 4-0 no-hitter at the Philadelphia Phillies. A paid crowd of 9,583 endured biting north winds on this misty spring afternoon, forgetting the chill as the drama unfolded.

Hooton yielded seven walks but no hits before stalking out to work the ninth inning, with the sun suddenly breaking through in a neat piece of stage setting. Leading off, Willie Montanez grounded a 1-0 delivery to Glenn Beckert's right, the second sacker gobbling it up smoothly to throw him out. Up came Deron Johnson and Hooton fell behind 3-0 while Regan and Dan McGinn heated up in the home bullpen.

Slipping over two called strikes, the right-hander got Johnson to foul a pitch into the right field seats before fanning him with his money pitch, a sharp knuckle curve. The final challenge was Greg "Bull" Luzinski, the burly youngster from Prospect Heights, who homered off Jenkins Saturday and came close to shattering the no-no in yesterday's seventh inning. He got all of a Hooton fast ball, bashing it high and deep to left center.

It would have bounced on Waveland Avenue, but the wind brought the ball back into the park, enabling Rick Monday to snare it in front of the 368-foot sign. In this spot, Luzinski had no chance to see smoke. Instead, Hooton flipped him a couple of knuckle curve strikes, amid anticipatory bellows from chilled, enthralled spectators. The cool kid didn't waste time getting them in out of the cold.

Luzinski struck out swinging on the next pitch and Hooton got engulfed by a swarm of Cubs. They pounded his back and ruffled his curly blond hair in jubilation at the first no-hitter by a National League rookie since Jeff Tesreau of the New York Giants did it to the Phillies in 1912. It was the eighth by a Cub hurler in this century and the first in Wrigley Field since Ken Holtzman throttled Atlanta 3-0 here on August 19, 1969. Holtzman also no-hit the Reds 1-0 in Cincinnati last June 3.

Besides Luzinski's blast, the only serious hid by the Phillies was Denny Doyle's third-inning wicked liner. It was a sure double, except that shortstop Don Kessinger timed his leap to foil Doyle.

"First one I ever caught," Hundley chortled of the seven-strikeout masterpiece. "If we were only 1 run up with the count 3-0 on Johnson in the ninth, I might have had to call for a fast ball."

Taking in the furor swirling around him, Hooton sat poker-faced in Durocher's office—available because Leo the Lip was home with a virus—facing a post-game grilling.

"I started fooling around with the knuckle curve when I was 14," he said. "Fatigue wasn't a factor because I pitched seven innings against (University of) Texas hitters on each of the last two Wednesdays. In the second turn, they got seven hits and a homer off me."

When he'd had enough, Hooton cut off the questions and eased offstage. It was his second remarkable performance of the day. A Cubs coach summed up the first one, a seven-walk, seven-strikeout triumph.

"Seven and seven and Burt Hooton," he said. "I'll drink to that."

The postscript to this brilliant start for Hooton's career was all too familiar to Cub fans.

Hooton was asked a few days later to assess his chances to emulate Johnny Vander Meer, the Reds' lefty who tossed back-to-back no-hitters in 1938, against Boston on June 11 and Brooklyn on June 15. He's the only big-league pitcher to do so in consecutive starts.

"Never heard of him," the rookie responded. "Reporters were looking at me like I was some kind of a fool because I didn't know who Vander Meer was. I'm not a baseball historian."

Not a superstar, either. Hooton went 10-14 after the no-hitter, making 1972 a lost year for both him and the Cubs. His career record in Chicago was an uninspiring 34-44 before he got shipped to Los Angeles in 1975, promptly becoming a winner for the Dodgers. That's the way it seemed to go for the Cubs, especially in '72, when Durocher finally bowed out after six-plus stormy seasons. New skipper Whitey Lockman couldn't get them into the playoffs, either. Ironically, the only other season highlight was an 8-0 Milt Pappas no-hitter against San Diego on September 2. Pappas came within one pitch of a perfect game before walking Larry Stahl on a 3-2 serve with two out in the ninth.

Just like Durocher—and the Cubs—close, but no cigar.

Belle of the Basebrawl

The Cubs have had their share of characters over the years, notably superflake Dave "Kong" Kingman, who could have been a superhero, but elected to emulate super recluse Howard Hughes. Then there were eccentric relievers Turk Wendell, Mitch "Wild Thing" Williams and Dick "Dirt" Tidrow, along with sometime starter Bill "Evil Eye" Faul, a self-proclaimed hypnotist. Throw in clubhouse cutup Jay Johnstone, third baseman Bill "Mad Dog" Madlock, who lost a war of words with Cubs owner P.K. Wrigley, then add the North Side's transient hippie, first baseman Joe "Pepi" Pepitone, and a couple of minor characters.

It adds up to a fairly impressive list of semi-weird stuff. Regardless, the off-the-wall roster is a lot longer on the South Side.

Leadoff hitter for that spaced-out squad would have to be Albert Belle, a big hitter with a bigger scowl and attitude that made Bad, Bad Leroy Brown seem like good 'ol Charlie Brown. Belle's previous personality problems at Cleveland were well documented, but the Sox needed a slugger, so he spent two seasons here, racking up MVP-type numbers in 1998, with 49 homers, 152 RBIs and a .326 average.

But Belle wasn't a bell-ringer in the playoff chase and the no-man's land around his locker made the clubhouse a cold, clammy place. He led the league in controversy, as in the corked-bat caper that enlivened a Sox-Indians Comiskey Park series. It didn't prevent them from failing to make the 1994 playoffs—there weren't any, because the owners locked out the players, ending the season and Chicago's best chance in 35 years to host a World Series on the South Side. All it accomplished was to further embarrass baseball with the comic-opera antics aptly described by this headline:

Holy Botched Burglary, Batman! Belle's Bat Back
(Daily Herald, July 18, 1994)

No Watergate-style smoking gun needed to solve this Comiskey Park batnapping.

A smoking bat will suffice.

Albert Belle's elusive war club reappeared Sunday almost as mysteriously as it had vanished after being confiscated Friday from the Cleveland outfielder. Before it could be tested to see if Belle illegally had corked the bat, the evidence vanished in a midnight burglary of the umpires' dressing room. Now the elusive bat is back in custody, en route to American League headquarters in New York —presumably by Batmobile. If X-rays show it was corked, Indians slugger Bell could be suspended.

"Kevin Hallinan (Commissioner Bud Selig's security director) came to my hotel room this morning with the bat," said Dave Phillips, crew chief for this weekend series. I had to confiscate the bat when (Sox manager) Gene Lamont asked me to check it, but when I got to the park Saturday, it was gone."

The AL then stepped in, pressuring the Indians to round up more than the usual suspects. Bat-corking is a baseball ritual, almost as time-honored as hazing rookies, but the break-in raised the possibility of burglary charges.

"My intent was not to minimize the situation," said John Hart, Cleveland's general manager, hastily backing away from his original claim that "calling this a criminal event is ludicrous." "We're satisfied the bat taken from Belle was the one we have," said AL media chief Phyllis Merhige. "Some tiles were removed from the ceiling in the umpires' room, so it looks like that's how the bat switch was made."

A bat signed by Indians infielder Paul Sorrento was left behind by the cat (oops, make that bat) burglar, who made off with the impounded shillelagh. Sox GM Ron Schueler stopped short of summoning Sgt. Joe Friday from the LAPD to bat down this Comiskey crime wave, but allowed as how the whole thing looked mighty suspicious.

"Somebody thought there was guilt, or he wouldn't have gone to all that trouble," Schueler theorized. "No way anybody could have gotten into the umpires' room (via the sneaky, overhead ceiling tile route) from our clubhouse, but from the other side, yes, they could."

Belle battled, or perhaps batted, his way to Baltimore in 1999 —presumably by Batplane—for a couple million more bucks than he got from the Sox, an unlamented departure. The vacuum he left behind didn't take long to get filled to overflowing, first by right-handed pitcher Jaime Navarro and then by left-handed pitcher David Wells. In just one season, Wells caused more dissension on the injury-riddled 2001 Sox than Belle and Navarro combined.

Mainly, Wells proclaimed himself a team leader without backing up his mouth on the mound. If he'd brought the same numbers from a two-year, 37-win stint in Toronto or come close to his May 17, 1998 perfect game for the Yankees, 4-0 over Minnesota, Wells' bluster would have been written off as the sort of eccentricity expected from lefties. But his belly overshadowed his braggadocio, bringing back recurrent lumbar woes.

So the rotund southpaw sank into non-story status, along with the rest of the 2001 Sox. At least Frank Thomas, the veteran taken on by Wells in a battle for the role of clubhouse Bigfoot, had a reason for missing the season after tearing a forearm muscle in April. Wells was equally ineffective in action or on the disabled list, triggering sighs of relief when the Sox dropped his 2002 option, enabling the portly portsider to waddle back to the Yankees for a living wage of $7.5 million.

Fiskal Responsibility

In his own way, catcher Carlton Fisk created more waves in the Sox clubhouse than Wells. Yet, Fisk was an all-time Sox fan favorite, except for team brass. His long-playing feud with Sox chairman, Jerry Reinsdorf only made him more popular on the South Side. Their ardor was apparent from this tribute to Pudge in old Comiskey Park's final night game:

Carlton Fisk (mask atop head) is not a happy camper while Toronto runs prance across the Comiskey Park plate. Combative catcher Fisk didn't back off from anyone, even Sox Chairman Jerry Reinsdorf.

No. 72 is no. 1 For Comiskey Fans
(Daily Herald, September 30, 1990)

No doubt about the identity of No. 1 in the hearts, and on the film, of fans at the last night game ever to be played in this historic setting. The overflow Comiskey Park crowd of 42,800 voted with their flashbulbs for White Sox catcher Carlton Fisk illuminating him more brightly than President Bush's 1,000 Points of Light.

Brighter than Saturday night's comeback 5-2 victory over the Seattle Mariners, the seventh-inning salute to Fisk lit up this extraordinary event. The incandescence was a glaringly visible "Thanks, Pudge" to the 42-year-old Hall of Fame inductee-to-be. The Sox already had taken the lead for good in the seventh when Fisk came out to hit for Rodney McCray.

Flashbulbs popped and fans roared for the veteran whose mental toughness played a starring role in the 1990 turnabout from AL West pretenders to contenders. Fisk masked his emotion when the media reached his clubhouse cubicle, but he knew what it all meant.

"That was bizarre, very strange," he said of the Kodak moment, blazing away from everywhere in the stands on every pitch to Fisk. "It wouldn't have been much of a photo if I'd punched (struck) out. They probably would have thrown the flashbulbs at me."

Sox manager, Jeff Torborg, saw it for what it was.

"There was a special feeling in this park tonight," he said. "They were waiting for a chance to show it for Pudge."

Aside from the affectionate attack of glaring bulbs, not one unruly incident marred the closing of this chapter in Chicago baseball. The fans' decorum was so faultless that another ninth-inning invasion by mounted Chicago policemen looked like embarrassing overkill.

"I hope the fans acts like that again tomorrow," said Sox shortstop, Ozzie Guillen of today's farewell game, after 80 years. "The players won't miss this park, but we'll miss the fans."

Can't Stop Wilt, Even with Stilts

I first saw Wilt Chamberlain play when he was a sophomore sensation at Philadelphia's Overbrook High School.

With this human beanstalk towering over the other nine kids on the court, it should have been Overpowering High School. Or Overbearing or Overmatched or something similar. Young Wilton Norman Chamberlain was in the process of destroying my guys, Northeast High School, in the Public League title game. Still four inches and maybe 100 pounds short of the giant who would dominate in high school, college, pro and even for a brief stint with the Harlem Globetrotters, he was awesome.

I never really had the one-on-one, two Philly guys talking hoops session with Chamberlain that I tried to set up at various places around the NBA. Chicago was not his favorite town—"Too cold" he told me with that imperious shrug he used to close conversations. And out-of-town writers were not his favorite people. He would huddle with George Kiseda, a *Philadelphia Bulletin* hoop scribe with a touch of the poet in his pen, or Stan Hochman, a very funny Philly *Daily News* columnist. But when I climbed way, way up in the Chicago Stadium stands one night to seek Wilt's opinion on how the NBA-ABA legal battle might affect players, he was noncommittal.

"I try to stay out of those things, my man," he said, employing that catch phrase the same way the Babe Ruth said, "Hiya, kid" to everybody he met. It was their way of recognizing people without knowing them, a necessary survival technique for superstars.

But there was an air of sadness about Wilt, for all his vaunted total of female conquests. He claimed it topped 20,000, and after seeing almost that many groupies around the LA Forum players' entrance on game nights when Wilt was their Main Man, who knows? The only time I felt sorry for the Dipper, as he preferred friends—not writers—to call him, was after the Lakers lost a seventh-game emotional orgy to the Knicks in the NBA finals on May 8, 1970. It was the night Madison Square Garden went wild when injured Willis Reed limped out of the tunnel and onto the court, an unlikely David, ready to slay the Lakers' Goliath.

In that setting, Wilt, Bill Russell and George Mikan combined probably wouldn't have stood a chance. Sure enough, the Knicks won a rare NBA championship and along with a posse of other writers, I elected to work the Lakers' dressing room rather than take a champagne soak in the winners' bathhouse. The bearded giant sat stoically on his stool, exchanging stares with us. Silence reigned. Finally, almost plaintively, Chamberlain rumbled, "Somebody ask me a question, so I can get out of here."

The loss wasn't Wilt's fault, but he got the blame. Neither were the playoff ousters pinned on Chamberlain and the 76ers by Russell and the Celtics. After all that frustration, the Big Dipper was weary—and wary—of the way those games were turned into one-on-one confrontations between himself and the Celts' Russell, a master shot-blocker. He left us too soon, so I won't have that talk with him about Philly playmakers—Wilt was one himself, delighting in dealing out assists—until a higher league, if we both make the cut.

In the meantime, I have the memory of the way Wilt the Stilt played Conan the Barbarian against the Bulls on this Chicago Stadium visit:

Wilt Snacks on Bullburgers
(Chicago Tribune, December 17, 1967)

Wilt Chamberlain is the best basketball team ever to appear in Chicago Stadium.

At his customary calm, businesslike pace, the 7-foot-2 center of the Philadelphia 76ers is a fearsome scoring machine. When he's mad, as he was last night, he destroys the opposition.

The Bulls happened to be in the Stilt's path this time, so he stomped them with a 68-point blast, the highest individual NBA scoring spree staged in this toddlin' town. Nobody did this much damage to the Chicago Stags (1946-50) or the Chicago Packers (1961-62) and Chicago Zephyrs (1962-63), a couple of one-year wonders. Actually, the Pack-Zeph double disaster was the same franchise, masquerading under those aliases while combining to lose 117 games in two seasons, mostly for empty seats.

Nobody noticed when they fled in 1964 to become the Washington Bullets. It's highly unlikely that the combined roster of the Bulls/Bullets/Packers/Zephyrs, or maybe even real bullets, could have corralled the enraged Chamberlain. Chances are this semi-superhuman force would have deflected them, just like he did to would-be Bulls' defenders.

As it was, the hapless duo of 6-7 Jim Washington and 6-8 Erwin Mueller ended up with footprints on their chests. The rest of the Bulls mostly stood and watched from a safe distance, sensibly declining to deter Wilt from stuffing, dunking, plunking and just plain dropping 30 of 40 shots into the basket, most from point-blank range. If not for his usual mediocre 8 of 22 at the foul line, the Big Dipper could have dipped into 70-plus-points territory for the seventh time as a pro.

Chamberlain's pique at referee Jack Madden made trivia buffs in the house wonder if he'd go for his all-time mark of 100 points, inflicted on the Knicks on March 2, 1962, in Hershey, Pa. In that same season, just a few months earlier, Wilt welcomed the pitiful Packers to the league, dousing them with a 73-point tidal wave.

"Hey, man, I don't keep count of my points," Chamberlain said, stepping out of a shower in the visitors' dressing room after settling for 68 this time. "The matchups were favorable tonight, so I went for it."

Actually, he just went at it with unstoppable zest. The Bulls crept off the court, wondering if anyone got the number of that truck, although they weren't responsible for provoking him. The guilty party was Madden, who whacked Philadelphia with three first-quarter technical fouls when his vision got questioned. One of them, with an automatic fine of $25, went to Chamberlain. Though that's mere tip money for the bearded giant, he took offense at Madden, venting his displeasure with offensive gestures to the Bulls—68 of them.

"Why doesn't Wilt do that every night?" pondered John "Red" Kerr, coach of the victims. "He can, and if he doesn't, he's cheating the fans."

They got their money's worth here. Chamberlain chucked 14 first-quarter points into the pot, 15 each in the second and third and 24 in the final 12 minutes. At one stretch, be hammered home 12 straight shots, like a man casually feeding quarters into a jukebox.

While leading the 76ers to the NBA title last year, their 31-year-old adding machine disdained such easy pickings to concentrate on rebounding and dealing out assists. If anyone suspected he might be getting too old to locate the basket, Chamberlain proved them wrong last night by shooting out the lights.

Actually, maybe he was aging. The Big Dipper never again scored that many in a game, topping 60 points just once more with 66 for the Lakers at Phoenix on February 9, 1968. But Wilt cracked the 60-point barrier four times against Chicago teams—three of them in 1961-62, the Chicago Packers' only season, and one more with the spree of 68 that victimized the Bulls in '67.

The Real Benny the Bull

When the Bulls needed a mascot, naming the red-suited, hoofed and horned critter Benny the Bull was an easy choice. Their own Benny, crackerjack publicist Ben Bentley, played a big part in keeping Chicago's NBA franchise alive long enough to draw sufficient fans for a mascot to have a Bulls' market during games. Ben's upbeat, offbeat personality, along with his experience, street smarts

*Ben Bentley (right), last of the P.T. Barnum-style press agents, was
a boon to the Bulls when the NBA newcomers struggled for survival
in Chicago.*

and endless store of media contacts, made him a natural to thump the tub for pro basketball's breakthrough in a town where the odds were against it.

Benny kept plugging away, making the daily rounds of all four Chicago newspapers to press the flesh, exchange small talk and seek the little breakthroughs that eventually paid off in big headlines. When fiery coach Dick Motta came aboard in 1968, Bentley's groundwork made it much easier for the suddenly controversial, but most of all, surprisingly watchable Bulls to become the hottest ticket in town.

Rows of empty Chicago Stadium seats filled as if by magic while the Bulls battled, brawled and Bulldozed opponents into submission. While that astonishing turnabout took place on the court, Benny's promotional expertise made sure Chicago knew all about what was happening. The blend of the Bulls and Bentley proved irresistible. It was good for him, too, revitalizing his career.

A boxing publicist and promoter by trade, Ben knew and worked with the big-time fighters from Joe Louis, Jersey Joe Walcott, Rocky Marciano, Sonny Liston, Ezzard Charles, Smokin' Joe Frazier, Sugar Ray Robinson, Sugar Ray Leonard, and on to the storybook career of Cassius Marcellus Clay, a/k/a Muhammad Ali. He wanted to, but was too busy, to get around to writing a tell-all book about the Sweet Science he knew and loved, whimsically titled "Behind the Leather Curtain."

Too bad Ben couldn't find the time, because it would have been a valuable—and immensely readable—contribution to sports history. Ben's stories of such wheeler-dealers as Arthur Wirtz, James D. Norris, and Uncle Mike Jacobs, impresario of the 20th Century Sporting Club, regaled all of us on those seemingly-endless Bulls' road trips.

Later, as ringmaster of "The Sportswriters," a long-running radio and TV verbal free-for-all, Ben's skill at keeping the pot boiling became apparent to a new generation of watchers and listeners. He also played the fascinating game of Chicago power politics in his role as spokesman for the Park District, a hotbed of intrigue. When the army of Ben's media and other friends gathered for a farewell tribute to this lifelong Chicagoan, I looked up this story I wrote after his seven-year stretch as the Bullhorn of the Bulls came to an end:

Bulls Lose Their Voice
(Chicago Tribune, July 24, 1973)

The Chicago Bulls lost yesterday.

They lost a press agent, flack, call him what you will, who got more done for this franchise in seven years than a think tank full of drip-dry spin specialists could have. His name is Ben Bentley, one of the first hires by owner Dick O. Klein, when NBA expansion created the Bulls in 1966.

Since then, Ben's genius for calling attention to the often-overlooked fact that there was a basketball team in Chicago deserves credit for the reality that the Bulls still are here. Bentley's leaving to become an administrative aide to Edmund L. Kelly, Chicago Park District supervisor. Since Ben customarily announces what he had for breakfast, it took a while for the news to sink in on his legion of newspaper pals.

As usual, he was not handing out what Damon Runyan used to call "the phonus bolonus." The new job title sounds a trifle starchy for a down-to-earth guy, but things figure to get less formal at the Park District office before long. Bentley is a Chicago civic asset, like the lakefront (and just as breezy), so it'll take more than a label to restrain his enthusiasm.

"I had terrific rapport with the Bulls players," Ben said, waxing nostalgic. "They're a sweet bunch of guys."

It might not matter who the Bulls get to sit in the PR office close to the front door of their Chicago-Sheraton headquarters. No way they can replace Ben Bentley. They don't make his kind anymore.

10

TV or Not TV

I'm not through with newspapers yet.

Whether they're through with me is another question. After almost 50 years in this fast-changing business, it could be we're both unraveling too much to be compatible anymore.

One thing you learn in just the business of living—if you stick around long enough—is that everything changes. The easy way out is to growl "And not for the better," stomping off with a supercilious smirk.

Sad but true, the newspaper game I knew no longer is fun and games. Like the rest of our economy, it's been computerized, depersonalized and sensitized to the point where freedom of speech is only a figure of speech. That last tendency concerns me most, although points 1 and 2 make working for almost any newspaper lots less fun than it used to be.

When the electronic technicians took over and the production process evolved from hot type to cold computer screens, newspapers made a giant step in an uncertain direction. Now, instead of space for a story, the pagination process provides a "news hole." Maybe George Orwell's *1984* was prophecy, not fiction.

Anyway, the rewrite man in the office and the reporter on the beat, breaking a story on the run, are vanishing species, like all the old-fangled utensils Meredith Willson lamented the loss of in "The Music Man." It's a new millennium, so the old way of looking at things no longer works.

Unfortunately, that includes reading and writing, to a painfully large extent. We don't seem to have time for that in today's frantic pace. I'm unaware if anything can be done about it. Probably not much, but I don't want to come down with a case of creeping old fogeyism right now, so I'll save the sad stories for some other setting. Writing this book has been too enjoyable to end it with a glass of whine.

My trip through what Howard Cosell accurately dubbed the toy department of life was so much fun that I have no complaints. Well, almost none. It went by too fast, but that happens to everybody, including those who haven't been as lucky as me.

Going where I've gone and seeing what I've seen for all these years would have been enough of a reward by itself. Especially since I got paid for writing about Al Kaline getting his 3,000th hit in Baltimore, Nolan Ryan winning his 300th game in Milwaukee and 1,000 other players doing 10,000 remarkable things in a lot of other cities.

That brings us back to Chicago, where I always wanted to be. I didn't know that until I tooled into town in 1961, in search of a job. Actually, I thought I had one when I left the *Illinois State Journal Register* in Springfield to drive to Rockford, where I'd been hired—or so I thought—to work on the Star's sports copy desk for the princely sum of $160 a week. By the way, the *State Register* and the *Rockford Star* are long since defunct.

I'm not folding yet. If I had known what a wild, wonderful ride awaited in Chicago, I'd have headed there sooner. It was a kick traveling around the country, except for the blizzards, fog, bumpy landings, solo midnight departures from pitch-dark arenas and lonely, indigestible dinners in 24-hour beaneries.

Still, the best part was seeing the lights of Chicago under the wing of a descending airplane. To paraphrase something I said in my first book, written over a quarter-century ago in actual time,

Diamond scribe Bob Logan doing what he's been doing since 1970 in Chicago press boxes—telling newspaper readers what happened and why. This time, he's pounding away on his trusty P.C. in new Comiskey Park.

but more like 25 seconds ago the way I figure, "If you make allow-ances for an occasional spell of beastly weather, there is no more exciting city on this imperfect earth."

It remains so, even if the Rush Street scene has managed to survive for some years now without me around anymore, tossing those 50-cent tips to bartenders at the 4 a.m. joints. It's been prac-tically a perpetual Christmas morning. As it goes for all of us, there have been tough times, bad times, troubled times along with all the good stuff. My friend Ben Bentley summed it up aptly: "Nobody walks in clover all the time."

All I'm saying is that people who love their job and the city they do it in are fortunate fellows or females, as the case may be. And I haven't even mentioned the two best parts yet.

One is being able to turn to the sports page every morning, read some brilliant, incisive analysis of a hard-fought contest be-tween two evenly-matched squads and say to myself, "I wrote that." It's the kind of psychic income that doesn't show up in a weekly paycheck, but the IRS hasn't slapped a tax on it—at least not yet.

The real reward is the people you meet. For somebody who hasn't been home often enough to live a normal, 9-to-5, Saturday mow-the-lawn lifestyle, those friends I've collected here, there and everywhere have been my family. Too many of them are gone, espe-cially two of the best—Dick Mackey of the *Kansas City Star* and George Cunningham of the *Atlanta Constitution*. Lots more Good Guys and Gals, in and out of Chicago, deserve mention without unintentionally slighting some of them.

Memories rekindled in researching this book proved once again what a lucky stiff I've been. A working stiff, to be sure, because sportswriting is not the 24-hour-a-day, 7-day-a-week freeload many people figure. For me, though, it's been a labor of love. And fun.

The way I always looked at it, sports is entertainment. It both-ers me that a lot of today's fans regard shrieking obscenities at the opposing team as an essential, in some cases major, part of rooting for their team.

The complaint department stops right there. I'm not the lead-ing literary light in the press box or the brightest bulb in the arc lights, but I'm also not dumb enough to figure my outdated notions will change the way anyone acts, or reacts.

The pace is probably too fast nowadays for a sentimental sort like me to fit in anymore. But I've enjoyed being a witness—though some might say witless—observer/interpreter of the Chicago sporting scene for this long. Lots of people helped make my job a 40-year walk in the (ball) park.

For instance, Roland Hemond and Bob Grim of the White Sox, John McDonough of the Cubs, Tim Hallam of the Bulls and three of the nation's top college publicists—John Heisler of Notre Dame, Kent Brown of Illinois and Mike Korcek of Northern Illinois.

Covering college basketball is easy when you work with coaches like DePaul's legendary Ray Meyer, his son Joey, and Lou Henson and Bill Self at Illinois, the late Gene Sullivan at Loyola and Jimmy Collins and Bob Hallberg at Illinois-Chicago. NIU's Jerry Pettibone was one of the classiest college football coaches, but this would be a book of lists if I kept adding to it.

So I'll stop after saluting a few of the newspaper pals who've been in the front-line trenches with me for 40 years, dodging bullets from both sides—unhappy readers and impatient editors. The *Tribune* once had a great sports copy desk, before most of us moved up—or perhaps down—to become writers. Spence Sandvig was the slot man—so called because the copy chief sat in the closed end of the horseshoe-shaped desk to deal out his notorious "puke packs" of short filler items to plug gaps in pages, along with the main stories we edited and wrote headlines for.

With me at various times on that rim were Don Pierson, now the nation's best pro football writer; John Husar, the late, great outdoors columnist; Cooper Rollow, who became the Trib's sports editor; Bob Markus and Roy Damer, a couple of old pros; and Bob Rockafield, the office cutup, who combined with Bernie Colbeck, czar of the phone desk, to take the heat off with their zany antics. Coming along later were first-rate writers Neil Milbert, Mike Conklin, Fred Mitchell, and Bob Verdi, still Chicago's most literate, entertaining sports columnist.

George Strickler was the sports editor then, taking over from Arch Ward, founder of baseball's All-Star game and the long-playing classic College All-Star football game, pitting collegians against the NFL champs in Soldier Field. Strickler knew about big games, because he was the genius who posed Notre Dame's Four Horsemen on four horses in 1924, creating one of the world's most recognized and most reproduced photos. Young George was an Irish sports information assistant then, and went on to be instrumental in the success of the Bears by seeing they got enough *Tribune* headlines to compete with Ward's pet project, the Chicago Rockets of the All-America Football Conference.

The *Tribune* had assistant sport editors then who had come up through the ranks. They knew every phase of the business and especially the people they directed every day. That's why it was a pleasure to work for guys like Ted Damata, a certified hockey nut, Jimmy "Mate" Segreti, who covered the Hambletonian, harness racing's Kentucky Derby, and Dave Moylan, one of the last of the great writers' editors.

Strickler, a football man, had little interest and even less faith in the future of pro basketball in Chicago. So when a risky, shoestring venture called the Bulls inched the Windy City back into the NBA in 1966, he wanted to cover only home games, and then on a rotating basis, without a permanent beat writer to cover the club daily. Rollow, the assistant sports editor, talked him into putting me on the beat, and from there, the Bulls in particular, and the NBA in general, became my personal responsibility, night and day for most of the next 18 years.

It was a whirlwind blend of people and places, names and faces, airports and alarm clocks, elation and depression, fun and frustration. You must be strapped in to survive that sort of nonstop roller-coaster ride. The only human emotion lacking on this beat was boredom. Most of the time, I was too busy to think about how I did it. Since then, I sometimes stop and ponder two things: a) How DID I do it? and b) I'm glad I did.

But I grew up with baseball. I know the pattern, rhythm and style of this game. Covering it in places like Wrigley Field and old and new Comiskey Park since 1970 has been pure pleasure, aside from the occasional blown deadline and embarrassing error in a story. When it's too late to get a fact straight in the final edition, writers learn to live with it. Most people don't understand, much less tolerate, mistakes made under deadline pressure, when you pick the wrong figure or name or exact sequence of events from the jumbled maze of information in your head, scribbled on your notes and quotes pad or in the computer printouts piled around your cluttered press box workspace.

Technically, editors who read the copy on their computer screens when the story is transmitted to the office are supposed to correct such muffs. No telling how many times editors have bailed me out by doing just that. When they don't, I blame myself, not them. That's not a feel-good copout. It's a basic fact of newspaper life: If my name is on the story, I'm responsible for everything in it, right or wrong.

One way to make sure of the facts is to double-check them. If time allows, triple-check. A slogan posted for decades in Chicago's City News Bureau, where generations of cub reporters learned their trade, tells how: "If your mother says she loves you, check it out."

On the sports beat, the best method is to check with other reporters. In most cases, we help each other. Anything out of the ordinary is sure to be discussed at length while the game goes on. It helps to put things in perspective, an essential part of accurate reporting.

And regardless of the obsession some editors have about changing newspapers into magazines, I stand by what I always thought was the main mission for any reporter on any beat. What we're there for is to tell you what's happening as honestly and accurately as possible. It can and should be done entertainingly, of course.

Yet, the notion persists now that wire service copy can give readers the facts. Writers are urged to use the game as sort of a backdrop for featurized spinoffs, trying to ferret out what one misguided editor described as his mission; "When I read a story, I want to find out something I didn't know."

The fluff some editors and a minority of readers crave can easily be added in places where it won't distract from the section's real purpose.

That's the way it should be done. Fortunately, I never wanted to be an editor. I would have lost enough arguments with those office-bound, swivel-chair commandoes to find myself out on a street corner, peddling papers instead of writing for them.

Actually, the lively rivalry between writers and editors is effective, if stressful. It keeps us on our toes, though it's not easy to write in that position. Conflict gets the juices flowing, so writers vs. editors could rank up there with Republican and Democrats, cats and dogs or maybe even baseball players and baseball owners on the all-time file of famous feuds.

It would be an oversimplification to say editors believe writers are on a permanent vacation, scarfing down free hot dogs in the press box, swilling postgame libations with the players and making out with the groupies who hang around clubhouse exits. Writers figure editors reluctantly break up their nightly gin rummy game on the copy desk to grab fire axes and commence chopping concise copy from a scribe who actually saw the game he's writing about into their version, sight unseen, of how they think it should read.

There's a touch of satire in this not-quite-true-to-life narrative, along with a grain—or maybe even a gob—of reality. For some reason, I can't fathom, many newspaper readers are convinced that writing stories for the *Daily Bugle* is sheer, unadulterated enjoyment. To swipe a line from George Gershwin about such hallucinations, "It ain't necessarily so."

So this is the right time to recommend some light reading for them and especially for the young people who've asked me this same burning question over the years: "How do I break into the newspaper business?" What they really mean, of course, is "How do I get a baseball writer's card or whatever else is needed for me to walk into the press box, munch those semi-edible but totally free hot dogs and tell my envious friends that I'm a big-time sportswriter?"

They're still asking that question, blissfully unaware of two new, painful realities of the sportswriting dodge: 1—The hot dogs are no longer free. The Cubs now soak the writers $5 and the White Sox $7 for a pregame meal. 2—Newspapers as we knew them are a dying industry. Consolidation decimated competition across the country, everywhere except in the biggest cities, including Chicago. Here, the competition that produces outstanding sports pages can thrive only if they're willing to put reporters on the scene.

Sadly, it's become bottom-line business for even the biggest papers. The corporate mentality has been a silent partner for decades; now it's a noisy presence.

Well, that's how the shrinking minority of old-time, front-line reporters feels. Since nobody in editorial boardrooms or accounting offices seeks or cares about our opinion, it doesn't matter. End of sermon. Now for the free advice I promised before climbing up on the soapbox.

For anyone wanting to understand the newspaper business in general and sportswriting in particular, glom onto a book called *Sports Page*. It's by Stanley Woodward, former sports editor of the late, lamented *New York Herald Tribune*. Written more than a half-century ago, it still crackles with the truth, common sense and wit that all newspapers should emulate. And although Woodward was in sports, he knew news, and especially what the whole business is all about, inside out, top to bottom.

His book should be required reading in every journalism school. Most young journalism grads yearn to land a TV job. It makes sense, because that's where the money is. But television also inflicted the star system on newspapers, instantly elevating the sensational, one-shot story above the patient, time-consuming method of making contacts, going one on one, building trust and being on the scene.

There are no secrets to becoming a good newsperson. It's a tough, grinding job. You can't fake it, because if the story is not there every morning in the papers—the real story, with names, dates, places and above all, what really happened—everybody knows it. That won't be until you know your sources, how to evaluate what they tell you. Fitting the pieces together can be fascinating, but your first obligation is to get it right. The urge to be a star by breaking a story is tempting. It's also the road to half-baked "scoops" that erode readers' trust in the printed word.

So the best way for those willing to pay the price is to find a job on a smaller paper and get out there to learn the hard way. We all make mistakes, and it's the only sure way to test your limits. It adds up to a lot of work for low pay and less recognition, plus confrontations with people who don't like the way you describe their activities. If you're lucky—and your editors are supportive— the facts will speak for themselves. I wouldn't discourage any ambitious youngster from taking the plunge, if only to find out how shedding illusions about the so-called glamor of newspapering might convince them to go get a normal job. Whatever else the news profession might be, it's not the standard definition of normality.

A lot of first-rate professionals make the same decision I did— to stick with it. I've been lucky enough to work with some of the best on the sports beat in Chicago, plus occasional dealings with crackerjack news side men and women. I'm not handing out grades here, especially for an earlier generation of sports guys who went out of their way to show me how to survive in the daily pressure cooker by watching the way they operated.

David Condon and Charlie Barlett of the *Tribune*, Jim Enright of the old *Herald-American*, Ed Sainsbury of UPI and Joe Mooshil of the AP were Chicago stars and good people, too. I was fortunate to know Jack Griffin, a legendary *Sun-Times* columnist, and other friendly rivals from that side of Michigan Avenue. (We used to call it Boul Mich, maybe because the Boul Mich Lounge, along with the Radio Grill, were late-night spots for writers to blow off steam and revile their editors.)

For instance, outstanding columnist Ron Rapoport, baseball writers Dave Van Dyck and Joe Goddard, and Toni Ginnetti, Chicago's top woman sportswriter. The list goes on in the suburbs, although those papers can't compete with the in-town Big Two, either in circulation or quality. There still are some big-league writers out in the boondocks, notably all-purpose Tim Cronin and columnist Phil Arvia on the *Daily Southtown* (technically a Chicago product, it's popular in the south suburbs) and baseball writer Jeff Vorva of the Northwest Herald. John Mutka, a Gary *Post-Tribune* veteran, covers Chicago teams and Hoosier sports for Northwestern Indiana towns that have become bedroom suburbs for a constantly expanding metropolitan area.

*Jim Enright (second from left) made an impact as a big-time bas-
ketball referee and a long-time Chicago sportswriter. Enright's handing out plaques to P.K. Wrigley (left), pitcher Virgil "Fire" Trucks
and ex-Cub manager Charlie Grimm at the baseball writers' annual bash.*

The *Chicago Defender* also has been a respected part of Windy City newspaper tradition. I've been friends with the *Defender* sports editors, especially Larry Gross. Larry and I are former Philadelphians, so we have a long-playing, jovial dispute about whether the ballpark where we rooted for the A's (me) and the Phillies (him) was Shibe Park or Connie Mack Stadium. It was both, as we're aware, but Philly fans will argue about anything—as will Chicago fans.

The Northwest suburban *Daily Herald* has Chicago's best hockey writer in Tim Sassone and a sharp, seasoned columnist in Mike Imrem. I reserve the final backpat for Bill Gleason, required reading for a couple generations of Chicago sports fans. More importantly, World War II veteran Gleason is a man of integrity, along with the Irish wit that made him Chicago's Toastmaster General at hundreds if not thousands of dinners, banquets, award ceremonies and every other imaginable event on the rubber chicken circuit within a hundred miles or a few thousand Tums' distance. I saw Gleason keep rowdy, raucous fans in line with his brilliant barbs year after year, regardless how overserved some were at the annual dinner of Chicago's baseball writers.

Bill and I didn't' always agree, especially about his long-playing feud with White Sox chairman Jerry Reinsdorf. But he always said what he thought, verbally and in print, and I never saw him back down from anyone.

Newspaper chains have been an increasingly dominant, and in my opinion, unfortunate force for opinion-molding in America. My experience working for a chain was limited to a year in Springfield, Ill., at the *State Journal-Register*, part of the Copley empire. It was a short, albeit illuminating stint. I started as the *Journal's* assistant sports editor, soaking up a crash course in effective newspapering from my boss, Ed Alsene, a master of the telephone interview technique.

I can still hear Ed artfully keeping a reluctant source from hanging up with an all-purpose line: "Well, coach, lemme ask you one more thing . . ." About 15 minutes later, Ed usually was the one to hang up, though not without enough scrawled notes to write a telephone operetta.

But that was in 1960, with the John F. Kennedy-Richard M. Nixon presidential campaign raging across America. Somehow I got drafted to be the *State Journal's* Page One, main news section editor.

If Nixon had been elected, the word was out that Jim Copley, boss of the whole nationwide chain, would be Secretary of the Navy. He sent Herb Klein, editor of the Copley flagship paper, the *San Diego Union*, on tour, presumably to let us rustics know which side we were supposed to be on. Klein, who would have been Nixon's press secretary, was a decent, genial man, and he never gave me the slightest hint about learning in any candidate's direction.

Still, the unspoken word filtered though the grapevine that the Nixon campaign story should get equal or better headlines and space with his opponent every morning, when I made up the front page. I tried to keep things balanced, and got few complaints until the day JFK came to Springfield for a massive torchlight parade as Election Day loomed in a neck-and-neck race. The mob choking Sixth Street in Springfield was enormous when I looked out the window to see Kennedy's motorcade go past.

If memory serves, Nixon was in Alaska that day, speaking to a half-dozen or so Eskimos while keeping his pledge to campaign in every state. The impact of Kennedy's visit was so emotional that he got a banner headline with a huge picture of semi-hysterical supporters storming his limousine. Nixon's promise to keep whale blubber flowing north to Alaska was duly reported on Page One, but I often wonder what would have happened if I had made that the lead story.

Anyway, I wanted back in sports—writing, not editing—so that Kennedy-Nixon frenzy was merely an intriguing interlude on the way to a 16-year, all-expense paid NBA journey. That merry-go-round began spinning in 1966, and before it ended, I had been to almost as many whistlestops as those presidential rivals.

Best of all, the only speeches I had to make were delivered to irate editors to let them know why an occasional deadline slipped by with no Bull story in sight. One of those adventures, a harrowing blizzard-bound Chicago-New York-Boston trek, is recounted in Chapter 3 of this book, but there were lots of other near-misses and frantic cross-country dashes.

Before I was ready to survive, let alone handle, that daily treadmill from panic to hysteria and back to tedium, I had to find out what life was like amid big-city deadline pressure. Fortunately, I had some extraordinarily good, kind and patient teachers. One of them at the *Chicago Tribune* was David Condon, an outstanding columnist and an extraordinary man. He hobnobbed daily with Chicago's power elite, including legendary Mayor Richard J. Daley and a bevy of politicians. Many were Irish and Notre Dame die-hards, so it was an easy transition for Dave between the make-believe world of sports and the power games played by Chicago's movers and shakers in smoke-filled rooms.

Somehow, he found time to be a friend and advisor for a bewildered rookie on the Bulls beat. This tribute to him was both overdue and incomplete, but Dave would understand:

There Won't Be Another Dave Condon
(Daily Herald, Dec. 21, 1992)

The season to be jolly was the right one for David Condon to go out on.

He left us laughing over our morning coffee for so many years. It's only fitting for his epitaph to include Christmas lights and bright spirits, a few of them the liquid variety.

Omit flowers, please, along with the funereal music and phony eulogies. Remember only that Dave's daily column brightened the Chicago sports scene for decades, just like his Irish gift of gab and endless array of merry mischief made him fun to know.

Condon ribbed everybody, from officious owners to preening players to unaware editors. If anybody got a pass from that barrage, it was his colleagues, especially young writers scuffling to gain a foothold in the newspaper business.

I fit into that category 30 years ago, so I had a front-row seat for Condon's skirmishes with stuffed shirts, leaving a trail of bruised egos in his wake. Actually, he staged a sort of Irish wake every day in his Wake of the News column, and one of the first things I noticed was that he made fun of himself as much, if not more, than his targets.

The self-styled "Rush Street Fats" wrote the classic "My Name is Barbara" episodes, allegedly penned by his daughter. They lampooned everybody and everything in and out of the sports world, including himself. Those who deserved to be taken down a peg or two got their comeuppance, although not in the mean, sneering style many columnists employ now. If someone needed a pat on the back, that was doled out freely, wrapped in Condon's unique gift of verbal verve.

Last time I heard, Barbara had moved from Rush Street to Crystal Lake. I hope she gets to read this overdue Christmas card to her dad. It's something I waited too long to send.

When Dave got the Good Guy plaque at the Chicago baseball writers' banquet some years ago, I lobbied to make the presentation, outracing the daily I-94 demolition derby to get to the dais on time. The audience of noisy drunks wasn't in the mood to listen to a tribute, even for someone who made their mornings more enjoyable for a lot of years. If Dave had been at the mike when one would-be wit (he was half right) bellowed "Gimme a break!" Dave would have shot back, "Sure, pal. Which arm or leg would you prefer?" bringing down the house the way he knew how.

Instead of delivering some such putdown, I took the easy way out, handing the hardware to Dave. It's something I regret, because he deserved better. Before returning to his chosen Madison Street doorway with a bottle of muscatel in a brown paper bag, the heckler needed to be told what Chicago fans lost when Condon's column vanished from the *Trib*.

Summing up the man and his era wasn't easy. Nobody's replaced him on Chicago's sports pages since then. The other thing you couldn't help noticing about Condon was his choice of heroes. Along with winners like Bill Veeck, Jackie Robinson, and Notre Dame, he loved losers, underdogs and characters. If you were down and out, you had a friend in his column. Dave's kind of event was blue-collar treasures such as the Illinois Derby at Sportsman's Park, within sight and sound of Cicero mob hits, not upper-crust affairs like the Kentucky Derby.

He dubbed that Cicero charge of milk-wagon rejects the Dash for the Dandelions, not the Run for the Roses. The Illinois Derby's official snort, he proclaimed, was a shot and a beer, not a mint julep in a frosted glass.

If you deserved a rap, Condon dispensed it with equal-opportunity justice. There was not a racist bone in his body. But the best of his writing always came funny side up. Dave's wrestling columns were satirical gems, worthy of an S.J. Perelman. They recounted in hilarious detail how Vern Gagne would strive to make the world safe for democracy on next week's International Amphitheater card by vanquishing that baddest of all Bad Guys, Baron Von Raschke, the Beast of Berlin.

That's how I'll remember Condon. His newspaper saluted 30 years of splendid sportswriting by tossing him unceremoniously out on the street. Condon was hurt, but he didn't whine bout it. He always had more class than the people who profited from this old pro's craftsmanship. We used to have long talks, where I saw his reflective side, but his public image was burlesqueing Leo Durocher for ducking out on the Cubs to make a furtive Camp Objibwa visit or sabotaging the sports establishment with literate, entertaining essays.

It was all part of a colorful gift package we won't receive this Christmas. God rest you merry, Dave.

Anyway, the advice and encouragement of the Condons and Gleasons and Wendell Smiths enabled me to enjoy this kind of, ahem, fun around the Midwest in general, and the Big Ten in particular for many moons:

Have Press Pass, Will Travel
(Daily Herald, Feb. 19, 1989)

If it's Sunday, this must be Bloomington.

Illinois or Indiana? Search me. I'm too busy reliving my misspent youth on this wild weekend junket. Imagine covering five basketball games in four states in six days. First, whisk to

Wendell Smith (right) talks it over with Bill Veeck. Smith blazed sportswriting trails to become one of Chicago's—and America's— best-known and best-liked sportswriters and editors.

Wisconsin on Wednesday for NU-Badgers, then to Michigan the next night for Illini-Spartans. Do not pass Go, collect $200 or waste much time sleeping before skeddadling back to Wisconsin for Saturday's Illini-Badgers basketbrawl. After verifying the casualty list from that interstate hate-in, head out on the long haul to Indiana for a Sunday matinee (Wolverines-Hoosiers) and wind it up back in Champaign for Monday night's Illini-Purdue late, late show on ESPN.

Sound like something you'd enjoy? I do, but then I've always been a trifle peculiar. An occasional weekend odyssey like this might make you wonder if that job offer from the pickle factory, as assistant foreman, dill division, is preferable to writing dill hoop stories. Anyway, the grind begins excitingly enough in Madison, where NU's last-ditch rally ends as Wis-ful thinking.

The snow has stopped, so no need to book One-Wing airline's morning flight across Lake Michigan to East Lansing. After the long drive, it's time to clamber up all those steps in Michigan State's ancient Jenison Field House, to the creaky wooden shelf at the top, laughingly known as the press box.

Heart pounding and knees knocking, you squeeze into a seat and peer groggily at those dim figures on the court, far below. It's Illinois in orange and MSU in white, all right, though they resemble ants with numbers. Concentrate, scribble down notes and try to figure out what's going on down there.

Unless you're a sentimentalist like me, a consoling thought is that you'll never again have to strap on an oxygen tank to climb Mt. Jenison. It'll be replaced next season by a spanking new Breslin Events Center. No time for fond farewells after the game story (but not you) goes to bed. Put your Edsel on automatic pilot and point it back toward Madison, where Wisconsin and Illinois will shoot it out Saturday at high noon.

Still think hoop, grid and diamond scribing is ball-to-ball glamor? Don't rush to judgment. We're just getting warmed up. Now hop on the overland one-car wagon train, retracing the Donner Party's route, from Madison to Knight's Landing, a/k/a Bloomington, Ind.

If the urge to go into a trance emerges by now, the electric atmosphere inside Indiana's Assembly Hall will blow away the cobwebs in your brain. When Michigan and the Hoosiers go at

it, they personify the mutual loathing between rival coaches Bill
Frieder , UM's resident eccentric, and Bobby Knight, the Baron
of Bloomington. This confrontation could breathe new life into
the comatose Big Ten race or chair-toss it into the deep freeze.

Either way, you still have to write and run, veering back
onto I-74 and turning toward the familiar flat central Illinois
landscape. Before you flee Knight's clutches, remember to finish
your weekly AP Top 25 rankings and phone them to New York.
If you can't imagine which collegiate powerhouse should be No.
14 on your ballot, guess.

When that unmistakable giant mushroom, the U of I's
Assembly Hall, finally looms up ahead, you begin to think you
might survive this leisurely weekend foul-o-rama. All that's left
is waiting until the TV moguls rake in enough loot from beer
commercials to start Monday's Purdue-Illinois game at 8;30 p.m.,
only a few minutes before it should be ending.

Now you're faced with relentless deadline trouble. Little
time left for banter or double-checking stats. Just get it right the
first time, sending two complete stories to meet early and late
press demands. At last, the final version is in print, worthy of a
Pulitzer Prize for fiction (just kidding, folks). You can relax,
munch a mooseburger at the local ptomaine palace, Cholesterol
Unlimited, and grab a few Z's. Just don't unwind too much.

You have to rise and recall your name early Tuesday morning before tuning in on the weekly Big Ten coaches' teleconfer-
ence. While you're at it, write another story and then head for
home—if you can remember where it is. The places you've been
and the games you've covered are just a blur, but it's all in a
week's work.

Now hustle your buns back on the road and do it all over
again.

Robbing St. Peter's to Pay DePaul

I could have used Jim Rockford to help dig up the details on
the confoozin', amoozin'—as L'il Abner would say—case of Fishman
vs. Wirtz. Before it was over, a lot of lawyers made plenty of yacht
payments from their hefty fees in a legal free-for-all that spilled

over two states, a couple of NBA franchises, and a myriad of intriguing characters.

One of them, a shadowy Milwaukee source with an ax to grind in this intriguing affair, tried to convince me that perhaps, just maybe, a couple of hitmen lurked in the background. I'll save the juicy details for another book. It was a bitter legal fight for Marv Fishman, a home builder once known as "the Cape Cod king of Milwaukee" for his architectural style. Fishman also was an avid basketball fan, joining the Wes Pavalon group that landed a 1967 NBA franchise in Milwaukee.

When Fishman tried to buy the Bulls in 1972 he ran smack into the NBA's basketball-hockey power elite, personified by Chicago bigfoot Arthur Wirtz. Owner of the NHL Blackhawks, only a fraction of this multimillionaire's interests, Wirtz was used to controlling whatever he got involved in. What everybody figured what that Wirtz-Fishman would be a replay of the 1940 Bears (73) vs. Redskins (0) NFL title game.

The Wirtz group got the Bulls, all right, with Fishman seemingly getting the shaft. But the intrigue was just beginning, a trail of deceit, deception and back-stabbing that dragged on for years. I wrote lots of stories about the whole affair, though some of the most enjoyable stuff never made the paper, because the threat of a libel suit was not far off. Both sides had sharp lawyers, hungry for any scrap of dirt to use as ammunition in this down and dirty deadlock.

So sources from opposing camps called me almost daily with updates on the latest attempts to cut this tangled Gordian knot. After seven years of wrangling, it ended up in court anyway. And when I wrote this story, I was unaware it would lead to another adventure, one that was a lot more fun:

Fishman Blows Whistle on Wirtz
(Chicago Tribune, June 9, 1976)

MILWAUKEE—The first step in a courtroom drama as intriguing as it is complex unfolds here Tuesday.

Eventually, it could become a $9 million lawsuit against Arthur Wirtz, owner of Chicago Stadium and emperor of a far-flung financial empire. Among Wirtz' extensive holdings is a chunk of the Chicago Bulls. According to Marvin L. Fishman, a Milwaukee realtor, Wirtz twisted arms in the NBA to influence the sale of the Bulls in 1972.

Fishman made a deal to buy the club from the original group that paid $1.5 million for the expansion franchise in 1966. He was turned down when he sought approval from the league for that purchase, normally a routine matter.

Court proceedings here will assess evidence from lawyers for Fishman and Albert (Ollie) Adelman of Milwaukee, who shifted allegiance to the Wirtz camp during the ownership wrangle.

"The vote on my group was 12 for and five against, with 13 votes needed for approval," Fishman said. "Other owners told me how outrageous it was to let Wirtz and his National Hockey League interests reach into the NBA and control its destiny. The votes against us were influenced by Wirtz' power to award hockey franchises.

"The heartache I went through made me determined to let the truth come out. The full story will be heard in court and I'm going to push it as far as it takes."

Fishman did just that. His case finally went to trial early in 1979, and I covered it until one day in court, when a lawyer hinted I'd be subpoenaed to testify in the trial about the sources for my stories on these backroom dealings. Newspapers do not want their reporters to get on the witness stand, for understandable reasons. If informants (we prefer to call them "sources," because it sounds more dignified than "snitches" or "blabbermouths") can't be assured their identity will not be revealed, they'll clam up.

Unwittingly, Chicago mogul Arthur M. Wirtz, owner of the Bulls and Blackhawks, gave author Bob Logan a press pass to cover the classic 1979 NCAA Tournament matchup between Larry Bird and Magic Johnson.

Lots of people on various levels of government do not want others, especially voters, to know about the deals—and the corners—they cut. In sports, owners, coaches, managers, players and especially agents get on the same high horse over alleged "unsubstantiated charges" from sources. The climate of political correctness is a fertile breeding ground for the notion that all sources are suspect. True, they have to be used both sparingly and carefully, but in the notebook of an experienced reporter, they're an indispensable tool.

So when I called George Langford, then the *Tribune* sports editor, and told him my sources were in danger of being unmasked, his response was prompt.

"Don't go back to the courtroom," George told me. "Get out of town and we'll see what develops."

That's how I got to cover the 1979 Final Four in Salt Lake City. The overwhelming people's choice for that memorable NCAA Tournament was unbeaten Indiana State and its reclusive All-American, Larry Bird, the Hick from French Lick. Bird carried his team to a narrow victory over hard-luck coach Ray Meyer's powerful DePaul in the national semifinal.

The championship game, the first of many meetings between Bird and Magic Johnson, saw his Sycamores fall to Michigan State. I saw it, too, thanks to some legal shenanigans in far-away Chicago. I'd still rather watch Philadelphia Eagles than legal eagles, but the lawyers did me a favor that time.

Winners are Where You Find Them

I could rant and rave for another chapter or another book about newspapers, the people who work for them and the things that make such work seem like it's not really work. I know it is, because bashing my head against deadlines for the better (not bitter) part of a half-century sometimes wore me out more than the limited—very limited—use of my muscles.

But there are young people out there who still want to work on a newspaper, despite all the gloomy forecasts that soon there won't be a newspaper to work on. I don't think I'd go back and ride that magic carpet again, if I somehow could, but like Chicago teams' all-too-brief playoff appearances, it sure was fun while it lasted.

I want to close this plethora of rambling reminiscences with a few words about two interesting people. One of the best parts about being a sportswriter is that when the game is over and you've somehow survived the dressing room/clubhouse crush to gather quotes and notes, the moment of truth arrives. It happens when you trudge back to the press box and sit down to tell the world all about it in a limited number of words and an ever-shrinking time frame.

It's a daily battle I've fought over and over with mixed results—won some, lost some, tied some. That sort of constant challenge is a welcome test for me. I could have done it better most days, but not for lack of effort on my part at the Philadelphia *Inquirer*, the Levittown, N.J., *Times*, the Illinois *State Journal-Register*, the Chicago *Tribune* or the *Daily Herald*.

Another thing that kept my motor running at all those places was the endless array of characters who play roles, major and minor, in the sporting whirl. Team and league schedules are just about the only semblance of organization I've ever detected in the disorderly jumble of practice, travel, self-serving pronouncements from coaches afflicted by terminal tunnel vision, child-man athletes with overstuffed wallets and overinflated egos and an extraordinary array of extras.

Those faces in the crowd include street agents, drug pushers and users, professional leeches, yes men and hangers-on, groupies, hustlers, con men and just plain fans. Trying to sort out this bewildering lineup and batting order can be a time-consuming ordeal, but it's impossible to describe the game without identifying the players. After a while, it resembles a perceptive theater critic's review of the Chicago telephone book; "Not much of a plot, but a heck of a cast."

I've tried in this book to concentrate on the entertaining side of such nonstop pileups, blending names, faces, facts, figures and fantasy into a piping hot or perhaps ice-cold recipe that never cooks up—or tastes—the same way twice. We all know there's a dark side of sports. It started taking the fun out of our games long before I came to Chicago. Now it seems the scandal-sheet tabloid tidbits are standard fare on every sports page.

That's the way our society is heading, I guess, if it's not there already. How we got to this state in all 50 states beats me. A lot of American attitudes changed on 9/11/01, of course, and sports won't seem as deadly serious until—or if—that shock wave wears off. But life goes in cycles, so the pendulum will swing again. How far and in which direction? Like you, I wish I knew.

What I do know is that a lot of people we don't read about every day are the ones who make life easier for the guys and gals, including me, who get the bylines and the recognition. I mentioned some names elsewhere, but a few others deserve my thanks. So here's to Wayne Duke, Jim Delany, Mark "Rudy" Rudner and Rich Falk at the Big Ten; Tab Bennett at Illinois; Lisa Juscik at Northwestern; Tim Hallam, Bulls; Bob Grim and Scott Reifert, White Sox; Chuck Shriver, Sox and Cubs; John McDonough, Bob Ibach and Sharon Pannozzo, Cubs; Ken Valdiserri and Bryan Harlan, Bears; Steve Malchow, Wisconsin; Don Canham and Bruce Madej, Michigan; Jim Vruggink, Purdue; John Lewandowski, Michigan State; George Wine and Phil Haddy, Iowa; Steve Snapp, Ohio State; Gregg Elkin and Kit Klingelhoffer, Indiana.

And, before I rudely interrupted myself, some deserved recognition from me to Bob Rosenberg and Wayne Embry. Their paths crossed occasionally on the NBA trail, but these good guys from opposite ends of the sports spectrum also are the poster people for what's still good about sports. Take Bob Rosenberg, for instance— and I didn't say "please."

If anybody has played anybody for the last 30 or 40 years, it's a good bet Rosey kept score for it. As the official scorer for the Bulls, Bears and Blackhawks, he'll soon be adding up the numbers for his 5,000th pro game in Chicago. He's also the scorekeeper for a lot of Cubs and White Sox home games, fattening that imposing total.

Rosenberg calls 'em as he sees 'em, and not just when he's hunched over his press box scoresheet. He's been around the games

Bob Rosenberg, doing what he does best at Comiskey Park. Chicago's official scorer, Rosey is the fastest figure Filbert in the Windy City.

and players and the games the players try to play with him long enough to know what it's all about. Every conceivable unusual, weird or bizarre situation, play or once-in-a-lifetime incident has been scored, ruled on and described by him. Even more entertaining is Rosey's supersized stock of stories about the whines, complaints, threats, curses and laments he gets from players, trying to get scoring decisions changed.

Moaners and groaners have as much chance of influencing Rosenberg as a Republican of convincing Chicago's alderman to pass an ordinance prohibiting anyone named Daley from running for mayor. That won't stop them from throwing fits or even hints of retaliation.

"Sometimes a player or manager will phone the press box from the bench during a game to yell at me," Rosenberg said. "It gets crazier when I make the hit/error decision in a close call. The pitcher gets mad if it's scored a hit, because that can make a difference in his earned run average. But the batter and the fielder both get sore if I call it an error."

The only really big threat of violence Rosenberg can recall was really big, indeed, in the intimidating personage of 7-foot, 2-inch, 300-something pound Wilt Chamberlain. Late in his career, the Big Dipper decided to transform himself from the fearsome force who scored 100 points in an NBA game to a Philadelphia-style playmaker, dishing off assists. He was leading the NBA in that category one night when the 76ers faced the Bulls in Chicago Stadium.

By this time, Wilt was used to friendly Philly scorekeepers inflating his assists total. Honest John—make that Bob—Rosenberg was not into chalking up phony numbers, though, so when Chamberlain came over at halftime to check the stat sheet, he was enraged to discover it gave him only his actual count. Next thing Rosenberg knew, Chamberlain's enormous hands were around his throat, while the piqued pivotman pleaded his case.

"Fortunately, Wilt didn't squeeze my neck," Rosenberg said. "I told him he wasn't getting cheated and he finally went to the dressing room."

The moral of this story: To get it right, Rosenberg isn't afraid to stick his neck out.

Another man with integrity is Wayne Embry. A standout college and pro player, Embry's blend of class and character made an impact wherever he went, in and out of the NBA. He and John Steinmiller turned Major Goolsby's Milwaukee saloon into a postgame playpen for visiting writers when Embry was the Bucks' general manager and Steinmiller, fresh out of Marquette, was their able publicist. Right across the street from Milwaukee Arena, The Major's offered such intriguing sights as 6-foot-9 Johnny "Red" Kerr dancing to a disco beat on one of the circular tabletops. Those were the days, my friends, but the good times were better because Embry was there to liven things up.

So I can't think of a better way to end my book than telling this tale of the Big Guy, a big man in lots more than just his imposing size:

We Can Learn a Lot from Wayne
(Daily Herald, Nov. 12, 1993)

All over America, race relations are strained.

Some white and black people are afraid to talk to each other, let alone play together. The communication that builds bridges of friendship, trust and respect is sadly lacking. One bright spot could be on four college campuses, where four young men with leadership potential quarterback their football teams.

They are Johnny Johnson at Illinois, Kevin McDougal at Notre Dame, Len Williams at Northwestern and Charlie Ward at Florida State. On the field, it's incidental that all four happen to be black. What matters is the way they've taken charge of their lives and their teams.

When I get discouraged about what's happening on city and urban streets, I think about those players. I also think of another black man, Wayne Embry, now general manager of the NBA's Cleveland Cavaliers. From his playing days as one of the toughest rebounders and defensive bulwarks in the pros, and up the ladder to the executive suite, Embry paved the way for these quarterbacks.

The Big Guy, a solid 6-8 and 260 pounds, never considered himself a victim, although lots of opponents wound up in that category after trying to drive the lane on him. As GM of the Milwaukee Bucks, Embry brought Kareem Abdul-Jabbar out of his shell. Freed from the suspicion that white writers and fans were out to get him, Abdul-Jabbar added maturity to his ability, becoming the NBA's all-time center, in my opinion.

Maybe I'm prejudiced because Kareem was Embry's pupil. Too bad the Big Guy didn't go into politics. He would have stood even taller in comparison with some of the mental midgets we keep electing.

"In the NBA, talent matters more than anything else," Embry told Abdul-Jabbar. "If you're the best, you'll get the recognition you deserve."

Now if only we could induce some of our so-called leaders to preach that message. Finding a way to transfer the pursuit of excellence from playing fields to neighborhoods should produce generations of Johnsons, McDougals, Williamses and Wards. I wish I knew a way to convince all kids that struggling for success like this quartet of quarterbacks is worth the effort. Those lessons are worth much more than football or NCAA victories, or even megabuck NFL and NBA paychecks.

Wayne Embry has been delivering that message for decades, both face-to-face and by example. Not enough of us took time to listen, but the parents of Johnny Johnson, Kevin McDougal, Len Williams and Charlie Ward obviously did.

Spending 40 years with people like that provided me with lots more tales to tell. I'm anxious to deal out still more pun-ishment to the best fans anywhere.

Chicago fans.

Celebrate the Heroes of Chicago Sports
in These Other Acclaimed Titles from Sports Publishing!

Jimmy Mac's Chicago Stadium Restaurant

The Chicago Stadium Restaurant

is a mecca to any sports fan. It is a first-class restaurant within a Hall of Fame museum. The Stadium is the proud home to some of the most treasured sports memorabilia in history. This 440-seat eatery and bar is a replica of the old Chicago Stadium.

You have the choice of enjoying a dry aged steak in Jim McMahon's Steak House, located on the third

level in the private sky boxes or a burger and a gourmet pizza in the Dugout, surrounded by jerseys, bats and balls from some of baseball greatest players. The VIP room is a comfortable hideaway for Jim McMahon and his celebrity friends. You can also catch Jim in the Game Room with his kids playing their favorite video games.

Like the grand old Chicago Stadium, this restaurant is the place of making great memories with family and friends.

**3315 N. Milwaukee Ave.
Glenview, IL 60062
(847) 803-0009
www.thechicagostadium.com**